D0893596

ENDORSEMENTS

"Ryan Sprague takes you onto the field, into the huddle and inside the heart and mind of a Florida State football player, offering both the unique perspective of a passionate walk-on and the life-long lessons and unforgettable memories of a national champion."
   - Dave Glenn, Editor/Publisher, ACC Sports Journal,
      ACCSports.com

"Among the many awards and tributes in his office, Florida State coach Bobby Bowden always kept an empty picture frame. It was his dream to someday fill that frame with his first undefeated, national championship team. That dream came true in 1999 and Ryan Sprague was a part of it. Sprague takes us inside one of the great programs in college football history and tells the story of a coaching icon as only a former player can. There is the joy and laughter that winners feel. But there are also sadness and tears, especially when the great man has to leave the stage. Ryan Sprague knows that both are necessary to tell the story. And he tells it very well."
   - Tony Barnhart, CBS Sports

"Anyone who played for former Florida State coach Bobby Bowden will tell you he was more than a great motivator and tactician, which helped him become one of the most successful coaches in college football history. They will also tell you that Bowden was a great mentor, role model and father to the thousands of young men who played for him. In GRATEFUL: From Walking-On to Winning it All at Florida State, Ryan Sprague tells Bowden's story as well as anyone through his own unlikely journey from walk-on to starter on a national championship team. GRATEFUL is a must-read for anyone who loves underdogs and college football."
   - Mark Schlabach, college football analyst, ESPN

Photos Provided by: The Florida State University Photo Lab
                        The Florida State University Sports Info. Dept.
                        The Tallahassee Democrat
                        The Tampa Tribune
                        Ryals Lee
                        Bill Fax
                        Colin Hackley – www.colinhackley.com
                        Ross Obley – www.rossobleyphoto.com

Front cover photo courtesy of Colin Hackley.

Back cover photo courtesy of Ryals Lee.

Cover Layout and Design: Jared Pervis

Page formatting: Darlene Melcher

This book is available in quantity at special discounts for your group or organization. For further information: www.ryansprague.com

Library of Congress Control Number: 2010911329

ISBN: 978-0-9828763-0-5
Printed in the United States of America

www.ryansprague.com

DEDICATION

The word dedicate has multiple definitions. One of them is "to offer formally to a person, in testimony of affection or respect." This is what I aim to do here; I dedicate this book to my dad and mom, Larry and Candi Sprague.

Interestingly enough, my motivation for honoring them in this way is found in a second definition of the word dedicate; "to devote wholly and earnestly, as to some person or purpose." I represent that person or purpose and my dad and mom were the ones devoted wholly and earnestly.

Mom & Dad,

Choosing to give me life, staying married and providing for me as I grew up are reasons enough to honor you with this dedication. But, as I reflected back, I was impressed and humbled by your tireless commitment to support and encourage me while at Florida State.

Thank you for choosing to drive 40,758 miles over five years to share the experience with me. Thank you for believing enough in me to let me leave Georgia and go chase the dream at FSU. Thank you for making the financial sacrifices to get me to school and subsequently follow me around for all those years. Thank you for tolerating me. Thank you for personifying the ideal of "being there."

I offer this dedication to you because of your dedication to me. Thank you dad and mom; I love you very much!

- Ryan

GRATEFUL

From Walking-On To Winning It All At Florida State

Ryan Sprague

TABLE OF CONTENTS

Sophomore: August of 1998 thru July of 1999

Junior: August of 1999 thru July of 2000

Final Season: August of 2000 thru January of 2001

INTRODUCTION

My name is Ryan Sprague. I played college football at Florida State University and I am humbled that you would be interested in my story. Had this story occurred at a different time, at a different school, or with a different coach, this story would be "run of the mill." But because it did occur at FSU, in the last five years of one of the great dynasties in the history of college football, and under the watchful eye of the greatest football coach the game has ever seen, it has significance. I appreciate that this story is not just my own but the collective stories of many.

In 1914, work was completed on the Panama Canal making it possible for ships to pass through and avoid the treacherous voyage around the southern point of Argentina. The construction of the canal was arduous and cost many people their lives. The canal was a remarkable effort of dedication, ingenuity, and collaboration that produced arguably the greatest man-made structure in the world. Once the incomparable masterpiece of engineering was finalized, it was time to test the waters. The first "official" ship to make the passage was the Ancon, but prior to her crossing a concrete ship named Cristobal made the actual maiden voyage[1].

The journey that the 1999 'Noles completed had been made before. Much like the Cristobal made the journey before the Ancon, the 1993 Seminoles won a national championship for FSU before we did. But the story isn't in the ships that made the voyage; the story is found in the anonymous people who made the voyages possible. At FSU those were people like the late Bill Peterson, the personable coach who laid the foundation of greatness in Tallahassee. He hired Bobby Bowden as an assistant, convinced the first wave of great players to suit up in the garnet and gold, and could give Yogi Berra a run for his quote-worthy status.

INTRODUCTION

Unassuming players like Dan Whitehurst, Bill Cappleman, and Ed Pritchett were winning games in Tallahassee before the players on my teams were born. Stars like Ron Sellers, Fred Biletnekof, and Ron Simmons won awards that helped make FSU a desirable college for up and coming stars to attend. Athletes like Edgar Bennett, Brad Johnson, and the Ostaszewski brothers who fell just one year short of winning a championship at FSU. All these men who didn't get to be the Ancon or the Cristobal were the ones who made our accomplishment possible. Without their efforts and sacrifice our team couldn't have achieved what it did.

Of course the whole project was the product of the vision, dedication, and excellence of our chief engineer, Bobby Bowden. He was the man who could see what we were to become and had the leadership skills necessary to take us there. The players have been great and the awards plentiful but Coach Bowden is the transcendent icon that has become synonymous with FSU football. His accomplishment makes my story matter. And his accomplishment was achieved upon the work of all those men who were represented above. Our stories are connected.

I will tell stories about the guys who played at the same time I did, but really it is the story of all the guys who ever played for Coach Bowden. We all played with great players, some of us were those great players. We were all a part of historical games. Each of us has stories to tell about Coach Bowden. I am a fortunate member of a great fraternity of Seminole players spanning decades and it humbles me to be included in that group. I hope that this story makes you all, my fellow 'Noles, proud. I hope that it inspires great conversations recalling the good old days, the battles won and lost, and the vibrant memories of sharing in the pursuit of greatness.

Over the course of five years there were many players with whom I shared the locker room, but they will not all be mentioned in this book. There were many coaches, trainers, equipment managers, sports information folks, graduate assistants, videographers, and many more who all contributed to the stories in this book and they deserve credit but there simply isn't room within the covers. Please know that I remember all of your work and I appreciate you. You were each as much a part of the dynasty as any of the players.

As you read through this book you will find stories you haven't heard before and some that you have. You will find yourself wishing that I had talked about a memory that you had and I am sorry if I didn't include it. I could only write about what I had firsthand knowledge of and I chose to write the book with a positive spirit. You will not find criticism in this book, nor will you find any player or coach shown in a poor light. We all have our issues and we all lose some games but to waste any time or ink on the negative, in light of what was one of the most incredible runs in college sports history, would be an injustice.

This book is for fans. It is my desire that fans of FSU enjoy this book with pride and feel that much closer to the program that they love. I hope that fans of other universities who love the tradition rich game of college football will find this appealing and satisfying as well. While we may wear different colors and sing different songs, we are all part of the pageantry of college football. My desire is that you would enjoy this story regardless of your loyalties as a fan.

This book is also for my teammates. If you are a player or coach who shared in these experiences, I hope you find this retelling accurate and enjoyable. It was scary how much I had forgotten and how much I had remembered incorrectly. The years had blended together and my memories had become foggy. Hopefully, this will refresh your memories and provide a written

INTRODUCTION

slide show of some of our awesome times together as Seminoles.

If my story were a painting, the canvas is college football, the frame is Florida State University, and the color of my life is but one of many colors used to create a magnificent portrait of greatness. The stories are shared from my perspective but don't let that impede your view of the bigger, more impressive picture. I hope that you enjoy this book like you would a themed ride in an amusement park and that at the end you feel like you have experienced the story. My desire is that you would be able to hear the sounds, see the sights, and feel the emotions as a group of kids came together for a great run, under a great leader, and achieved great things. The greatest compliment that I could receive would be for you to feel in reading this book the way that I felt writing it... grateful.

-Ryan

Tyler Jones, "The Panama Canal: A Brief History," May 31, 1990, www.ilovelanguages.com/tyler/nonfiction/pan2.html

FOREWORD *by Bobby Bowden*

Ryan Sprague's book is a documentary of success that every aspiring youth will want to read. It is the story of an overachiever that wouldn't give up; a young man that would not accept the term, "you can't," as an out in life.

I coached College Football for 57 years, which means I mentored thousands of young men. During this time, there were always two categories of players I dealt with. In one category were the players on football scholarship and in the second were boys not on scholarship trying to obtain one. Each year I coached, during my 34 years at Florida State, I would have 80–85 players on scholarship plus anywhere from 30–50 walk-ons. "Walk-ons" is a term used to identify players on the team without a scholarship. I told my staff to call them "free agents" (a pro football term) to help add dignity to the walk-on title. There is a high percentage of free agents in pro football that make it and become starters. Out of the 30-50 free agents on our team at FSU each year we probably averaged two a year that went on scholarship, Ryan Sprague was one of these. When he came out for football he was moved from center to fullback and then found a home at tight end. Ryan became a starter and started on our National Championship team of 1999. This team is the only team in Division 1A football history to be preseason #1 and remain #1 every day of the season until the last day! They were 12-0.

I have always had a secret love for my free agents and expressed to my staff many times that these are the guys that really love to play football. It's like working seven days a week and not getting paid... But, hoping it will pay off in the future. Even to this day, I will give my former 'walk-ons' as high a recommendation as I will any of my former scholarship players because of the price they had to pay. Florida State could never have had the success they had through the years without the contribution of walk-ons; thirty-three years without having a losing record.

Ryan Sprague's years at FSU were during the 90's, where we won more games in that decade than any team before or after. We just edged out Nebraska. Ryan had the physical tools to start for us... but barely! He was big enough, tall enough, fast enough, strong enough, and tough enough... but just barely! However, Ryan had a heart as big as any player I coached. He had pride and resolve that wouldn't let him quit. He had self-confidence that he could play winning football at a major college level and he possessed the greatest virtue of all winners... persistence! Persistence is the will not to quit. He never cried for mercy though I know he wanted to. With this attitude, Ryan honed his skills along with his desire and made the cut. The moral of the story? You can do it if you believe you can and are determined not to quit.

I am proud Ryan chose Florida State to get his college education and play football. I will never forget his contribution to our success. We put 14 consecutive years together where we were in the Top 5 in the nation by Associated Press polls. If you include the Coaches' Poll, we were in the Top 4 in the nation for 14 consecutive years. I have always felt that the character of the team was just as important as the physical ability of the team. Yes, there is a physical standard you must meet to play Division 1A football but without character you probably won't reach your goals. A big virtue in all religion is sacrifice. You can't play football if you won't sacrifice your body for your team. There is no "I" in team.; it's about us, we, our, and not about me. Our team motto in '99 was, "it's not about me." When players start thinking about their own statistics and putting self above the team, you better watch out.

Of the many free agents I've coached through the years, only about one of twenty earned a scholarship. That doesn't mean that the other 19 failed in life. Most became successful in other fields after graduation. After all, you go to college to get a degree. Ryan Sprague became successful in both categories.

-Bobby Bowden

Prologue

BOWDEN WALK

It was a perfect day, but for all the wrong reasons.

When this day was envisioned, the temperature was to be in the 70's and the sky would be a gorgeous blue totally absent of clouds. It would be a day marked with joy and celebration as a legend voluntarily stepped away from the game that he loved. But when the day actually arrived, the weather was an appropriate metaphor for the reality of the moment.

It was freezing. Well, not literally, but close enough. The weather was something out of a Herman Melville novel. The sky looked like the brush of a chimney sweep after completing a cleaning and the rain was constant. Not heavy, just unrelenting and cold. If the atmosphere could speak it was singing a dirge and early in the morning on Jan. 1, 2010, many Seminole fans were singing the same song.

Ten or fifteen years ago, when talk began about the imminent retirement of Bobby Bowden, the script would have been for him to walk away from college football at the peak of his greatness. He would be standing in front of another of his great teams, hugging his wife, Ann, and hoisting one more National Championship trophy. But the story didn't go that way, and a day marked for joy was instead marred by melancholy.

GRATEFUL

The dynasty Coach Bowden built in Tallahassee had fallen in recent years and a program once synonymous with excellence was now tarnished with mediocrity and an academic scandal. Instead of celebrating another ten win season and a major bowl, we were thankful to be 6-6 and eligible to play in the postseason. This particular year was more reminiscent of Coach's first years at Florida State than of the glory days, and it was sad. I don't use the word "sad" in a pathetic sense, but with a sense of longing and heartache. The circumstances weren't sufficient to honor the man who had reinvented the game of college football, so an idea was born to bring some of that greatness that marked his career into the present moment and provide a proper send-off.

Most of us had arrived at Jacksonville Memorial Stadium about 90 minutes earlier. I was huddled underneath a 10x10 party tent with about fifteen former Seminole football players. A group of guys I played with, including Chad Maeder, Josh Baggs, Chris "Birdseed" Walker, and Jarret Gardner shared stories and caught up while the players under the other tents did the same. Over 300 men who had played for Coach Bowden over the decades made the pilgrimage to Jacksonville, Fla. to honor the man who had so impacted our lives. I looked around and saw James Coleman, Matt and Todd Frier, William McCray, Chris Weinke, Kurt Unglaub, Clay Ingram, and Derrick Brooks among the crowd. Players who hadn't seen each other in years were in familiar territory as we huddled shoulder-to-shoulder just like we had thousands of times before on the Seminole practice fields. We were all there for one purpose... to be present the day Bobby Bowden, our coach, coached his final game, in the Gator Bowl against West Virginia.

Thankfully, I was living in Tallahassee at the time so the three hour drive was inconsequential. However, I would have been there if Seattle, Wash. was my home. This was simply a moment that I wouldn't have missed. There were guys from Bowden's days as a community college coach in Georgia in the 50's all the way up to guys who had graduated the year before. There were NFL hall of famers, Heisman trophy winners, doctors, teachers, pastors, salesmen, and politicians in the mix but on that dreary morning in Jacksonville, we were all just Coach Bowden's players. I considered myself privileged to be there.

We could barely hear the instructions to form the line and head to our places because of the rain pattering on the tents and the vibrant conversations. Imagine you and your friends getting together to rehash old stories of the glory days. Now, multiply that a few times and you will have an idea of the noise level. When we finally heard the instructions, we moved from the protection of our little tents, stepped into the rain, and began the march towards the "Bowden Walk." We made a processional from our location across the façade of the stadium for about 200 yards until we came to the team's entrance to the field. We turned to our left and found ourselves staring at an inspirational sight of thousands of Seminole fans eagerly awaiting the legend.

The Seminole Nation had been lining up for hours on the street to be a part of this event . Fans were standing up to ten people deep and covering a distance of 300 yards. About 100 yards into the corridor of Seminole fans I found my wife and her family. They were soaking wet and shivering while they attempted to shield the cold, stinging rain off of our four little boys. The other players and I had to continue walking and a little further up I was able to find more of my family. My parents, my sisters, and my brother were squished into a set of bleachers not unlike the ones found in Herald Square for the Macy's Parade. They were joined by a crowd that would have made a fire marshal cringe and the engineer who designed the bleachers boast. The drenched and devoted fans

GRATEFUL

waited for a chance to offer their support to the living legend as he led his team to battle one last time. Thousands of Seminole fans were braving the elements and it was obvious that they were all paying a price to be a part of this event. While the former players had been under the cover of tents and enjoying space heaters, the dedicated fans were unprotected from the elements and uncomfortably cold. Kickoff was still hours away and on any other day these people would have been in their cars or maybe even still at home; but this wasn't any other day. This was Bobby Bowden's final game as a college football coach and a little inclement weather couldn't keep them away.

I felt bad for these committed and passionate fans as the players were loosely divided in half to form human walls for Coach Bowden and the 2009 Seminoles to pass through. Unfortunately, we also became a barrier between them and the man they were there to honor. The only consolation was that they got to see some of their favorite players from over the years up close and personal. The guys were laughing and teasing one another, hugs were being exchanged, and there was a sense of joy that transcended the weather and the weight of the day. It was like a second reunion as we connected with teammates who had been huddled in different tents than the ones we were in. While we were, in a sense, special guests at the walk; in our hearts we were just like the fans, eagerly anticipating the arrival of our hero.

A roar erupted from the crowd nearest the street and thousands of heads turned like spectators tracking a serve a Wimbledon. The flashing blue lights of the Florida Highway Patrol car leading the convoy of busses were to Coach Bowden what a horse drawn chariot would have been to Caesar. The cruiser pulled to a stop at the beginning of the human tunnel and without delay the back door opened. The Seminole faithful erupted as Coach Bowden stepped out of the car while we began standing on our tip toes and hopping up and down to catch a glimpse of our Coach. Already the chill produced by the weather was being supplanted by the warmth of the moment.

He shook the hands of his escorts and the FSU administration that was waiting for him before he began his stroll down a very literal memory lane. Coach Bowden said himself that this moment was the toughest for him. Seeing his old players from decades of coaching all there to support him was emotionally overwhelming. I believe that many of us shared the sentiment. The guys instantly closed the gap that the directors had worked so hard to create prior to Coach Bowden's arrival. It looked like a levy breaking as the guys poured from their place of containment to rush Coach Bowden for a chance to shake his hand or give him a hug and I don't think the directors minded a bit. So what if kickoff had to be delayed a few minutes; this is what the "Bowden Walk" was all about.

As he made his way through the thicket of humanity, the Seminole fans surrounding the area roared every time they caught a glimpse of their coach. They cheered to say "thank you." They cheered to say "beat West Virginia." But mostly, they cheered because they loved this man. This is the man that had paced the sidelines of Doak S. Campbell stadium for over three decades and the only coach many of them had ever known. He brought big time college football to the little town of Tallahassee in the form of Atlantic Coast Conference championships, Heisman trophy winners, national championships, and even one undefeated team.

That team, the first team in the storied history of college football to go wire-to-wire and win the National Championship, was my team, a team that Coach Bowden led to his only undefeated season. This was the team that came together for a special run of greatness that highlighted the magnificent career of Bobby Bowden, and a team that I was fortunate to play for as a junior at Florida State. But the story doesn't begin there. This story begins in Augusta, Ga., with me watching the "Game of the Century" between Florida State and Notre Dame in 1993… cheering for the wrong team.

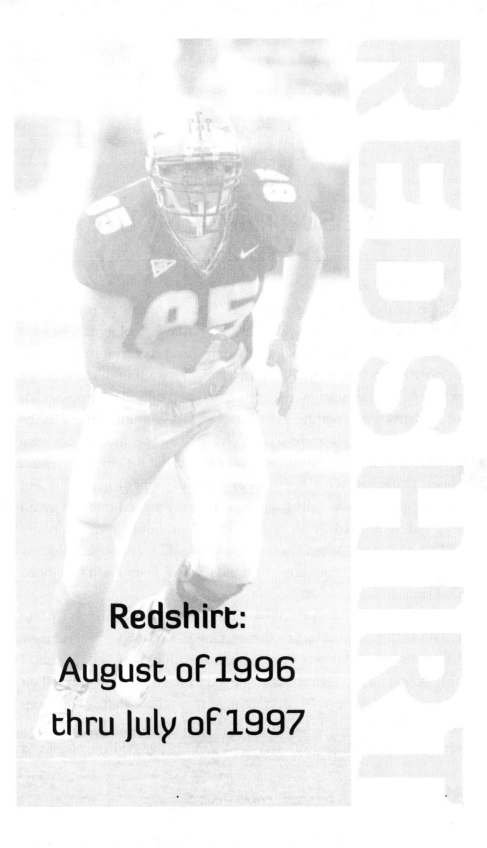

Redshirt:

August of 1996

thru July of 1997

01

THE SURPRISE OF MY LIFE

U p to this point, the most significant moment of my football career occurred in the Lakeside Middle School gym. The only reason I was on the team was due to the head coach offering a favor to my dad and on a Friday afternoon, I was waiting in the hallway with my Panther teammates for my first pep rally. The thousand or so students were creating a disproportionate amount of noise as the coach prepared to introduce the team. One by one, the players were announced, they would run to center court, and the students would cheer; that's just what happens at a middle school pep rally. But when my name was called and I awkwardly jogged into the gym I was rudely greeted by an unmistakable and humiliating chorus of "BOOOOO!!" I wasn't a very popular kid and much to my surprise, my token placement on the football team hadn't changed that fact.

I managed to survive middle school and continued on to Lakeside High in Martinez, Georgia, just outside of Augusta. Lakeside wasn't known as a football recruiting hot bed. In fact, I only knew of two guys who played college football after their careers at Lakeside were over. We were a school that was known for a strong debate team, solid golf, and good baseball. But, we were in the midst of a pretty good run on the gridiron. I played tight end, linebacker, and defensive end. Our quarterback, David Rivers, was a great high school QB and ended up with a full scholarship to play for George Welsh at the University of Virginia. I was able to ride his coattails and because many colleges were scouting him, I began to garner a little attention as well. My best guess is that the interested colleges saw that I was 6'5" and hoped I might mature into a football player. Outside of that there was really no reason to recruit me.

Towards the tail end of my junior year, recruitment letters began arriving from schools like Presbyterian College, the Citadel, and Furman. David had been invited to the University of Georgia for a summer camp and somehow I got an invite too. Ray Goff and the UGA staff recruited me fairly strongly but that recruitment abruptly ended when Goff was fired. Jim Donnan was hired to replace Coach Goff and I apparently didn't fit into his plans with the Bulldogs. In spite of Georgia's interest in me dissolving, I was still getting attention from those smaller schools. As my senior season began two new schools entered the discussion; Wake Forest University and for reasons still unknown to me, Ronnie Cottrell, the recruiting coordinator for Florida State University began to regularly call.

The only thing I knew about FSU was that I didn't care for them. I was a rabid fan of the University of Notre Dame. My dad grew up in Big Ten country and he liked the Irish. When I first took an interest in college football, I remember looking up national champions, and when I saw that Notre Dame won it in 1977, the year I was born, my blood turned Irish green. I had historical books on Irish football, owned all kinds of Irish clothes, and even owned a Notre Dame letterman jacket! I had been to South Bend, Ind. to see the campus and ran the length of the field with my brother, Daniel.

I could name their coaches in succession, all their Heisman Trophy winners, and recite the "win one for the Gipper" speech verbatim. I was every bit the fan that Rudy Ruettiger was. This devotion is what found me cheering loudly when the Irish defense was able to stop Charlie Ward and the Seminoles, to hang on for the win in "The Game of the Century." Of course, I also remember standing in the mall and watching the TV in a shoe store when Boston College defeated the Irish the following week, allowing the 'Noles to slip back in and win their first NCAA championship.

When I began hearing from the Seminoles I still had aspirations to suit up for Notre Dame. But, Notre Dame never called and I wasn't willing to live in the groundskeeper shed and attend the local community college so I put away my shamrocks and considered other options. I ruled out the Citadel instantly because I was not interested in the discipline associated with being a "knob" in Charleston. Bear in mind that nobody was offering me a scholarship and when it came down to it I was considering walking-on at Wake Forest or doing the same thing in Tallahassee. Both universities invited me to come to their campus for an "unofficial visit." (An "unofficial visit" is an NCAA term that means that I had to pay my own way.) My parents and I jumped on the invitations to visit the schools and our first trip was to Winston-Salem, N.C. to visit the Demon Deacons.

Wake Forest is on a beautiful piece of God's creation and is a quintessential college campus; gothic architecture, large quads within an intellectual fortress of dorms and academic buildings, complete with a world class library. I loved the campus and I loved the fact that incoming freshmen received a new laptop computer. The game I attended, however, reminded me of high school playoff games in Georgia, without the robust passion. The stadium only held about 30,000 at its capacity but it was nowhere near capacity on that day. There was no real atmosphere to speak of and the game experience was quite forgettable. Our trip to Tallahassee was a couple weeks later and while it wasn't as picturesque, the football was like nothing I had ever experienced before.

I remember actually thinking Tallahassee was unattractive. Of course it didn't help that essentially every road in Tallahassee was under construction and orange cones obscured every view. The huge live oak trees stood out and we were impressed with the campus architecture, but the view that was most memorable was of Odell Haggins' hand when he showed me his 1993 National Championship ring. We had toured the coach's offices and looked out over the vacant Doak Campbell Stadium turf before Coach Cottrell had us sit down with Coach Haggins. Odell was responsible for recruiting my part of the state of Georgia and I remember him telling me, "If you come here, you will have a chance to win one of these (pointing to his ring) every year." The trip could have been over at that moment because I was sold. If I was going to pay my own way to school and walk-on to the football team, I might as well do it and get some cool rings in the process!

While it was all icing at this point, my recruiting trip continued with a trip down to the Seminole locker room. I don't remember a whole lot about the locker room, but I do remember walking up to a locker with a No. 44 Seminole jersey (*I was 44 in high school*) hanging inside and my name on the placard on top. Coach Haggins' rings were cool, but my name on a locker was amazing! They certainly knew how to make a guy feel important. The feeling I can most closely relate it to would be when I was a little boy walking into the Magic Kingdom for the first time. I was giddy and proud to be taking pictures in front of *my* locker and *my* Seminole jersey. But, it didn't end there.

The next step was to enter into *the* cathedral of college football, Doak S. Campbell stadium. We woke up and joined over 80,000 garnet clad Seminoles on their way to see the 'Noles play. No offense to the folks in Winston-Salem but there really was no comparison. The crowd was three times larger, the stadium itself dwarfed the one at Wake, and when those fans began bellowing the War Chant while the Marching Chiefs provided the cadence, I had chills running down my spine. The War Chant is awesome but when Chief Osceola rode across the field mounted on Renegade and planted his spear into the turf, Florida State became planted firmly into my heart. The 'Noles dominated their opponent that afternoon and I was totally sold on being a Seminole. I was even willing to overlook the orange cones.

I headed back to Augusta feeling like I was the man. I had just spent a couple of days on the campus of FSU as a prospective member of their football team. That was a long way from being in the gym of Lakeside Middle School being booed by my peers. Things had changed since those middle school days but I still felt like I had something to prove. As my senior season progressed, Odell Haggins called and told me that he was going to come to Lakeside and see me play. A member of the Seminole coaching staff was going to drive past those orange cones all the way to Augusta and watch me play football! Regardless of what anyone else believed, I crowned myself the coolest person at Lakeside. I remember being envious of David because he had bought a bunch of cool UVA gear since he knew he was going to Virginia. Since I had not received a scholarship offer, I wasn't sure I was going to FSU so I was not bold enough to declare that I would be a Seminole. But this visit from Odell changed everything. I went ahead and told the world about my impending visitor and gloated all week... well, until Friday morning.

When I got to school that day I was eagerly anticipating Coach Haggins' arrival and our game that evening. But when I walked into the locker room that morning there was a big problem. I had been demoted to second string! The rest of the morning was a blur; but I remember groveling to my position coach, David Machovec, and begging to be placed back into the starting lineup. "FSU is coming to see me play tonight!" I pleaded, and mercifully Coach agreed to let me start. I don't know what that sudden demotion was all about, but it certainly got my attention. With that crisis averted I went about my day, but with a sick feeling of anxiety.

After school, the second major problem of the day reared its ugly head. Coach Haggins had called and he wasn't going to be able to make it to Augusta after all. I never found out what happened there either, but I do know that it was humiliating. It wasn't that Odell couldn't make it that was so humbling, but the fact that I had been so pompous. Here I had been boastfully telling anyone who would listen about the Seminoles being interested in me only to be promptly deflated by Haggins' absence. Thankfully, my coach still let me start and my friends weren't too hard on me.

Coach Haggins' inability to see me play was not a reflection of FSU's interest and I continued to receive letters and phone calls from Coach Cottrell throughout the year. He continually encouraged me that if another school offered me a scholarship I should take it, but if not they would love to have me. Apparently, being an "honorable mention" on the all-county team isn't very impressive because no scholarship offers came. So that spring I applied and was accepted to be a student at FSU. After my graduation and a long summer of anticipation, in August of 1996, I was driving down Georgia highway 319, past thousands of orange cones ready to begin my career in the Garnet and Gold.

02

TALLAHASSEE

There are two kinds of walk-ons who can participate with a football team; a non-recruited walk-on or a recruited walk-on and I arrived in the panhandle as one recruited. The only practical difference is the day the NCAA allows you to begin practicing with the team. For a non-recruited walk-on, you aren't allowed to join the team until the fall semester begins, but the recruited walk-ons can suit up at the same time as the rest of the team. While the extra two weeks of practice provide a huge physical advantage, the real benefits are relational and mental.

Showing up to campus a few weeks early for practice is great, if you have a place to live. It's a non-issue for the scholarship guys because they are in the football dorm, Burt Reynolds Hall. Burt Reynolds played football for the 'Noles back in the day and went on to become a Hollywood success story. I had the opportunity to tour "Burt" on my pseudo-recruiting visit and I was eager to move in. When I received my admission packet from the school, one of the first things I did was select *Reynolds* Hall as my first choice for housing. My first big surprise as a freshman was learning that Burt Reynolds Hall and Reynolds Hall are different housing facilities. I had selected and been approved to move into Reynolds Hall and instead of being across the street from Doak, I was across the campus.

As miffed as I was by my oversight, living in Reynolds turned out to be an amazing opportunity for me at FSU. I made and became great friends with my "second floor boys;" and we are still very close today. But, it made my daily commute to practice brutal; especially for the pre-dawn mat drills. The eventual long commute

"The second floor boys." L-R: Jay Miller, Me, Dave Perales, Jayme Johnson.

to practice was the least of my issues upon my arrival on campus. My room was reserved and I was ready to unpack but it was August and the dorms hadn't opened so I wasn't able to move in to Reynolds yet. So me and my fellow walk-ons lived out of suitcases for a while in a temporary dorm that was vacant with the exception of a handful of wannabe Seminoles holding on to a dream. Welcome to Florida State... sort of.

The first couple days of fall camp are non-contact preparation for the bludgeoning we are about to endure. Freshmen arrived a day or two before the upperclassmen for a series of physical tests to determine what kind of shape we were in. It is similar to the NFL combine but on a much smaller scale. We performed vertical and long jumps, ran different agility drills, and were given medical physicals. They were performed to gather athletic information and to establish a medical baseline to measure our health as we proceeded through two-a-days. I felt special being there with the scholarship guys and I held the hope that I might be able to pass myself off as one of them; just give me a uniform and a pack of Mentos and I was going to be fine.

My hopes were dashed as soon as I entered the locker room to find my locker. The room was organized by position groups, the linemen in one section, linebackers in another, etc. So I went and found the tight end section. I saw Melvin Pearsall's, Myron Jackson's, Kamari Charlton's, and… that was it. I was looking for the nameplate that I saw on the recruiting trip, "Sprague 44", but it was nowhere to be found. I walked up and down the aisles looking for my locker but trying not to embarrass myself in front of the scholarship guys who had quickly located theirs and were already getting changed. Finally I came to the last row of lockers and learned that apparently "walk-ons" are a position group unto themselves because there were my brethren and there was my locker.

There was no sneaking into the club now; we were officially on the "other side of the tracks" and there was no denying it when I saw my gear. The walk-ons had the same shirts and shorts as the scholarship guys but there was one glaring difference. Every player on the team had their numbers stenciled on the left thigh of their shorts. This was done primarily for the sake of sorting laundry;

every piece of equipment we used had our number on it to make sure it all returned to our lockers. But in the land of the walk-ons, numbers are not promised. Since numbers 0-99 were attributed to the 85 scholarship guys, the walk-on numbering began at 100. Stenciled onto my left thigh was the number 138 and I felt like Hester Prynne shamefully walking around Boston when I had those shorts on. As alienating as the triple digits made me feel, it was nothing compared to the shame associated with my shoes. As soon as I saw the clods that we had to wear, I wanted to just put the shoes I wore to the stadium that day back on, but mine were Adidas so that was out of the question.

FSU is a Nike school and part of the deal is that they outfit the team with brand new shoes every year. The schools get the top of the line shoes with the specific color pattern of the team. The scholarship guys were lacing up their sweet cross trainers while we were trying to figure out whether or not we were being pranked. The shoes were bad. They were boxy, bland, awkward shoes that looked to be designed in the 1980s. I couldn't believe Nike had actually allowed their swoosh to be embroidered on these "shoes." I'm sure that they were safe and effective cross-trainers but if there were such a thing as a "lame stick" these shoes were piñatas and that stick had been in the hands of an entire class of second graders. The luster had quickly worn off and the reality of my place in the athletic caste system had settled in. I was a walk-on.

In spite of my self-consciousness and fear of being shunned by the rest of the team I was able to begin to develop some relationships. It was tough for the first couple of days because I was the only tight end on campus; but when the upperclassmen reported I began to connect with my segment. I believe this is the primary advantage to being a recruited walk-on; being there with the guys as we battle it out through the toughest part of the year.

34

GRATEFUL

Those preseason practices are wielded by the coaching
blacksmith wields his hammer while crafting a sword. Sharing in
that sharpening experience with the team helps to meld you into
the fraternity and permits you to be one of the guys.

My first season of two-a-days in Florida was shocking.
Augusta can be hot and humid but it might as well be Winter Park,
Colo. compared to the sauna that is Tallahassee. The heat was
overwhelming at first but eventually it became a motivator for me.
I prided myself on not letting it get to me and every time I saw a
player throw up or have to get iced because of the heat, I felt
stronger. I was not going to be like every other freshman; I was
going to overcome the heat and that made me feel good. I actually
began to take pride in how much weight I would lose in each
practice. One of the rules imposed by Athletic Trainer, Randy
Oravetz and his staff was that we had to weigh in before and after
each practice so that our weight could be monitored. Losing double
digit pounds in one practice happened all the time and I wore it
like a medal of honor.

The other startling aspect was how little I actually knew
about football. We ran a pro-style offense in high school which was
pretty sophisticated but it wasn't a college offense. Learning the
Seminoles' play book was the most information I had to learn in
any one time in my life. Absorbing all that terminology and all the
assignments was daunting but my ignorance of the technical side of
the game was laughable. I'm sure all freshmen go through this
process of having to relearn technique and I would imagine that
my learning curve was the same as everyone else's, but it felt like I
had never played the game before. I was taught a new stance, new
foot work, new hand placement, new body positioning, new ways
to run routes, hold the football, and how to stand in a huddle. It
was *football 101* but it felt like an advanced placement course to me.

This isn't a poor reflection on my high school coaches; it simply reflects that every coach has a way they want things done and if you want to play for them, you do it their way. When in Tallahassee, do as the Seminoles do.

By the time the fall semester began, I had started to embrace my role as a walk-on. I was able to move out of my suitcase and into room 227 at Reynolds Hall. School was in session and my life as a collegiate student-athlete had begun. No longer would I just play football all day long, now my days would be filled with classes and home work to go alongside my football responsibilities. I had begun to settle into my place on the team but now I was going to need to discover my place on the campus as well.

03

NEW ROUTINE

Two-a-days lasted about three weeks, and for those days we ate, drank, played, and slept football. But, our lives as full time football players ended when school began and our morning practices were replaced by dreaded morning classes. Eight a.m. is early. School started for me in high school around 7:30 a.m. and as I write this, my routine gets me up every day at 6 a.m., but as a college freshman 8 a.m. was unbearable. Most of my civilian friends (non-athletes) started their days closer to 11 a.m., but for the football team eight was normal. Most days our pre-practice meetings began at 2:15 p.m. which required guys to be there around 1 p.m. to get taped and ready for practice before they went to meetings. I didn't like being at the stadium any longer than absolutely necessary, and I never got my ankles taped, so I tended to arrive about 1:55 p.m. those days. The point is, we had to be done with classes before 1:30 p.m. so we had them all early in the morning. Had I been on scholarship my mornings would have been even worse.

The scholarship freshmen were required to be in study hall at the stadium before classes began. My $20,000 in student loan debt might have been worth the extra hour of sleep every morning! The upperclassmen that needed it had study hall in the evenings after practice. Even though I avoided the pre-dawn study hall I still loathed my Monday, Wednesday, and Friday 8 a.m. classes, but there wasn't much I could do about it.

MONDAYS

I rarely took showers before classes. One reason was because it was so stinking early and I liked to roll out of bed at the last possible minute. The other was that I took a shower every day after practice so I felt that I was sufficiently hygienic. As a freshman, I had three classes in succession beginning at eight in the morning. Normally, after class I would meet one of my friends from Reynolds in the student union and have lunch. Oh what a glorious day it was when Chick-Fil-A opened there! Our practice schedule was different on Mondays so my afternoon was wide open. Many, many of those uncommitted hours were spent playing Mario Kart, Golden Eye, or NCAA football on whatever gaming system was current. We logged more hours in our college football dynasties than we ever did on any other hobbies combined.

When it was finally time to turn off the video games, I would head to the Moore center for dinner. On Mondays, we would begin our time together as a team with our meal. Nobody was worried about getting sick because Monday practices were the lightest practice of the week. After dinner, we would breakdown the film from our previous game and get the scouting report for our next opponent. After the indoor portion of the session was complete we would head outside to run our corrections.

The coaches would have us run through the plays that we executed poorly from the last Saturday and we might get a look at anything new we were going to install for the upcoming game. Upon the last scripted play, Coach Bowden would call us all together and he would address the team. He would talk about the goals we had set for the game we had played and point out if we met them. He would call out the players who performed particularly well and as he said each name, we would respond with a singular, united clap of our hands. He would get a nice rhythm going but also liked to hesitate every once in a while to see if we were paying attention; you didn't want to be the lone clapper. Once all the accolades were handed out, it was time to focus on the errors.

This is the only time that any of us didn't like Doak Campbell Stadium. We would have to run stadiums for different errors committed in the game like missed assignments and penalties. If you knew what to do but were beaten on the play, you didn't have to run, that's part of football. But, if you went the wrong way, made the wrong read, or blocked the wrong man an evening running stadiums was in your future. You had a reservation in section five with your coach and 86 steps.

When practice was finally complete, some of the upperclassmen headed to study hall and the rest of us went back to our homes. Monday nights were always a favorite with my roommates. In the prime of our entertainment gluttony, we had four televisions going at 9 p.m. each week. One tuned to the WWF, one to the NWA, one to Monday Night Football, and one hosting the video games. If Willy Wonka had designed an entertainment factory, he would have used our living room as inspiration.

TUESDAYS and WEDNESDAYS

The mornings during the week were basically the same, and on Tuesday and Wednesday the afternoons were as well. No more post lunch free time because we had to be dressed, ready to practice, and in our meeting rooms by 2:15 p.m. Our day would begin with roughly an hour and a half film session before we would hit the fields. These two days were always the longest and toughest practices of the week, with Tuesday being the worst because it was the longest and most physically grueling.

Walking out of the locker room was miserable. One second it is 71 degrees and you can see; the next second you are blinded by the sun's glare and it's a scorching 97; that was always the worst hit of the day. After walking about 70 yards across the parking lot we would reach the tunnel that ran underneath Pensacola Street and led to both Dick Howser Stadium and the Seminole football practice fields. The tunnel was only about 6'7" tall, so many of the guys had to hunch over to keep from smacking their head on the roof. It was corrugated steel much like the tunnels you will find on golf courses. That was appropriate because often times you would have to scrunch yourself down into the ribbing of the tunnel because a jolly old man would come whipping through that tunnel in his golf cart. Often times, just to be a nice guy and spend some time with his players, Coach Bowden would give one or two of the players a ride out to the fields. One time I got to be that guy. I don't

remember what we talked about; I was just glad to be conserving the calories I would need at practice.

Upon exiting the tunnel, we would take a sharp left and take the short walk to the first of three practice fields. We would enter the fields by passing through a gate with a steel, garnet and gold banner across the top of it that said, "Enthusiasm." To our left was the famous Sod Cemetery holding the grass from all the different "sod victories" from over the years. Depending on how early you got to the field, you would have a few minutes to toss a ball around or get some last minute equipment repairs before Dave Van Halanger, our strength and conditioning coach, would blow his whistle signaling that it was time to go to work.

Some days we would stretch on field one, in the shadows of Dick Howser and some days we would stretch on field two. Field one was the special team's field where our kickers and punters would spend most of their day. Field two was primarily used for the offense and field three was the domain of Coach Mickey Andrews and his defensive staff. The fields ran parallel to one another and were separated by about 10 yards and about two feet of elevation; field one being the closest to sea level. Between fields two and three sit two Seminole icons; the shade tree and Coach Bowden's tower.

Coach Van would have us in lines with the starting offense closest to the 50-yard line, then five yards behind them the second string defense, and so on. The defense would be facing us in the same pattern on the other half of the field. During our stretching period, the position coaches would make their rounds trying to get guys ready for the day at hand. The day was divided up into five-minute periods and one of the equipment managers had the responsibility of staying in the camera tower, also between fields two and three, monitoring a stop watch and sounding the siren on a mega phone every five minutes. He would then call out what the new period was and turn that number up on his flip chart, "period four, period four."

Towards the end of practice, you would always see veteran players trying to talk the manager in charge into trimming a few seconds off the periods, thirty seconds never felt so good. After stretching, we would have about three periods of pro-bono work. It was in these pseudo-periods labeled alphabetically that we would work on our kicking game. It was basically a prolonged warm-up but there would be some hitting going on. These drills normally occurred on fields two and three because when the last faux-period was over, Coach Bowden would blow his whistle and we would all surround him under the smaller of the trees next to his tower.

Coach Bowden would use this brief time to get us focused on the day's practice. He would say "remember to get some juice in ya men," referring to the PowerAde that the trainers had with them. FSU was purely a PowerAde school since the other sports drink is associated with our rivals in Gainesville. After our little meeting we would split up, offense on field two and the defense on field three. We were now under the direct leadership of Mark Richt and Mickey Andrews, the offensive and defensive coordinators respectively. In the meantime, Coach Bowden would retreat into his observation tower and begin taking copious notes of the day's activities to reference when he met with his coaches later that day. Our mid-week practices were normally 22 periods with four or five kicking periods prior to period one, labeled A-D or E depending on how many there were; a practice might have looked like this.

Periods one, two, and three were spent in "individual drills" which were performed in position groups. The tight ends would be working on routes, footwork, or driving a sled while the running backs worked on securing hand offs, etc. For periods four – six, we would form larger groups. The offensive line, tight ends, and running backs would come together to work on the running game while the QBs and receivers would be working on the passing game. After that the tight ends and running backs would head up to field three for some work with the linebackers, in a drill called "Dallas" during periods seven – nine.

Dallas was a passing drill with the linebackers playing against the tight ends and running backs. This was a competitive drill and one I always enjoyed. We would line up in our formation without the offensive line and the line backers would line up to defend. An equipment manager would snap the ball to the quarterback and we would run the play. After Dallas, for periods 10 and 11, and only really during two-a-days, the tight ends, running backs, and linebackers would join the offensive and defensive lines for "board drills." "Board drills" were all about getting low and being tough. There was a 2x6 board lying on the ground and an offensive player would line up opposite of a defensive player while they both straddled the board. The coach would blow a whistle and the battle was on. The object of "boards" was to drive your opponent off the back of the board without compromising your straddled foot placement. I was never very good at this drill but I loved it. "Boards" always made for the best video in our film sessions.

Occasionally, early in the season or during the Miami week we might be asked to do a period or two on the boards, but most of the time within a season we would do some other blocking drill to minimize injuries. After pounding each other for a few periods, about period 12, we would experience the best period of the day, the break. The whole team would run over to the big shade tree, actually sit down, drink PowerAde, and sometimes eat popsicles. The only thing bad about the break was having to get up from it. It ranks up there with getting out of a warm shower in the dead of winter and setting an alarm clock; all of them being things you just don't want to do. After our five minute break was over and we had plenty of liquid in us, we would head out to finish practice.

Periods 13-17 were spent with the offensive and defensive lines working on pass protection and pass rush while the rest of us ran something called, "Pass Skeleton." Skeleton was a passing drill with everyone involved except the lines in a full speed simulation of our aerial plays. We would spend quite a few periods here because we relied heavily on the passing game in our offense. After Pass Skeleton, in periods 18-20, we would begin our 11-on-11 scrimmage. This was always the liveliest part of practice. Partly because of the authentic competition and partly because only 22 players at a time were participating, which left the other 80 or so guys to become fans. There was more trash being talked than at a Waste Management stock holders convention. We would even have the offensive coaches jawing with the defensive coaches. It was great. After 11-on-11, for the last periods of the day, 21-22, we would head to the goal line. This would be the most intense five or ten minutes of practice because everyone wanted to finish well and win at the goal line. A touchdown and the offense wins, a stop and the battle belonged to the defense. Because the coaches wanted it too, normally there was extra conditioning on the line if we lost. Pads would be popping during these drills and the guys loved every minute of it.

Coach Bowden would begin working his way down the steps of his tower and onto the field where his whistle would mark the end of practice. We would all surround him again, under the same tree and he would deliver our post practice notes. He would point out players he thought stood out for good or bad reasons, mention team wide announcements, say "good practice men, get with your coaches," and then blow his whistle. Quickly we would surround our respective coordinators, either coach Richt or Andrews. They would briefly address us and then release us to our position coach who would inform individuals of any responsibilities they had to take care of, things they might have done well or poorly in practice, and then what running we had. The close of the little segment meeting signaled the beginning of "Gassers."

A Gasser is simply lining up on a sideline, running across the field, touching the opposite sideline, returning back to where you began, and then doing it again; that would be one. We had to make them in certain times based on our position, and had to do however many Coach Richt felt we needed. The tight ends and quarterbacks had to make them in 42 seconds, while the linemen had a few more seconds and the little guys a few less. If a player failed to complete his run in the allotted time, the Gasser didn't count and he had to do it again. Eventually we would wrap that up only to have our "discipline running." These would be extra Gassers earned from dropping passes, jumping off sides, being late for a meeting, etc. About two and a half hours after Coach Van blew his opening whistle, we would be dragging ourselves back through that tunnel and into the locker room to hit the showers.

Dinner would be waiting for us in the dining hall known to us as "Ms. Betty's." Ms. Betty was the lead chef for the athletic training table. Some guys would grab-and-go while others would slowly enjoy their meal, trying to regain enough energy to make it home again. On Tuesdays, many of the guys would return to Ms. Betty's around 9 p.m. for the weekly Fellowship of Christian Athletes huddle, but other than that, the two days were nearly identical.

THURSDAYS

Thursdays looked just like Tuesdays and Wednesdays until 2:15 p.m. We had a shorter time on the field on Thursdays so we made up for it by having longer film sessions. We would look at the film from Wednesday but get to spend a concentrated amount of time looking at our opponent's game film. Thursdays is normally when Coach John Lilly would point out one of the mascots doing something ridiculous in the background of the film; the inflatable Cornhusker was always good for a laugh.

The transition to the fields wasn't as miserable as the previous days because we didn't wear shoulder pads or football pants on Thursdays. We would wear our helmets, shorts, and practice jerseys but not always our own. There is a tradition at FSU of switching jerseys with teammates on Thursdays like opponents after a World Cup match. If you weren't paying attention you might think quarterback Chris Weinke was playing running back or offensive lineman Jason Whitaker was playing wide receiver but upon further review you would see that it was just running back Nick Maddox wearing the no. 16 jersey and wide receiver Robert Morgan sporting the no. 68.

The practice was devoted to repetitions against the scout teams; no contact and no work against our guys. Everything we did was against defensive fronts we would see the following Saturday, to be sure that we were mentally prepared for anything that they might try against us. As long as we were executing well, Thursdays were enjoyable practices filled with enthusiasm and laughter. Should our execution drop, the hammer would too and we would find ourselves doing up-downs until Coach Richt felt we had developed the proper focus.

After practice we would shower, change, and head over to Ms. Betty's but we would have an important stop before dinner.

Thursday was the day that the ticket office would set up shop for us to sign our families up for their tickets. We had to put the names down of each person using a ticket, so the ticket people could get them organized before the team left town. With a full stomach and our tickets reserved, it was time to head home and anticipate Friday. For me, as a walk-on freshman, Friday was the day that I felt the most disconnected from my team. If we had a road game, they would be jumping on a plane and heading to the game location. If we had a home game, they would take the bus to Thomasville, Ga., 30 miles away, to get ready for the game on Saturday. But, in either case, I was hanging out with my friends back at Reynolds Hall wondering what happened on those trips. I would find out next year, but this year I needed to focus on my role as a member of our scout team.

04

SCOUT TEAM

Being on the scout team is grunt work. You are charged with "representing" the opponent for the coming Saturday by running their plays the best that you can. Prior to each play, we huddle up and the scout team coach, John Lilly while I was on it, would hold up a sheet of paper with a play drawn on it containing general blocking assignments and routes for the receivers. We got to see it for three seconds and then we had to go execute the play. We also would wear the number for the player that we represented so that our starters saw a better picture of what to expect on game day. For instance, our first game of the 1996 season was against Duke, so the scout team quarterback wore the same jersey number of the Duke quarterback. The number recognition especially helped our linebackers recognize formations by identifying the tight ends by number and seeing where they lined up on any given play.

While the representation we provided with our jersey numbers and formation helped, it was the execution of the play that was of utmost importance. As a scout teamer you can't win here. You can learn some great life lessons about being true to yourself and not yielding to the desires of others, but in the process it is hard to make friends. If you go 100 percent you might please the scout team coach, but you make the world class scout-team-eater on the other side of the ball unhappy. If you go all out, the man you are going all out against might decide you need to be taught a lesson. If you hold back to avoid the pummeling from your teammate, the coach of the starting unit will lay into you about not providing a "good look" and hurting the team's chance for success on game day. If the coach is really feeling froggy, he might even threaten to keep you from dressing out on game day or to take away your scholarship if you have one. It all proved to be "coach-speak" because they weren't cold-hearted men, just coaches attempting to motivate. No one lost a scholarship on account of poor effort as a scout teamer. But, those same coaches who clamored for maximum effort didn't *really* want maximum effort, just ask Jean Jeune.

Jean was playing linebacker for the scout team in 1996. He was supposed to be running a blitz that the opposing team would regularly run. Warrick Dunn was playing tailback at the time for Coach Sexton. At this time, Warrick was a senior and one of the top players in America so he rarely saw heavy duty on the practice field. Nobody wants to have a star player injured in practice. But, this particular drill was vital because he needed to see the different blitz looks to be prepared for the game. Coach Billy Sexton coached the running backs and if Coach Andrews was like a hurricane where you knew the wrath was coming and could expect it; Coach Sexton was a tornado. You never quite knew when Sexton would go off and when he did, it could be over just as quickly as it began.

Dunn was lined up in the backfield, prepared for the snap and Jeune was the linebacker opposite him, holding a blocking pad about the size of a baseball strike zone ready to go as well. Quarterback Thad Busby set the play in motion with his cadence and Jeune came through the gap between the left guard and left tackle just like the play was written up. He slowed as he was about to make contact with Dunn so that Dunn could get into position to block him just like what happens almost every time. But the skies grew strangely dark all of the sudden and an F-3 Sexton tornado tore across the offensive practice fields. Jeune was the unfortunate player in the path of the storm. Coach Sexton laid into him about not going full speed and not giving Dunn a proper look. He threatened to never let him play, that there were hundreds of guys out there who would trade places with him and give maximum effort, etc. He screamed at Jean and told him that he better give 100 percent or he would send him to the sidelines. So, they reset the play and Jean did what any wide-eyed freshman, walk-on football player would do; he did exactly what Coach Sexton said. At the snap, Jean tore across the line of scrimmage and drove into Dunn with everything he had. The next thing we knew, Dunn was blown off his feet and onto his back, much to the delight of the coach... the scout team coach. Because an F-5 Sexton Tornado was suddenly spotted... "WHAT DO YOU THINK YOU'RE DOING?!?! DO YOU KNOW WHO THAT IS?!?!" (Referring to the all-American running back lying on his back) Jean was instantly removed from the scout team defense and sent to the sideline as confused and frustrated as any man could be. Sexton assigned an unsuspecting player to be the new linebacker and demanded that he "better not go full speed and try to win a scholarship by hitting his running backs..." tornado warning.

Well, back to my time on the scout team. Because there was no one else to do it, I was playing center on the scout offensive line at a whopping 210 pounds. The rest of my scout team line mates averaged around 6'2" and about 250 pounds; while our assignments averaged about 6'5" and closer to 280. Bear in mind that I wasn't burdened with the full responsibility of playing center because I didn't have to snap a real football. In an effort to eliminate the fumbles between quarterback and center, keep the plays running, and avoid broken fingers I slid a deflated, folded over and taped up football across the ground. This helped my cause because I could get a head start on the D-line since I didn't have to worry about a fumble. We needed all the help we could get since we were blocking one of the best defensive lines to ever play college football.

On one end was Reinard Wilson and he was complimented by Peter Boulware on the opposite side. Both guys were all-Americans and eventual first round NFL draft picks. The interior was a rotation of Andre Wadsworth, Greg Spires, Julian Pitman, and Connell "Spanky" Spain. These men were not only much larger and stronger than us; they were also faster and just better football players. Wadsworth became the third overall selection in the draft, Spires played nine years in the NFL and won a Super Bowl ring. Pittman was a fourth round pick of the Saints, and Spain was signed by the Bengals and played five seasons in the Arena League. I think our scout team line would accrue a combined four months of NFL experience coming from Justin Amman and myself getting into training camp and then quickly cut.

During the grind of one of our practices, we had a little tension develop between "Spanky" and the scout team guard playing beside me. We were getting pushed by Coach Lilly to give everything we had and really challenge the defense. At the same time, the defense was trying to get us to give "just enough." Well, "Spanky" took issue when our guard really got after him and on consecutive plays would yell into our huddle and threaten to beat us if we didn't cool it. I think that my helmet must have been malfunctioning because for some reason that is outside the realm of logic, I decided to call "Spanky" out. I would compare this to David and Goliath but I didn't even have a stone to throw. I don't even know what I said to him, but I know he didn't like it. I just remember that after I said it, I looked straight at my coach in hopes that by averting my eyes "Spanky" would just let the insubordination slide. It didn't work.

I have never been to Africa, but I think I know what a charging rhino sounds like. It was so sudden. The pounding of his Nike clad hooves into the turf, the looks of shock and fear in the eyes of the guys who were looking at the carnage about to unfold, and the terror motivated reaction that occurred. I spun around just as "Spanky" was about to unleash his fury upon my guilty body and I didn't have time to think. I just reacted. As he uncoiled his wrath, I grabbed his right arm with my left arm and pinched it against my rib cage. Simultaneously, I shot my right arm under his left arm pit and began to roll backwards. As a high school wrestler I learned this life saving little move called a "lateral drop." His momentum carried both of us to the ground and I just continued the roll until I found myself on top of him, chest to chest, with my body perpendicular to his. I now had the bulk of my body weight pressing against his right arm and I was holding onto his left arm with everything I had. Nothing followed from me; I had no idea what to do next, I just knew I didn't want to let him up or he'd kill me. The whole "fight" probably lasted no more than five seconds but it felt like an eternity while I was on top of "Spanky" waiting for someone to intervene. My rescuer ended up being Odell Haggins. Thankfully, Odell is pushing 300 pounds himself and as a former NFL defensive tackle for the San Francisco 49'ers he was able to both separate "Spanky" and me while providing a wall for me to hide behind as well.

Like a lottery winner, my life was changed instantly and I was a scout team legend. As soon as Odell got us separated "Spanky's" line mates began harassing him for getting whipped by a man with "three numbers on his shorts." Their ribbing defused the situation and rescued me from a second attack. Not only did those man-mountains harangue him, they also celebrated me as I just created months of fodder for them to use to tease "Spanky." An equipment manager on our field radioed his co-workers who began relaying the story to the players within earshot and word of the incident spread like a brushfire. When the "fight" occurred the team was spread over all three practice fields, but by the time we were all together on field two for live scrimmage situations, everyone knew. I was the talk of the team... well "Spanky's" humiliating loss was the talk and I was the goofy kid who pulled the upset. In just a few short minutes, the legend grew from a fear motivated survival move, to a Mike Tyson beat down. I was being lauded like a heavy weight champion and guys who previously didn't know I existed were patting me on the back. Even Warrick Dunn, who was very soft-spoken, gave me a compliment. I went from a no-name walk-on with three numbers on my shorts, to one of the guys in about five seconds. I had earned the team's respect. I believe with all of my heart that was the moment that opened the door for me to earn my scholarship because I was no longer nameless.

As we ran off the field that day, "Spanky" ran up beside me and simply said, "good shot man," with a joyful grin and quickly followed it with, "I'll get you next time!" Thankfully, there never was a next time. Instead, I became a sort of a mascot for the D-linemen and I loved it. As we watched game and practice film together those guys would tease me along with each other and call out when I did a good job. I had moved from a nameless walk-on to a part of "the seg." In spite of my offensive roots I became a huge fan of the defense that year and they didn't disappoint.

They were stout in the first six games of the season as we rolled out to a 6-0 start, but the game against Miami was their watermark performance. Miami entered the game with the number one defense in America so our guys arrived in Coral Gables with a chip on their shoulder. They shut Miami out for three of the four quarters, sacking UM's Ryan Clement six times, forcing three turnovers, and even scored a touchdown. Our offense made sure there was no doubt about who the best defense really was by posting 17 points on the 'Canes in the first quarter and the final score read 34-16. We played Virginia the following week before our trip up to Atlanta to play Georgia Tech. The game itself was far from newsworthy but it marked a major milestone for me, my first road trip.

05

ATLANTA

I had dressed out for the four home games up to this point but hadn't traveled to any of the road games. Coach Cottrell had promised me that he would try to let me dress for one of the road games and he proved to be a man of his word. "Ryan, I've got good news. Since you are from Georgia, I am going to let you dress out for our game up at Georgia Tech." The coaches decided to "redshirt" me that year, which meant that I could practice but not play. Redshirt years are used to help kids develop and get acclimated to college without costing them a year of eligibility. It wasn't customary for redshirts, much less redshirt walk-ons to travel with the team so this was an incredible treat. We were set to play the Jackets on Nov. 2 and my birthday being Nov. 3, it was about as good a birthday gift as I could have received. Little did I know that my turning 19 would lead to near humiliation.

I had a lot of work to do. There are eight people in my family and thankfully I also had a lot of friends interested in following me too. Not to mention we were ranked no. 3 in the country at the time and people just wanted to see a great football team in action. Needless to say, I had to round up a bunch of tickets. The way it worked was that scholarship players received four tickets and non-scholarship guys received two. Depending on where the game was being played the guys would shift from having extra tickets to needing extra tickets. The guys in South Florida would trade their away tickets in North Carolina for tickets to the game down in Miami and vice-a-versa. So, that Thursday I was begging and pleading with guys to get as many tickets as I could because I didn't have any tickets to trade. Thankfully, with the help of my defensive lineman friends and the fact that we had already played UM, I was able to get what I needed.

On Friday, the team met at the stadium to catch our bus and ride to the Tallahassee airport. The support staff, the coaches' families, and a handful of Seminole supporters would join us on our charter flights to the game locations, this week being Atlanta. After only about one hour in the air, the plane touched down at Hartsfield International Airport. Four or five charter busses were there waiting on the tarmac with a full police escort to take the team to the hotel.

The escort was sweet! Coach Bowden was in a police cruiser leading the way, while about six officers on motorcycles flanked the caravan as it headed into town. As the buses neared intersections, two of the motorcycle cops would speed ahead and block the intersection so that the convoy didn't even have to slow down. Sometimes they blocked entire roads so that the busses could travel the wrong way down one way streets. This was always one of my favorite parts of the road trips.

Late Friday afternoon, the team pulled up to the Marriot Marquis in downtown Atlanta and everyone received their room keys and went to drop off their bags. But that isn't how it went for me on this trip. About the time the team was checking into the hotel, I was a couple hundred miles south in Tifton, Ga. riding in the back seat of a little sports car on my way to Atlanta.

Coach Cottrell had arranged things for me to be able to

dress out, but I wasn't able to travel with the team. I had to provide my own transportation, meals, and lodging. It was very similar to my recruitment and coming to FSU on an "unofficial visit." We can just call this an "unofficial road trip." I called on one of my friends from high school to crash in their Georgia Tech dorm while I was in Atlanta. That Friday evening I spent time with my family, reconnected with old friends from Augusta, and got a tour of the Tech campus from my high school friend, Cliff Richards. Friday felt like any other weekend trip to Atlanta to visit friends, but Saturday was a brand new experience.

Were I on an *official* road trip I would have had a wake-up call in my hotel room, and after rolling out of my plush bed I would have joined the team for a bountiful breakfast. Instead, I woke up with a sore back from a night on the couch and a classic, college dorm room breakfast of milk and cereal. We were scheduled for a night kick-off so I was on my own for meals all day. I met my parents, long time friend and Tech student, Kelly Points, and her parents for a birthday lunch; she and I were both born in Charlotte, N.C. on Nov. 3. We killed time around Atlanta until it was about time for the team to be wrapping up their pregame meal. Our plan

was to be at the hotel when the busses left so that we could join the caravan and make sure I was able to get into the stadium with the team. My mom had bigger plans though.

We arrived while the team was in the room eating and I went ahead to check in with Coach Cottrell. While I was in with the team, in a very professional environment, where I already felt like an imposter, my mother was doing what only another mother could understand. Coach had answered all my questions so I headed towards the door to find my parents. As I left the land of "cool and focused," I entered into the land of "you have got to be kidding me!" My mom was partially hidden but I could see her face as she stood in the lobby of the hotel beaming as proudly as a toddler with a brand new puppy. She was hidden by the object of humiliation that she held in her joyful hands... a Texas sized birthday cake for me. Her intentions were to bring this labor of love into the pregame meal to share with the team and have them sing "Happy Birthday" to me. I shuddered in horror as I stared into her hopeful eyes, and then considered the eternal shame inevitably associated with having my mom stage a surprise birthday party on a freshman year road trip. The lump in my throat was the only thing that kept the shock induced vomit from escaping as my face turned whiter than the icing on the cake. In the seconds that I had to think; I said what any mortified teenager would say... "Throw it away, now!"

Oh, my mom tried desperately to reason with me but every passing second brought another look over my shoulder to the dining room door. Were one of the players to walk out, it would all be in vain. I would have crushed my mother's feelings and had my future dreams of being cool crushed at the same time. Something had to happen and it had to happen fast. The decision was an easy one for me as I sacrificed my mother's love and devotion on the altar of fitting in, and insisted that she and the cake disappear. It must have felt like a love struck suitor being rejected while on a knee with a ring in his hand to her, complete rejection. She nobly acquiesced to my immature demands and the cake found its resting place in a hotel trash can, whew! The ride over to Bobby Dodd stadium was icy but we finally arrived and I was able to step back into the world of "cool and focused."

Getting into the stadium that day resembled the experience of a fan going to a game much more so than that of a player. Had I brought my own car, I would have been forced to find and pay for parking, but it was more like being in middle school and going to the movies because my mom and dad drove and dropped me off. So, as the team was smoothly stepping off the bus in the travel uniform, I was awkwardly sneaking around in street clothes hoping for Coach Cottrell to notice me before security did. I had to look like a crazy stalker, desperate for an autograph or something as I lurked in the shadows like Gollum. Coach spotted me and waved me over as he began explaining to the security guards what was going on. I imagine the conversation went something like this:

"Coach, if he isn't with the team party he cannot come in this gate; he will have to get a ticket like everyone else."

Coach Cottrell sympathetically replies, "Listen, he doesn't know that we know but, we all saw that his mom brought a birthday cake to the team meal and if he gets embarrassed again I don't know what he'll do."

"She did what!?" exclaimed the guard.

"Shhhhh! Keep your voice down. Just play it cool and let the poor kid in, he won't affect the game whatsoever, I can guarantee that much." Coach Cottrell pitched in full recruiter mode. With that the guard stepped aside and Coach Cottrell waved me in with his trademark grin. Blissfully ignorant, I strode through the gate and into the visitor's locker room.

I was glowing with enthusiasm as I began to get dressed, but I had a sick feeling when I pulled out my jersey and saw that there wasn't a name on the back. There was a better chance of one of the Yellow Jacket cheerleaders getting into the game and taking a snap for us than there was for me to play, so it made perfect sense that my name wouldn't be on the back of my jersey. But, for a teenager who was excited to be on the field in front of a bunch of his friends and family, "perfect sense" was perfectly depressing. Once I pulled my jersey over my shoulder pads and had them on I forgot about the name issue, but It didn't take long for the Georgia Tech student body to remind me.

Traditionally we go out onto the field to warm up in waves. The skill guys, consisting of receivers, defensive backs, running backs, and the quarterbacks, went out first. A while later they were followed by the bigger skill guys of fullbacks, tight ends, and some defensive guys. Finally, about an hour before kickoff, the rest of the team went out. Upon the arrival of the last group, we all came together for our stretches. Being on the 14th string placed me in the very last row of the stretching lines, which was in the back of the end zone, directly in front of the students. The last row also left me a full 55 yards from Coach Van as he was calling out our stretching routine. I was mortified of humiliating myself during the stretches because it was very hard to hear his whistle from where I was, particularly when we would do our back stretch. The Seminole method in '96 was to lie on our backs with our feet pointed towards midfield, and on the whistle we would roll our legs up over our heads and work to get our toes to touch the ground behind us. It was a very unflattering position but tolerable because there were 100, twenty-four carat behinds sticking in the air and not just my own. We would release from that position when Coach Van would blow his whistle again, but when we were in that yoga inspired contortion it was very hard to hear him. My strategy was to release early because it was better to be the only guy sitting than the alternative; my plan backfired though.

My premature uncurling caught the attention of the student section who unfortunately noticed that I didn't have a name on the back of my jersey. They offered a few generic comments but it wasn't too bad until we broke out for our position warm-ups. As the forgotten members of the 'Nole offense, the tight ends were relegated to about a ten-yard stretch of end zone right between the running backs and the offensive line. Of course, this left us right in the heart of the student section for about 15 minutes… plenty of time for the "little engineers that could" to get creative.

I was accused of sneaking onto the field, of winning a contest, and being a coach's son as the reason I was the only one on the field without a name on my jersey. They questioned my ability with unrelenting passion so it became game time for me. The tears I shed as a middle school football player being booed by my classmates prepared me well to withstand the jeers of a few uber-enthusiastic college kids. No matter how creative or crass they became, nothing they said could rival that middle school nightmare. I decided that I was going to be the best warmer-upper on the field and prove myself to those shirtless number-crunchers. If a pass was in the air, I was catching it and when I lined up to block, I was going to drive my unsuspecting teammate off the field. The first time I tried to hit Kamari Charlton he stiffened and very quickly put the fear of upperclassmen into my head which overwhelmed my desire to impress. I toed the company line for the rest of the blocking warm-ups and let the Tech fans have their fun. Melvin Pearsall heard what was happening and with a heart of gold took me under his wing like an older brother would a younger brother. He turned and said to me, "So, did you have to sneak into the stadium?" and smacked me on the helmet, just like a big brother.

Once we were done with our warm-ups, I was freed from the ridicule of the students and it was quickly my turn to gloat. Granted, I had about as much to do with the outcome of the game as they did but I was the one on the field while they were stuck in the stands looking at a 49-3 win for the Seminoles. Name on my jersey or not, I had the last laugh as we jogged off the field victorious. They may not have respected the back of my jersey, but after that game they sure respected the name on the front. They were gracious enough to call me out and try to make amends and I was gracious enough to tell them where they could find some cake.

After the blow out win in Atlanta, we had four games remaining on the 1996 schedule. A resounding win the following week against Wake Forest secured the ACC championship for us and the next two weeks followed a similar script to the previous two. Southern Mississippi and Maryland offered little resistance as Warrick Dunn, who finished fifth in the Heisman Trophy vote that year, led us to dominating victories by an average score of 51 – 12. There was one game left in 1996 and it would be historic.

06

EPIC

It never got any bigger than this. We played in some huge games during the five years I invested at Florida State. Bowl games, Coach Bowden's 300th win, and even a few national championship games but none were bigger than our end of the season clash in 1996 with the University of Florida. I was a wide-eyed freshman just happy to be in the stadium for this battle and I wasn't disappointed. UF came into the game undefeated, ranked no. 1, and led by eventual Heisman winner, Danny Wuerffel. We boasted an undefeated season too, a no. 2 ranking, and our own Heisman trophy candidate in Warrick Dunn. As special as Warrick was, he was overshadowed on this day by our typhoon of a defense, led by ends Peter Boulware and Reinard Wilson.

The setting couldn't have been better. A beautiful day in late November, two undefeated teams ranked no. 1 and no. 2 in the country, bitter rivals separated by only a two-hour drive, and 82,000 football fans drunk on the moment. Many Saturdays would have us running out of the tunnel and onto the turf at Doak to a partially full stadium, as our fans tended to arrive fashionably late. But on this Saturday every seat was full, aisle crammed, and box at capacity, well before kick-off. When we made our entrance there was no mistaking that we were a part of history.

As a redshirt player, I would not see the field that day but I dressed out as if I would. I wasn't about to witness my first Florida State vs. Florida game in street clothes, fans can wear street clothes. As long as I was on the team and allowed to dress out, I was dressing out. We were in our traditional home uniforms of gold pants, garnet jerseys, and the unmistakable gold helmets. UF was in their orange pants, white jerseys, and orange helmets. Of all the teams we played, I always loved the contrasting uniforms when we played UF; the smooth, classy look of garnet and gold as opposed to the loud, hunters-vest orange and sapphire blue sported by the Gators.

If a war had broken out around Tallahassee that day, those inside Doak Campbell would have been oblivious because we wouldn't have heard the first shot. The fans in that stadium reached record volumes and maintained it throughout the course of the game. Actually, the crowd noise played into our defensive strategy of "playing to the echo of the whistle." Coach Bowden coined that phrase in response to Florida's coach, Steve Spurrier's, complaints that our guys might hit his quarterback after the whistle. The intensity of the crowd provided a huge advantage with on the field communication as well. Our fans kindly allowed us to call plays and audibles from the line of scrimmage but screamed like they were in the throes of un-anesthetized child birth when UF tried the same; advantage 'Noles.

Led by Thad Busby, Warrick Dunn, and our defense, we jumped on UF and had a 17-0 lead as the first quarter came to an end. But the second quarter would belong to the team from Gainesville as they responded with a 14 point second quarter and we went to the half still leading 17-14 but UF holding the momentum. We came out in the third quarter and the team's defenses pounded the other's offenses and didn't allow either team to score. The fourth began very similar to the first as "Pooh Bear" Williams scored a touchdown and gave us a 24-14 lead. Wuerffel proved the nation right in considering him for the Heisman as he led the Gators on a long touchdown drive to pull Florida within three, at 24-21 and just over one minute left on the clock.

The stadium was a fusion, as hopeful energy from the UF fans collided with the nervous energy of the FSU fans when the teams lined up for the Florida onside kick attempt. If UF recovered, Wuerffel and company would have a chance to tie or win, but a recovery by us and the game was all but over. The tension reached crescendo as the ball was kicked and after an agonizingly long three seconds, the ball rolled harmlessly out of bounds. Our ball! Thad led our offense out for the last couple plays and as the final seconds ticked off the clock of this epic, the real commotion began.

I don't know if it had ever happened before but I know it hasn't happened since. Pandemonium ensued after we defeated UF and locked up a chance to play for the national championship. The brick walls and five-foot drop were not enough to keep the storm surge of Seminoles from flooding the field. The moment the game was final, Garnet and Gold clad members of the Seminole Nation were running wild on the turf of Doak Campbell. Not just one or two, but tens of thousands! The seats emptied and the grass quickly disappeared beneath the sea of humanity. It was the coolest thing I had ever seen. I totally forgot my responsibilities as a player and joined the party. The fans didn't care that I was a freshman walk-on. I was a Seminole. They congratulated me, jumped on my back, grabbed my helmet and screamed, and anything else you can imagine, to express their euphoria from seeing the Gators skinned.

Somehow within the thousands that were shoulder-to-shoulder on the field, my roommate and friend Jay Miller, was able to find me and we celebrated like I actually had something to do with the outcome. We didn't care about the details, we were just as excited as anybody else except I had a helmet and that made it all the better. Apparently there wasn't enough room on the grass, because our fans swarmed up the goal posts like ants on crumbs at a picnic. Within minutes both goal posts were snapped at their base and began crowd surfing around the field. Our fans totally lost their minds! The goal posts are 40 feet tall and our fans managed to dismantle them and carry them out of the stadium like Vikings returning with a kill. The legend of those posts being shouldered around Tallahassee and eventually sawn into little pieces for fans to hold onto is one of the great college football stories of all time.

I was so enraptured by the moment that by the time I got into the locker room, Coach Bowden had long since wrapped up his post game speech and some of the players had already showered and were headed home. I never missed another of Coach Bowden's post game speeches but I wouldn't have changed anything about that particular day. For the fans that were there that day it will go down as one of the great sporting moments of their lives, but for me, it was the explosive beginning to the most exciting five years of my life.

The cover of Sports Illustrated read, "Dunn Deal," with a picture of Warrick Dunn escaping the grasp of a Gator tackler. We had completed an 11-0 season capped by a victory over Florida while they were ranked no. 1. The Sugar Bowl awaited us, and as the newly crowned number one we controlled our own destiny… or so we thought.

07

DEFEAT

The Florida victory was one for the ages and had us floating as we headed into the college football postseason. We knew that we were going to New Orleans but we didn't know our opponent. That would be determined the following weekend by the conference championship games. Arizona State was ranked no. 2 and was set to play the fourth-ranked Buckeyes of Ohio State in the Rose Bowl. Nebraska was ranked third going into the inaugural Big XII championship game. They were heavily favored to defeat the unranked Texas Longhorns and meet us in the Sugar Bowl. College football has a way of creating unforeseen drama and Dec. 7 would provide the necessary stage.

Florida rolled in their championship game, beating eleventh-ranked Alabama 45 -30 and making itself an attractive team for the bowls to consider. That night, all eyes were on St. Louis where the matchup of the surprising Longhorns and the defending national champion Cornhuskers was being played. We thought we were scouting Nebraska to prepare for a rematch of the 1994 Orange Bowl when Coach Bowden won his first national championship. Instead, we were watching the resurrection of the Texas program and an unthinkable series of events that would lead to my first taste of defeat as a Seminole.

The 1996 season was the second year of the new Bowl Alliance, which had been established between Notre Dame and five of the major seven conferences, excluding the Big Ten and the Pac-10. The goal was to eliminate subjectivity in the naming of a national champion by getting the top two teams playing against each other in a bowl game. The Rose Bowl produced a wrinkle in their plans because Arizona State won the Pac-10, preventing the second-ranked team from playing in the Bowl Alliance. This left the anticipated matchup between us and Nebraska. Texas had other ideas and taught the Huskers a lesson on the dangers of overlooking an opponent.

In spite of their being unranked, the Longhorns stormed into St. Louis and upset Nebraska by a 37-27 score, sending the Bowl Alliance scrambling to pick up the pieces. Because we had just defeated the Gators, they didn't want to place them into the Sugar Bowl for a rematch. But, their hands were tied because the fourth-ranked team was the Big Ten champion Buckeyes who were also committed to the Rose Bowl. They would be unjustified to select the fifth ranked Brigham Young Cougars, and it would have been counterproductive to their goal of an incontrovertible national champion so the rematch was scheduled.

This was not the first time that Florida and Florida State would hold a rematch game in the Sugar Bowl. The 1994 regular season ended with an unfathomable 28-point fourth-quarter comeback staged by the Seminoles to tie the Gators. The "Choke at Doak" was appropriately followed by "The Fifth Quarter in the French Quarter" as the teams squared off to finish what they started. That rematch carried with it the residue from the previous game in Tallahassee and The Seminoles came away with a 23-17 victory. I feared The 1997 Sugar Bowl wouldn't be as sweet for us. I hated the idea of playing them again but I held onto the hope that they would only be playing for revenge, but we would be playing for the national championship.

The night before we were set to play the Gators, the Rose Bowl was being played and many of us were keeping a close eye on it. Every Seminole, fans and players alike, were rooting for Jake Plummer to lead the Sun Devils over the Buckeyes and eliminate any hopes that UF had for a championship. Arizona State winning would assure them the national championship were we to falter in the Sugar Bowl. We were ecstatic when "Jake the Snake" led the Sun Devils on a drive that gave them the lead with just over a minute remaining. That ecstasy was replaced by dread as Arizona State was called for two pass interference penalties, which led to David Boston's game-winning touchdown catch with just seconds remaining. Florida had to be celebrating because a month earlier their national championship hopes had been stolen by us but now the Buckeyes had given them a chance to return the favor and repair their broken dreams.

Had I been a contributing player I would have felt differently, but since I was nothing more than an overdressed fan for this game, I felt sick watching the end of that Rose Bowl and thinking about our game the next night. I felt like we had been set up to fail and instead of being rewarded for our over achieving victory to end the regular season, we were being punished in a cruel twist of fate.

The game got off to a fast start for Wuerffel and the Gators. He hit Ike Hilliard for a nine-yard touchdown in the first, and we exchanged field goals to cap the first quarter scoring at 10 – 3 in favor of Florida. The game stayed competitive through the second quarter as we stood toe-to-toe and went touchdown-for-touchdown. The Gators' Fred Taylor scored on a two-yard run which E.G. Green answered with a 29-yard reception for the 'Noles,

17-10. Wuerffel would respond with a second touchdown pass to Ike Hilliard, this time for 31 yards. Even though Warrick Dunn was fighting through an illness and only saw limited playing time, he managed a 12-yard scoring run towards the end of the half to make the half time score 24-17.

The second half began well as Scott Bentley nailed a 45-yard field goal to pull us within four at 24-20 but that would be the end of the scoring for us that night. Spurrier kept Wuerffel in the shot gun and kept extra blockers in the backfield to thwart the pass rush from our defensive line. We still got to him five times, but it wasn't enough. Following the Bentley field goal, Wuerffel hit Hilliard for a third time and stretched their lead to 31-20. Coach Spurrier then used the aggressiveness of our line against us and allowed the Gator tailbacks to rack up 168 yards on mostly draw plays. The

Gators scored three more touchdowns in the second half, all on the ground, to pile up 52 points and a convincing victory.

We lost. For the first time in my career as a Seminole, we entered the locker room in defeat. After Wuerffel scored on a 16-yard run in the third quarter, I felt like the loss was inevitable so I was almost numb as we entered the locker room for the last time that year. The Gators were celebrating an improbable championship while we were faced with "maybe next year." I hate that phrase. Sure, it has its place in the off season to motivate for the upcoming year, but in a locker room full of heartbroken warriors it doesn't belong. Many of them were seniors who hoped to provide Coach Bowden with his first undefeated team and a second championship. After an incredible run, including winning the ACC championship every year and a national championship in 1993, they were ending their careers with a loss. Thankfully this class would be remembered for the legendary "Choke at Doak" and the incredible defense of the home turf that season, but losing their last college game to the Gators was miserable. It didn't hit me as hard as it hit them, for obvious reasons, but I could see their pain.

There were a lot of tears in that locker room but like every other year, focus had to be quickly realigned on the next season. Coach Bowden had to hurt with the seniors, yet rally the underclassmen within the same post-game speech and with typical Bowden grace he did just that. He honored the effort and accomplishment of our graduating teammates and used their excellence to fuel those of us left behind with maintaining their legacy. We said goodbye to a group of highly decorated football players that night and began to embrace our new identity embodied by the rising seniors who would lead us into our off-season. For the first time since the Georgia Bulldogs' victory in the 1984 Citrus Bowl, the Seminoles entered an off season following a bowl loss and for the first time in my life, I began a Seminole off season. It began with the dreaded mat drills.

08

"GO BACK!"

GO BACK! The two words that any Seminole player dreads above all others. These two words make Trump's, "You're fired!" seem tame. At least when Trump tells a contestant they're fired, they get to go home. When Coach Amato or Coach Andrews yelled, "GO BACK!" we didn't get to go home; we got to do it again. One more time through the physically grueling, mentally exhausting, and character revealing trial; I'd rather be fired.

The night before mat drills begin, in February, is miserable. An agonizing, sleepless night of checking your clock every thirty minutes to make sure you don't oversleep. The previous year tearing through your mind as you try to think about anything wrong you might have done, and hoping against hope that your name won't be called by Coach Amato the next morning. The night drags on and races by at the same time. The constant ticking of the clock pounds in your ears and your stomach is in knots as you anticipate the spoon.

BANG, BANG, BANG, BANG. At first, the bone chilling sound of the metal spoon being rapped against the steel doors of Burt Reynolds Hall by one of the trainers is a distant sound, but you are alert. Even though the reaper is at one of your teammates' doors you are all too aware that the bell tolls for thee. Every five or ten seconds the shrill clanging would repeat and as the volume increased you could tell it was a few feet closer. Even though you knew it was imminent, the sound of the spoon meeting your door and penetrating the momentary silence was dreadful. Like somebody flushing the toilet with you in the middle of a warm shower and freezing the water; the knocking jolted you to attention. Mercifully, my self-placement into the other Reynolds hall would keep me from being introduced to the spoon until the next fall. By the time the spoon was alerting my teammates to wake up, I was already on my bike and cruising across the sleepy campus.

I arrived at the Moore Center under the dull illumination provided by the parking lot lights; even the sun knows to stay away from the Moore center at 5:30 a.m. in February. My teammates were moping down the concrete steps towards Doak Campbell stadium, which was the only motivating factor in sight. The thought of 80,000 rabid 'Nole fans packing that place in the fall provided just enough oomph to get us into the mat room. Once we were in that torture chamber, listening to the buzz of the fluorescent lights, and feeling everyone's nervous anticipation, the only thought we had about those 80,000 people was the fact that they were safe in bed!

We were told to assemble in one large circle. Everyone was in their team issued work out attire, consisting of garnet shorts with our numbers stenciled on the left thigh and FSU on the right, grey T -shirts with FSU printed across the front, and our shoes. These provided our only armor as we headed into this battle against our coaches, the mat, and ourselves. The awkward silence was broken by the sound of Coach Chuck Amato's enthusiastic steps as he walked to the center of the circle with his ominous black book. The pages of this book contained the offenses of every player in the room who had been late to a meeting, missed a class, talked back to a coach, needed an attitude adjustment, or just happened to be one of Chuck's "favorites."

This is the room where we did mat drills.

He would begin mercilessly shouting out names and if yours was called you had to enter the ring with him. I began to appreciate the subtle cushioning beneath my feet, in the form of an amateur wrestling mat, because I knew I was about to become very familiar with it. The next word out of Coach Amato's mouth would begin the month of agony for the Seminole football team, and with the maniacal grin of a villain taking pleasure in the pain he is about to inflict, he yelled, "FEET!"

The sorry souls in the ring began rapidly running in place until the next command pierced the air, "HIT!" On that word, each of those players rapidly dropped to their chests, letting gravity flatten their bodies on the mat before instantly popping back to their feet and firing their feet once again. This move, designed to be repeated at a coach's discretion, is known as the "up-down." The frequency of someone's name in Amato's black book or the severity of the offense written next to it determined how many "up-downs" they had to endure. Some had 25, a nice little warm-up, while others had upwards of 200, a miserable appetizer for the main course waiting to be served. Once the last of the guys, usually a linebacker because Amato loved pushing them, had managed to get to his feet, the fun began for the rest of us. Fun like running a marathon through the Amazon carrying two squares of shingles.

We were separated into three groups. The "skill" group, made up of receivers, defensive backs, and running backs. The "linemen" composed of the offensive and defensive lines. Finally, there was my group, the group in-between, consisting of tight ends, linebackers, quarterbacks, and the kickers. Just as soon as we were divided, we were sent to our three different areas of torture; two groups to the basketball gym for sprints and Coach Andrew's personal drill, while the remaining group stayed upstairs for "mats."

Mat drills are a vomit-inducing, coach-pleasing, hour of cardio-vascular brutality. They are the worst aspect of being a Seminole football player but at the same time, the tool the coaches used to make us special. We hated going through them but loved what they produced in us.

To perform mats we had to get in groups of five and spread ourselves across the mat end-to-end. The upperclassmen were usually in the first group with the freshmen in the rear. One of the coaches stood in the middle of the mat like a drill sergeant ready to break his new troops. One more coach stood at the far end of the mat. He was the man who determined when we could leave the mat. If you imagine trying to eat one of those two pound steaks to win a free meal, this coach would be the gristle you have to muscle down once the meat has been eaten. There isn't as much of it, but it is hard to swallow. Finally, the rope; the last barrier between us, oxygen, and the 40 seconds of rest we will get while the other groups roll through. Coach Bowden could often be found standing quietly to our left taking mental notes of how we responded to the pain, to the coaches, and to each other. He had a strong group of seniors to replace and he was learning who his leaders were.

Just like the "up-downs," mats began with one word... "READY!" Upon that command, the group on the mat jerked down into "football position." (Football position is simply having your feet about shoulder width apart, your knees bent almost to the point of your thighs being parallel to the ground, your back straight, and your eyes focused in front of you.) "FEET!" Now we began firing our feet like the pistons in a car, up and down as quickly as we could. "HIT!" Like Michael Phelps off the starting block, we leapt from our position, diving flat onto our bellies and as quickly as our chests hit the mat we sprung back to our feet and got them firing again. As we launched into our dive, the group behind us jumped onto the mat, filling the space we just vacated. They had to wait, in football position, for the eyes of the coach on the mat to focus on them.

While they enjoyed the lactic acid burn, we were sent with the flick of a wrist to the left and right until the coach felt that we were done. We had to maintain the rapid pounding of our feet as we shuffled in whatever direction the coach pointed. When he changed direction, we changed direction over and over again. Eventually the coach would have to let us go. He hated to do it, but would agree to let the next coach have at us because that meant he got to torment his next group. He would roll his two hands over each other, or just jerk one hand past his head signaling us to advance.

On his mark, we would dive into a somersault and then sprint to the "gristle coach." We funneled together until we were shoulder to shoulder and kept firing our feet in front of this coach. He would perform a similar hand rolling gesture once he determined we were allowed to sprint off the mat. On his release, we would sprint off the mat about 10 yards and run underneath a rope being held by two trainers. At this point, just like when kids finish their word in a spelling bee, silence is golden. Silence means rest. Silence means everyone in your group met the coach's expectations. But if anyone in your group fell short of perfection... "GO BACK!" We would then have to sprint around the mat back to the beginning, and the group standing at the ready would ever so graciously step off the mat and we would take their place. No rest, no water, no break, just "FEET!" and we would do it all over again. While on the mat the group of five would encourage one another to do the best that we could. But, when our teammates were out there, we hoped for them to fail because the longer they were on the mat the more we got to rest.

Normally, the upperclassmen had it easiest on the mats, and there were two significant reasons for this. First, they had experience on the mats which translated into good form. Second, they were not in the same lines as the young guys, who were being sent back all the time, which led to more rest. Because of the way the positions were separated, I never got to see the skill athletes on the mats. No doubt, those guys were something to behold. But, within my group, nobody out-performed Dan Kendra. He was the only player I knew that actually looked forward to February and mat drills. He was a machine. His natural athleticism and elite conditioning helped, but it was his masochistic infatuation with them that really made the difference. I would equate it to Lance Armstrong reaching the mountain stages in the Tour-de-France.

Dan set out to conquer them while the rest of us were just trying to survive. Dan didn't care what line he was in, but the rest of us were acutely aware of the guys in our group because they represented our fate and having the wrong guy could be brutal.

Being in the larger group with the linebackers was like playing with fire. If you ended up in a mat line with no linebackers in it, chances are you wouldn't go back too often. But, if you got the freshman linebacker, you better pack a lunch. You would be going back more often than a woman trying on wedding dresses. There was no escaping; you just had to find a way to get through it. After 20 of the longest minutes of your life, a trainer would blow the air horn and the rotation would commence. A group from the gym came upstairs, the group on the mats would head down for the wind sprints, and the group sprinting got to spend the next 20 with Coach Andrews... Thank God for wind sprints.

As crazy as it sounds, the wind sprint station was perceived by many as rest. The basketball gym was split in two, length wise, with the sprinting station to the left of center court and Coach Andrews' drill to our right. Our group collected in the left corner of the gym as Coach Sexton readied himself for us. Due to the limited space, we would be in groups of three or four for this drill. The objective was simple. We had to race each other across 75 percent of the court where Coach Lilly was waiting to be sure we were in a full sprint as we crossed the line. If we met his expectations we would jog to the opposite wall and wait for the other groups to finish before the coaches would exchange responsibilities and we would do it again. Twenty minutes of sprinting from one side of the gym to the other provided the necessary recuperation time to complete Coach Andrews' station.

Coach Andrews' station was actually a combination of drills led by multiple coaches but they were nothing more than trimmings; Coach Andrews was the main course. This final rotation was actually divided into three smaller rotations of about seven minutes each. In one part, we had to jump rope for the entire time. The next, was a series of sprints under about a three foot high chute. The last was Coach Andrews.

His drill was very similar to the mats but there was no diving because we were on a gym floor. There was a strip of tape on the floor, half way between the sideline and the free throw line for the hoop on that side of the gym, leaving about seven and a half feet on either side. In groups of three we had to sprint to the tape and face Coach Andrews in a single file formation. He would yell "READY!" and our feet had to start chopping, then without wasting any time, "GO!" and he would point to his left or his right. Whichever way he pointed we had to turn and sprint that direction. We would touch the sideline with our hand, turn 180 degrees and sprint across the expanse to touch the free throw line with our hand, followed by another 180 until we returned to our starting position. Assuming we hadn't totally made a mess of the drill, Coach would send us sprinting past him to make room for the next group. There were no more than three groups with Coach Andrews at any time because the other guys were jumping rope or under the chute. This meant that our rest time was miniscule and Coach got to work us many times. Each time in front of him we had a new variation of the original drill but the premise was the same. Stay low, run fast, and finish the drill. When the equipment managers signaled that the hour was complete, we had literally finished the drill, and we jogged back up to the mat room.

Mats would end with a post agony stretching routine and a few words from the coaching staff. The room was full of the sound of heavy breathing, the sight of thoroughly sweat-saturated T-shirts, and an exhausted sense of accomplishment. We had survived the morning. A quick shower was followed by an even quicker change of clothes so that we had time to eat some breakfast before reporting to our 8:00 a.m. classes. I remember arriving in those classes with my body still sweating and my heart still racing. The "civilian" students who were arriving, still wearing their pajamas and complaining about the time had no idea what had transpired in the early hours that morning. A group of student athletes had given everything they had, both physically and mentally to the cause of becoming great football players and a great football team.

The end of February marked the end of mat drills and the beginning of a season in the weight room and running ramps in the stadium. Our off season conditioning was in full bloom and it would produce immense physical change in all of us, but the spring of 1997 would produce another change in me that I could never have anticipated.

09

FOUR CHAIRS

(Before you read any further I want to preface this chapter. While this book isn't purely about football, it is framed by the context of the game. Up until this point the stories have involved players, coaches, or situations familiar to fans of football. This chapter consists of the same elements but not to the same degree. This book is about my life as a Seminole football player, and in the winter of 1997 my life was altered because of that fact. Before I attended Florida State I did not believe in God, but while there, I came to believe what the Bible records about Jesus Christ. This chapter is the story of how that happened. It involves our strength and conditioning coach, Dave Van Halanger, and it begins at our practices but beyond that the setting leaves the world of college football.

I have written this disclaimer to the fan who began reading this book expecting stories of football and might find this chapter out of place in a book about sports. I can appreciate that, but my faith is as much a part of my years as a Seminole as any game I played or player I competed with. I no longer play the game, I don't watch film, and I don't prepare my body like I once did but my faith is stronger than it ever was and that faith was nurtured under the leadership of Coach Bowden, Coach Richt, Coach Cottrell, Coach Van Halanger, and Coach Lilly. This book would be neither complete nor truthful to leave this chapter out so I would love for you to read it. I hope that I have written it in such a way that you find it as compelling as you have the book up to this point.)

"Hey, Hey Sprague-er, missed ya at FCA last night!" Back in the fall Coach Van would greet me at every Wednesday practice with that phrase. I would be outside with the other guys stretching or tossing a football and he would take advantage of that casual time to invite me and the other guys to F.C.A. Coach Van was the leader of the Fellowship of Christian Athletes huddle for FSU and they met at the stadium on Tuesday evenings. As a freshman Seminole I was obviously not attending those Tuesday night meetings which prompted Van's weekly invite. He didn't really push; but he did always remind me of the milk and cookies.

Some time during the fall, I took him up on his invitation. Even though I don't remember the first time I went, I do remember the chocolate chip cookies and the chocolate milk. The milk was nothing more than the simple little cartons that you see in schools across the country but when coupled with the decadent cookies, they made for a splendid combination. Every Tuesday night, a big platter of those discus sized chocolate chip cookies, made by the staff of Mrs. Betty's kitchen, and an iced cooler full of those cartons of liquid joy awaited us in the lobby of the Moore Center. Before the first word was spoken, the cookies and milk had me hooked and I vowed never to forgo free cookies ever again.

As it turned out, the students involved with FCA were pretty cool too and I thought I could be friends with some of them. There were athletes from the golf team, women's basketball and volleyball. A few baseball players were there, some of the softball girls, and a large group of "civilians." I liked to refer to the student body outside of the athletic departments as civilians because they didn't face the same time structure and physical commitment that the athletes did. Anyway, the people seemed nice and the food was right up my culinary alley so I made Tuesday nights a regular part of my schedule.

GRATEFUL

I don't know what the opposite of a wall-flower is, but whatever it is, I am that thing. From my first night there I made every effort possible to be noticed and make friends. I gave people nick names, shook hands, told loud stories, and volunteered to be in skits when they had them. To be real honest, I like attention and this was a positive environment for me to get some. Well, all that attention seeking proved to be the leverage that God would use to pry me away from myself and open my heart to Him.

Sometime in January or February, announcements began about an upcoming retreat for the high school students of Tallahassee. Every winter the North Florida FCA would hold this retreat and the college groups from FSU and Florida A&M, which is only a couple miles from FSU, would provide the leaders. They were having a hard time recruiting their necessary leaders and the announcements turned to urgent pleas and eventually to begging. In a moment of desperation, I became one of the athletes to whom begging was focused. It wasn't begging in the manner in which I was approached, it was begging in the fact that it was me who they were approaching. It was like a group of kids being forced to add the short kid to their basketball team because there was no one else available; I wasn't a Christian and I didn't pretend to be.

I liked the people at FCA and I loved the free cookies, but when I heard the word Genesis, I was thinking of Phil Collins and not the Bible. However, I was an athlete, I was not afraid of crowds, and I enjoyed people, so the director took a chance and invited me to come as a leader. While it was laughable to think of me leading a Bible study, my desire for attention trumped my ignorance of anything spiritual so I agreed to save the day. The last weekend of February, after mat drills had finished, I joined my fellow leaders and headed to Marianna, Fla.

The camp looked like an ant hill that had just been disturbed as middle school students swarmed all over. They were hauling sleeping bags, flirting, playing soccer, flirting, practicing cheer routines, and flirting. What else is to be expected from 300 sixth, seventh, and eighth grade kids away from home for a weekend? The combination of body odor doused in an inordinate amount of cologne produced a smell that was as oppressive as the fog in San Francisco. These would be the kids I would spend the weekend with and some of us would have the paths of our lives forever changed.

FCA does a good job with their camps. They are high energy and very athletic. The food was, well, camp food but that's part of the fun. Each day there would be a large group gathering where someone would teach from the Bible, and then us college students had the task of leading a discussion with the kids in a small group setting. It's funny how being given the responsibility of leading and teaching made me pay attention in the big group talks, I didn't want to look stupid. The small group times seemed to go pretty well; I felt like I was able to comprehend the teacher's points enough to answer the kids' questions but I knew I was walking blind. I didn't really have a clue at all, but I don't think the kids noticed.

Everything changed for me on the last night at the camp. The main teacher gave his talk and then he provided an illustration to bring the weekend home. The room was silent as he went and picked up four of those grey, aluminum folding chairs one at a time and placed them in the front of the room facing all of us. There was an apprehension in the place for fear of being asked to come and sit in one of the chairs. Thankfully he spared us that embarrassment, but his explanation of the chairs was harder to swallow than that embarrassment would have ever been.

"This is chair one, and chair one represents people like Billy

Graham. These are people who everybody knows as a Christian; people who leave no doubt about their faith. These are people who live as if they are going to Heaven when they die. They are involved in their church. They carry themselves with a forgiving and joyful attitude. They love people and place others needs and desires in front of their own. When you spend time with these people, you find yourselves drawn to them and curious to know why they are different. They are authentic and inspiring people who so impress us that we will even place these people up on pedestals sometimes. Chair one represents obvious, genuine Christians."

Walking past the two chairs in the middle, he focused his attention and ours on chair number four. "This chair," he explained, "is an obvious person too. This person doesn't believe in God and makes no bones about it. He doesn't go to church, doesn't pray, and doesn't care to. Beyond the absence of love and good deeds in this person's life, you would also find immorality. Where Billy Graham might be in a prison ministering to the incarcerated, chair four would be one of the convicted. As boldly as chair number one exudes faith, chair number four exudes disbelief. Chair number four represents someone who is obviously not a Christian."

Up to this point in the illustration I was following along just fine and taking copious notes. Chair one, Billy Graham; chair four, Freddy Krueger. But chairs number two and number three struck a little closer to home as the teacher moved away from the extremes and into my reality.

"Number two," he went on, "is a person who is a little tougher to identify. This person isn't a church person but seems to be a pretty good person. They don't steal from anyone and they love their family. They don't dislike the church necessarily and they might even go on the holidays. They probably wouldn't talk about church for fear of being rude or appearing judgmental to someone with different beliefs. Chair number two represents a person who isn't opposed to faith necessarily, and might even be leaning towards belief, but they aren't in active pursuit of it. If pressed, this person would tell you that they didn't believe fully in God, but they would be open to the idea."

Finally, he stood behind chair number three. He didn't speak immediately; he just looked down at the chair and let the silence marinate over us for a moment. Some people might have been reflecting on the previous three chairs and which one represented them, but not me. So far he hadn't described me so I was simply sitting comfortably and listening to him make his points while I considered questions to ask my group.

"This chair!" his shout rang through the room, shattering the tense silence. "This chair," now in a calmer but firm voice, "is the most frustrating chair. This person is the double agent, the person in disguise, the one who is deceiving everybody... everybody except God. This person behaves like a first chair but believes like a fourth chair. They go to church and attend the camps but they are playing games. They might enjoy Christianity like a businessman enjoys a Rotary Club but they have no faith. The trouble is nobody knows because they live two separate lives. On Sunday, they are the first person at church but just as likely to be the first at the club on Saturday night. They are walking contradictions; social chameleons. Maybe they aren't wicked, but they know in their hearts that they don't believe; yet they willingly participate in the charade to feel like they are in the club. They might know the lingo and wear the right clothes, but they knowingly don't believe."

All of the sudden he picked up the folding chair and threw it sideways against the cinder block wall. It was like the shrill sound of barking inside a dog pound. The room was not designed for acoustics, so there was no soft material to absorb the clanging and scraping of aluminum against concrete and tile. His move commanded our attention in much the same way as a man shooting a hand gun into the sky amidst a crowd of unruly people. My eyes were fixed on him.

Every word of description he attributed to this third chair could very easily be used for me as well. If I was a chair, I was this one. My family had attended a Catholic church until I was about 10 years old. But, about that time I was banned from the Sunday School program and that was about the end of my religious experience. My friend, Toby Watt, brought me with him to a camp my junior year of high school and it was eye-opening for me. Although attending the camp prompted me to go with him to his church youth group a couple of times, I really was no different because of it. In college, I had been "playing church" with the FCA group and presenting myself as a Christian when I knew that I didn't believe what they were preaching. I was that third chair. Needless to say, he had captivated me.

The teacher continued his illustration by explaining the consequences of living in the third chair. "The book of Revelation (the last book of the Bible) says that God vomits the lukewarm person out of His mouth." This explains why the chair was thrown into the wall. He continued, "If you believe that you are represented by this third chair, then I am speaking to you. You need to get off the proverbial fence and make a decision, either you believe in Jesus or you don't, but stop playing games. Don't try to make people believe that you are something that you're not, be real!"

I was stunned by the weight of his comments, and he continued. "Here's the bottom line, you aren't perfect, none of us are. God is perfect and you have separated yourself from Him by your sin. If you were to die that sin would leave you red handed before God. You would be separated from Him for eternity. The Bible tells us that." This truth was convicting. Thankfully, he didn't leave me in my guilt.

"This is the good news we call the gospel, Jesus came into the world to save sinners. Jesus paid the price that our sin demanded and upon believing that truth and trusting His saving work on the cross, our relationship with God can be restored. We can accept the debt canceling work of Jesus and live at peace with the Creator of the universe! The gift is on the table and the question you must ask yourself is, do you believe it? Better yet, do you believe Him?"

His words penetrated my heart and left it pounding. I knew I had never believed any of this stuff before, yet now I found myself believing it. What I had once seen as boring and pointless, I now was seeing in a new light. There was no arguing that I wasn't perfect. Even though I couldn't tell you anything about it, deep down I believed that there was a God. I was stuck. This God I couldn't describe had offered to love me in spite of myself and I had to do something with that. I believed it! I believed that Jesus' death on the cross could redeem me. So I responded. When he asked if anyone believed what he had explained to stand up, I considered it.

I was embarrassed. I felt stupid. I knew that there was nothing magical in standing up, but I also knew that I believed it. So, as a couple of the kids in my group stood up to make their new belief known, I stood up with them. A couple five foot tall middle school girls and a 6'5" college football player standing next to each other as equals in the sight of God, once lost but now found. I didn't know it then, but this moment in time would be more impactful on my future than any moment on the field. While I had the opportunity to test my wares in the NFL, that time was short lived. My faith, on the other hand, has been strengthened over the years so much that I am writing this book while serving as a minister of Jesus Christ.

Coach Bowden is obviously renowned as a football coach but many also know him for his faith. He never forced his faith on us while we played for him but he wasn't shy about sharing it either. His boldness and leadership created an environment for his coaches to practice their faith as well. It was this uncompromising commitment to God that paved the way for Coach Van Halanger to be so involved with FCA and invite us to participate with him. Coach Richt often included times of devotion and reflection on Jesus in his meetings. Truth be told, Coach Richt's faith in Christ stemmed from a conversation he had with coach Bowden after a Seminole player lost his life at a party. My position coach, John Lilly, would regularly have passages from the Bible on his board to inspire us and when we were challenged to articulate annual goals he always included spiritual ones right alongside our athletic and academic ones. Jesus Christ was simply part of the experience of playing football for Bobby Bowden. It never interfered with our preparation for the game we were there to play, but it was evident in every aspect of our lives as surrogate grandchildren of Bobby Bowden. Some of us came to share his beliefs while others did not but we all respected the fact that he was an authentic man who lived what he believed and many of us owe our lives to him.

Freshman:
August of 1997
thru July of 1998

10

FULL RIDE

With the retreat behind me and my head still spinning from all that had occurred, I had to jump right back into everyday life. There were just a couple weeks of classes before my first run at spring practice was to begin and I didn't even know what position I would be playing.

In my development as a football player, the previous fall did more for that process than any other time. I was grossly undersized; I felt like Olive Oyl with a whole bunch of Popeyes and Blutos around me. Every player on the field had more experience with the game of football and 95 percent of them were very, very good at it. Where I wasn't even the best at Lakeside High School, most of my scout team partners were big time high school stars simply paying their dues. The guys I was assigned to block were not just the best from their high schools or the best at FSU; these guys were the best in the Atlantic Coast Conference and a couple were the best at their position in the country! It was ridiculous to ask me to compete with these guys. But you know what, nobody ever apologized for asking me to block them and nobody entertained the thought that it was unreasonable. I was shown an assignment and expected to pull it off, that's life as a football player at FSU. You are expected to get the job done, period.

94

I spent more time in the backfield that autumn than some of the running backs as the two forklifts playing defensive tackle effortlessly planted me there time and again. Not that I arrived at FSU under the delusion that I was much of a football player, but those arduous months squeezed the last drops of pride out of me and prepared me for the rest of my career. I had chosen Florida State for the rings but I learned real quickly that those rings didn't come cheap.

God designed me as a bit of a late bloomer, and between the day I reported in August of '96 to the first day of spring ball in March of '97, I put on almost 40 pounds of good weight. At close to 250 pounds, my body looked a lot more like a prototypical tight end. After struggling through a full season on the scout team as an undersized center, the coaches approached me about actually trying to learn the position. Coach Sexton was the first to mention it to me. "Ryan, you have O.K. feet for a tight end but you could have excellent feet for a center." That's coach-speak for "Ryan, you're not very fast but at least you're not very quick either."

I had a tight end's body with a center's speed and agility, so the coaches played the odds and moved me officially to center. We had a veteran center in Kevin Long, who was going into his senior season and there were only two other centers on our roster. Eric Thomas was Long's backup and Jarad Moon, who was in my class, backed Thomas up. Both of those guys were over 280 pounds, could bench press small cars, and had played center for years. That's how much hope the coaches had for me to make it as a tight end. The idea was that I would keep putting on weight and learn the intricacies of the position well enough to give Moon a run for his money one day. But I had never played any real center in my life. In my 6 years of playing football, I had more experience as a quarterback than I did as a center. Seminole kickers are more comfortable lining up for field goals against Miami than I was with the prospect of playing center, but those were my marching orders, so I put on my boots.

I began spring practice as the fourth string center, which I guess is better than fourth string tight end. Spring isn't as intense as the fall because there are no games on the immediate horizon. We still watched film and practiced in the afternoons, but there was much more teaching in spring ball, and that's what I desperately needed. Day after day, I was working on the fundamentals of blocking under the direction of Offensive Line Coach, Jimmy Heggins. The tight ends have to run routes and catch passes so they don't spend anywhere near the amount of time working on blocking fundamentals as the offensive line. That spring provided a vitally necessary foundation for me in my development as a complete football player.

Spring practice was good because I advanced significantly in my technique. I believed I had a good session of mat drills back in February too. I always felt confident on the mats because of all the time I spent on them as a high school wrestler. There really are no skills that translate from wrestling to mat drills but psychologically I felt strong. Neither mat drills nor spring practice saw me advance on the depth chart, but I believed I advanced in the eyes of the coaches. Football was complete for that semester. We were still required to be in the weight room, but outside of that, we just had to finish up our spring classes and get ready for summer conditioning. The summer was college paradise. We would sleep in, go work out, hit the pools, and spend hours playing Mario Cart on the Nintendo 64. It doesn't get much better than that for a 19-year-old guy. The only problem was that I wasn't sure if I was going to be able to stay at FSU.

A "walk-on" is simply an athlete who is participating on a

college athletic team but does not have the benefit of a scholarship. There is both a stigma and a brotherhood associated with being a walk-on. We were treated differently than the scholarship guys and rightly so, but it is that "second class" treatment that bonded us together. Once we got over the humiliation, we began to take pride in the fact that we were number 138 or 115 instead of 44 or 83. We embraced our private uniforms made up of the shoes that Nike wasn't proud of and hand-me-down gloves. We also shared the dream of rising from the ranks of walk-on, to former walk-on, and receiving a scholarship.

For me, a scholarship represented being able to remain at FSU. The United States government happily loaned me roughly $20,000 to go to FSU as an out of state student for a year, but doing it a second year was highly improbable. My parents and I were struggling with getting more loans to chase the dream or enrolling at an in-state school that was more affordable. I wanted a scholarship bad but I never in a million years believed I would be given one. In spite of that, we decided to give it one more year.

Two-a-days cranked up that August and signaled the beginning of another football season. When preseason camp rolled around, I was given jersey no. 67 and my life as an offensive lineman continued. There is no denying that being an O-lineman is the least glamorous of all the positions on a football team and I could never get myself to embrace that lifestyle fully. Call it pride, call it self-preservation, but I never let go of the dream of playing tight end for the Seminoles. That's what I wanted and I would often catch myself watching the tight ends practice, resting on one knee with my helmet in my hands, while K. Long, E.T. and Moon worked at center. I wanted to be on the team more than I wanted my way, and deep down I knew the coaches' reasoning was correct so I gave everything I had in '97 to becoming a great center, but my career took another unexpected turn.

Early in two-a-days, Coach Cottrell began alluding to the fact that if I kept my effort up I might be in the running for a scholarship. At this point, I was practicing with the offensive line but still spent a little bit of time with the tight ends. Most days, I would stay with Coach Heggins for the day, but sometimes I would split time between him and Coach Cottrell. I just kept my head down and I kept the pedal to the metal at practice. If they needed me to snap, then I would snap. If they needed me spelling the tight ends, then I would do it happily. I viewed it all as opportunities to be on film and in front of the coaches. It gave me two coaches who were familiar with me and I certainly don't think that hurt. Day after day, Coach Cottrell would drop me a signal to keep it up because Coach Bowden was watching and every day I took him at his word.

Towards the end of camp, as we were walking off the field at the end of practice, Coach Cottrell told me I needed to go up to Coach Bowden's office after I got dressed. My heart skipped a beat. I was certainly hopeful that it was good news, but I had never spoken to Coach Bowden before and I was awestruck by the idea of going up to his office. I showered in a hurry that day and changed my clothes quicker than Superman in a phone booth. I scooted out of the locker room and went straight for the elevator. Normally I would press two because our meetings were on the second floor, but this time I pressed three. I was going to the coaches' offices; more specifically I was going to *the* coach's office.

I stepped off the elevator and into relatively familiar surroundings. Coach Cottrell's office was to my right just past the recruiting secretary, Carol Moore's desk. I had stood in this spot before and had been to Coach Cottrell's office, but in front of me was an open door leading into the bowl trophy room and the entrance to Coach Bowden's office. I never really felt qualified to walk through that door, but on that day I had been summoned, so I walked in. I was standing in a large room and to my right, were dozens of trophies representing all the different bowl games that the 'Noles had won under coach Bowden. Behind those trophy cases, about 30 feet away from me on the back wall, there was a huge picture of the 1993 National Championship team. On the wall opposite me were paintings of some of the great Seminole players like, Deion Sanders and Ron Simmons. To my left, within my reach, was the desk of the secretary for our Athletic Director of football, Andy Urbanic. His office was through the door behind her desk. Just past her desk was the desk of Sue Hall. Mrs. Sue was Coach Bowden's personal assistant, and she was wearing a great big smile on her face. She must have sensed my nervousness because she enthusiastically motioned for me to go on in.

I walked past her desk, past the painting of "Prime Time" and timidly knocked on his door. I waited for a response and when he said to come in, I slowly entered the room. His office was rectangular in shape with Coach's desk far to my left. In front of me, the long wall was almost entirely glass. Mostly windows but with a glass door, it overlooked the field of Doak Campbell Stadium from behind the end zone. His desk was dark mahogany, and the resting place for more trophies and memorabilia. Between me and the desk were about 15 feet of carpet and two garnet, leather chairs with their backs to me. On the floor, directly in front of, and centered against his desk was a large, triangular piece of slate. It had a gold hue and had been carved, leaving the word "SEMINOLES" and the iconic Indian head logo raised off the smooth surface of the stone. On the left side of his desk, there was a small grouping of books, including a Bible, and a book titled, "Bear," in reference to Paul "Bear" Bryant. The center of his desk held a pewter, half-football trophy commemorating the 1980 Orange Bowl where FSU battled Oklahoma. That game was Coach Bowden's first major bowl at FSU and first shot at an undefeated season. Unfortunately, the Sooners defeated the 'Noles 24-7. A little past that trophy sat a simple little name plate that read, "Mr. Bowden."

Behind his desk sat a built in display case that stretched from the floor almost to the ceiling. At the very top of the cabinet was an actual alligator head with an authentic Seminole tomahawk planted into it. Each glass encased compartment held a different item. There was a statue of Chief Osceola riding on Renegade with his famous spear held over his head, a couple trophies, some footballs, pictures of his extensive family, a sculpture of two hands pressed together as if they were praying, a crystal vase, a few historical military artifacts, and for reasons I would learn a few years later, an empty picture frame.

Coach was sitting behind his desk autographing footballs by the bag full. He looked up from his work, smiled, and in a matter-of-fact manner said to me, "Congratulations." He asked me to sit down and told me that he had noticed my efforts and he had decided to put me on scholarship. While I began dreaming of winning my Heisman trophy he said to me, "This is only a one year scholarship. You are going to have to work to keep it." Maybe the Heisman campaign was premature, but I had what I had been hoping for, a full athletic scholarship to play football for Florida State University! He offered his hand. I shook it, and babbled something resembling, "Thank You sir, you won't be disappointed," and I skipped out of his office. I was in there for less than two minutes before I quickly ran over to the compliance office to sign the scholarship papers.

Just like that, I had arrived. I was excited, so I called my parents to tell them the incredible news. When they were on the phone I told them that they wouldn't have to worry about paying for college that year. They dryly responded with, "why?" I boasted, "I got a scholarship!" My parents, God bless 'em, responded with something along the lines of, "yeah, sure, what's really going on?" I tried to convince them that I wasn't kidding, but the unbelievable story was just that. As the conversation ended they still didn't believe my account, but that didn't squelch my enthusiasm.

The next day when I showed up at practice, I had a new locker with the team and not in the walk-on corner. My number 138 clothes had been replaced with a double-digit number. Believe it or not, I do not remember what that number was. I wore seven in my first three years: 138, 67, 65, 39, 87, 82, and finally 85. I was practicing in the no. 67 but never wore that in a game, so I do not recall which one I initially received on my locker. The numeral was irrelevant anyway, what mattered was that it was no longer triple digits! My clunker shoes had been replaced with the authentic, team-issue Nikes. My locker room location had changed as well; no longer was I on the walk-on aisle. Now I was situated with the linemen and tight ends. I was a full-fledged scholarship athlete… in Tallahassee at least. My parents still did not believe I had earned a scholarship. The next morning, however, I was the recipient of a gleeful phone call from my parents.

The Augusta Chronicle ran a little blurb in the sports section from the press release issued by Florida State. It took the local paper writing an article for them to accept the truth, but they believed now, and they were proud! I was floating at practice that day and I was thrilled with life when I went to bed that night. Now that I was on scholarship, one of the first things I was required to do was move my stuff over to 215 Hayden Road, the address of Burt Reynolds Hall. A year overdue, but I was moving into the football dorm, just across the street from Doak Campbell. My new roommate was freshman tight end, Carver Donaldson.

Burt isn't exciting. There is a prestige about it, because it is the football dorm and many of the Seminole greats lived there at one time. Beyond that, it provides modest housing at best. The design is simple, featuring three, two-story buildings arranged in a "U" shape with the parking lot and a small pool in the center. They finished construction in 1988, and it was built primarily with concrete and cinder block. Each apartment slept two guys and contained a simple living room, small kitchen, smaller bathroom, and a bedroom that the roommates shared. The Seminole Boosters named the facility after former Seminole tailback and Hollywood star, Burt Reynolds. He has generously supported the university with financial gifts and by promoting the school in his different television and movie projects, and honoring him in this way was their way of saying, "Thank you." In spite of it being 20 years old and bland aesthetically, I was ecstatic to be living there. Reynolds hall, on campus, was newly renovated and much nicer, but living in Burt helped to unite me with my teammates and the generations of Seminoles who had gone before me. It's a part of the nostalgia of being a Seminole and I considered it a privilege to be moving in. It was a great day! But it's funny how quickly things can change. Just a few hours, later I would be on the phone contemplating quitting the team, running away from Tallahassee, and not saying a word to anybody.

11

SLEEPING IN

I went to bed beaming. I was a full scholarship football player for the Florida State Seminoles; are you kidding me? If you would have told me, as a senior in high school, that I would have played football beyond high school, much less possess a full-ride, much-much less for the dynasty that was Florida State, I would have called you crazy. But sure enough, as I laid my head on my pillow I was entering slumber as a full-fledged Seminole. Unfortunately, my slumber lasted a bit too long.

It was a Saturday morning and we had a kicking scrimmage scheduled. A kicking scrimmage was a glorified walk-thru so that we could work on the special teams while at the same time avoiding undue stress because we would have a full scrimmage that evening. That being said, the kicking scrimmage was much shorter than a traditional practice and that would loom large.

I turned over in my bed to look at my clock and if I hadn't been in bed already, I would have fallen over. I wasn't running late and forced to scramble to get to practice... practice had already begun! I had received a scholarship about 12 hours prior and now sat in my bed with my face in my hands, horrified and humiliated by the fact that I had slept in and was missing my first practice as a scholarship player. I was in shock! In fact, I actually began packing because I had every intention of jumping in my car and driving back to Augusta without a word to anyone. I felt terrible. I was mortified at the thought of facing Coach Cottrell, who had stuck his neck out for me and Coach Bowden, who ultimately bestowed the scholarship on me. Would they strip me of it? Would I be kicked off the team? Would I have to run a marathon of stadiums? Or would they contrive something even worse than I could imagine? I kept packing.

Is there anything more disrespectful or low than being granted a scholarship only to skip out, unannounced on your very next practice? I imagined the coaches responding like Clark Griswold in "Christmas Vacation" when he received his Christmas bonus of a membership to the jelly of the month club. I would be dragged in front of them in chains by one of the graduate assistants to face the wrath of the scorned legend. I kept packing.

In a moment of serenity and desperation I called my oldest sister, Jennifer, and explained my dilemma. To this day she has no concept of the game of football but she offered sage advice to this humiliated athlete that Saturday morning. Her counsel was simple and to the point, "go to practice and take it like a man," although those weren't her specific words. She managed to calm my nerves and assure me that they would at least obey the laws of Florida so I decided to stop packing and head over to Doak to face the reaper.

I was in Doak when we lost to NC State on homecoming in 2001. I was there when we lost to Miami on the last play in 2009. I was in the Orange Bowl when we laid an egg and handed the national championship to Oklahoma. By far and away, walking out of the locker room towards the field that morning was the worst I have ever felt in a football stadium. Pure misery.

I was wearing shorts, a T-shirt, and a pair of flip-flops. As I headed towards the turf I passed my armored teammates walking off the field and into the locker room. I received a comment or two from my teammates who lack the gift of tact or sensitivity. The first coach I saw was our offensive line coach, Jimmie Heggins. He had a reputation for mincing few words and unashamedly mixing character shots within the football critique.

I cringed as his eyes met mine. He quickly closed his eyes, dropped his head, and shook it back and forth as if he was saying no, and started chuckling. I wasn't quite comfortable with that response because it sounded much more like the maniacal laugh of a Hollywood villain before they would blow something up. Surprisingly, he did nothing more that laugh at me but the next man I saw was Ronnie Cottrell, my coach at the time.

I can only imagine how pitiful I must have looked with my glue pale face and melancholy posture, but I must have been a sight. Coach Cottrell dealt with me with the sensitivity of a dog lover finding a starving stray in their yard. He placed his hand on my shoulder and just asked, "What happened?" I shared my plight and told him of my packed bags and my willingness to take myself back to Georgia. He just laughed, put his other hand on my other shoulder and with his southern drawl said, "Don't do that, it's going to be fine. We all mess up sometimes."

I was speechless. I received a stay of execution! Interestingly enough, I didn't feel happy. I felt almost worse. Where was the yelling and screaming? Where was Cousin Eddie's Winnebago? I must have looked confused because Coach Cottrell eased my mind by saying, "you are going to become real familiar with those stadium steps." Sweet relief.

Now, I felt happy. I had been acquitted but I also got to earn my way back by running all 85 steps of Doak S. Campbell stadium many, many, many times. In light of what could have been, I smiled every time I labored up those steps. The remainder of preseason camp was uneventful, as we prepared for our first game of the season against the Trojans of Southern California.

12

PLAYING TIME

About three quarters of the way through preseason camp we began working on our special teams plays with regularity. Coach Sexton was the coach in charge of the offensive special teams which were the field goal team and the kickoff return (KOR) team. My involvement on the field goal team was almost a given because we would line up with four tight ends to perform kicks. Two would line up at the end of the line of scrimmage, right next to the tackles; and two would line up as either wing-back, angled just behind the outside leg of the tight end. I didn't expect to find a home on the KOR team but Coach Sexton decided to give me a shot there too, and that would give me the opportunity to be on the field for the first play of the 1997 season.

It's a good thing that I was given the scholarship because I doubt if I would have been able to drive all the way to Los Angeles. I had traveled officially with the team to the Sugar Bowl last season, but this was my first time traveling as a scholarship athlete. This trip would provide a string of firsts for me and my family. My first ever trip to California, my first time playing in a college football game, and the first game my parents weren't in the stands for. They made every trip to Tallahassee in '96 even though they never saw me on the field. The L.A. trip was simply cost prohibitive for them so we shared this moment through the miracle of television.

The game was a collection of firsts for Florida State as well. It was, of course, the first game of the season. This was the first time we began a season on the road since 1988. This was the first time we had ever played USC, and it would be the first close call of the year. We were ranked no. 5 in the preseason polls and the Trojans were ranked no. 21, but as is often the case in season openers, the teams played a sloppy game.

More than 72,000 fans crowded into the Los Angeles Memorial Coliseum to see us battle the Trojans that day and after the coin toss it was determined that we would receive the ball first; I was going to be on the field for the very first play! And this wasn't just any field. This field had been in use since 1923 and was rich with history. I was about to play football on the same field that O.J. Simpson and Marcus Allen used to win their Heisman Trophies, and Ronnie Lott used to launch his Hall of Fame career. I was going to run in the same place as Carl Lewis when he won four gold medals in the 1984 Olympics. This was the same site that football entered the world stage as an exhibition event at the 1932 Summer Olympics. I was treading on hallowed ground. History aside, I was about to play in a college football game, in front of more than 70,000 people at the stadium, and millions watching on the television. I was so revved up that I nearly hurt myself.

"KOR!! KOR!!" Coach Sexton began screaming as soon as the official signaled that we were going to receive. I strapped up my helmet and ran to him to be accounted for and hear the play call. The majority of the KOR team is underclassmen so Coach began counting helmets to make sure we were all there. Getting a delay of game penalty or being flagged for only having ten men on the field would have been a bad way to begin the year. Once he was certain that we were all present and accounted for, he gave us the play and we were ready to go. The officials signaled for the teams to take the field and we ran out to our positions. My location was just behind the front line of blockers on about the 40-yard line and when I arrived there I had a few moments to kill. I was amped and I couldn't sit still, so I began hopping up and down as I tried to identify my assignment. Once I had identified my man I thought it would be important to get in a last second stretch to be sure I didn't pull a muscle. I quickly spread my legs and flung my head down towards my left knee with such intensity that I strained my left hamstring. I came perilously close to pulling the thing in all my excitement, but I popped back up and got ready for the play.

The ball was kicked and I was off, sprinting like Carl Lewis and ready to truck somebody like Ronnie Lott but in reality, I just blocked my man while Germaine Stringer returned the kick about 24 yards and the 1997 season was underway. I would only see the field three more times that day, twice following our two touchdowns and once more on KOR after USC's lone score. We escaped the legendary Coliseum with a 14-7 victory but the score was irrelevant to me. We had erased the foul taste of our only loss from the previous year and I had just played football for the Florida State Seminoles!

Our next game was our first one at home and my first chance to experience a full game day routine with the Seminoles, and it began on Friday.

13

GAME DAY

On Fridays, before a home game in Doak Campbell, we would make our pilgrimage to Thomasville, Georgia, to spend the night and get mentally ready for game day. Many of the guys disliked this trip because it was designed to keep us away from the night life in Tallahassee and keep "distractions" away from us. I always liked the trip because it signaled the beginning of the game experience. We would meet around 3 p.m. at the stadium after everyone had finished class and get on board the team bus. This bus was a piece of work. It had to be 20 years old and was easily the most outdated resource in use by the athletic department. It had a single red stripe running the length of the bus on each side, and the rest was a shade of silver. The local Taltran buses would have been an improvement, but I still loved it. It was our bus, and it was the eve of game day!

Once everyone arrived, including Marvin "Snoop" Minnis in one of his trademark, sapphire blue zoot suits with matching sapphire blue shoes, we would be on our way. After about an hour long road trip, we would arrive at the hotel and get checked in. Check-in was fantastic! We would pick up our room keys from

Clint Purvis, the team chaplain or Randy Oravetz, the team's head trainer, and pick up our afternoon snack. The snack consisted of a Papa John's pepperoni pizza, a frosty from Wendy's, and a drink. This poor health content might be why Dan Kendra would pack his own food, but the rest of the guys loved this stuff. We would go by the rooms, drop off our bags, eat some pizza and kill time until the team dinner.

Dinner was pretty consistently grilled chicken breasts, baked potatoes, pasta, some veggies, etc. Normally I would eat with the O-linemen who turned me on to two great culinary delights. The first was dipping my chicken in ranch dressing and the second was to pour a little whole milk in our vanilla ice cream. Every calorie helps, I guess. Added fat or not, it was good and I ate it every Friday night of the football season. Nothing finer.

After dinner, Coach Bowden would address us as a team. This would be a very matter-of-fact speech going over the game plan, simple things like not turning the ball over, etc. One of the unique components of this time was when Coach would wrap up the football portion and share from his heart for about 10 minutes. At this time, he would read us a passage from the Bible and share some wisdom. More often than not, it had to do with the fact that football is a game, and life is much greater than the game we played. He would present the message of Jesus to the team and simply encourage all of us to seriously consider what Jesus claimed. No choir music, no emotional overtures, just a bare bones accounting and a challenge for us to contemplate life's biggest question; "what will happen when I die?" Granted, I am a Christian, but I always felt he did a good job of presenting his faith succinctly and sensitively so as not to alienate the guys who did not share his belief, and yet give plenty of opportunity for people to consider what Christianity was all about. Following this time, he would fold up his notes, point to the coordinators and tell us to, "get with our coaches."

We would split into our offensive and defensive teams and have a last minute crash course of our game plan. We'd go over any new plays we installed that week, the favorite blitzes of our opponent, and our overall strategy for how we would attack them. Often times, it wasn't a whole lot more complicated than our players being better than their players and we just needed to execute our game plan, simple yet effective. After that, we might have a meeting with our position coaches, but most Friday nights the position coaches would be at a high school game on the recruiting trail. So, we would meet with the graduate assistants for a brief meeting. Imagine a middle school classroom with a substitute teacher and you have a pretty good taste of what those meetings were like. When those wrapped up, the football portion of the night was complete.

About 9 p.m., some of us would attend a little Bible study that Clint Purvis always led. We would study God's word for a few minutes, pray for each other, laugh together, and remind each other of our priorities and convictions. Accountability is a much needed and beneficial tool within the context of a college football team. We'd break from that meeting and then head to our rooms.

Some guys would read, some would watch TV, some would go over plays, and others went straight to sleep. But we all were getting amped for tomorrow... game day.

SATURDAYS

The best 12 days of a college football player's year are game days. The night before is a combination of Christmas Eve and the night before a final exam; full of anxiety and eager anticipation. We would wake up in our hotel rooms, throw on our team issued jumpsuits and make our way to the dining room for our breakfast. The hotel would provide a buffet style breakfast with scrambled eggs, grits, sausage and bacon, bagels, oatmeal, and various other classic breakfast foods depending on our location. Other than being on time for the meal, we had no responsibilities during breakfast so many of the guys would eat quick and head back to their rooms. I always had cabin fever so I would linger in the dining room until most of the guys were done and reluctantly head to my room. Traditionally, we were up by 8 a.m. so there was plenty of time to kill before we would make our way to the stadium. If we had a dreaded noon kickoff, the whole morning schedule shifted dramatically, but those were rare occurrences.

Our practice was to leave the hotel about four hours prior to kick-off when we were in Thomasville. After the drive back to Florida, we would still have around three hours until game time and about 90 minutes until warm-ups began. The initial part of the game day drive was uneventful but as we crossed the state line the mood began to change. Overnight, the city of Tallahassee had been transformed into a college football wonderland and the anticipation was fantastic. Our police escort would lead us onto Stadium Drive and into a sea of Garnet and Gold. RVs were parked all down the street with fans lining the curb doing the War Chant and cheering as our bus cruised past. One time, on our trip in to play the Gators, we were taunted in a memorable way by a Florida fan. At around 45 years old, wearing a blue T-shirt, denim shorts, and a Gator visor she appeared harmless. She came running from her parking spot to be closer to our bus, and as we approached, she did a 180, dropped her pants, and mooned the whole team. We should have been speechless, but instead, the guys let her have it. I don't know what message she intended to send, but she certainly provided a laugh.

The closer we got to the stadium, the thicker the crowds became until we reached our destination and walked into Doak Campbell to the cheers of our fans. My pregame routine was a mix of superstition, time killing, and distraction. Linebacker Brian Allen's approach was totally opposite of mine as he affixed his game face the moment his feet touched the Earth in Tallahassee. He was ready to play and he allowed the waiting to stir himself into a frenzy. I didn't want to put my gear on and then just wait, so I would read the game day program. I milked it for all it was worth as I tried to burn as much time off the countdown clock as possible. When I ran out of articles I would begin the process of getting suited up for the game.

This was when the headphones would go on and the CD player would turn on. I am pretty sure that my pregame soundtrack was unique to my team and maybe to the entire football world. More often than not, I was listening to *NSYNC. *(Please don't put the book down. We all have skeletons in our closets, don't we?)* Sometimes I would listen to Creed but I tried to stay away from the intense stuff. My style was to try and stay as relaxed as possible, leading up to when I would actually put my helmet on. Once it was time to strap everything on, my mood would change drastically so I delayed until the last minute.

About one hour before kickoff we would make our way onto the field for the warm-up sessions. This was always a favorite time of mine because we were on the field, in our gear, but didn't have to be completely focused on the game. It was in this time that I could really absorb my environment by listening to the crowd, searching the stands for my family, and marinating in the reality that I was actually on the field and about to play.

Our warm-ups were pretty standard stuff with the exception of three Seminole traditions. The first was when the entire team had assembled on the field and we performed our pregame stretching routine. The stretching itself was no different than any other team in America, but when we were finished Coach Bowden had installed a unique exercise we called the "flip drill." On a whistle we would snap down into "football position," accompanied by more than 100 voices shouting, "hah!" Another whistle and we would drop into a squatting position with our hands on the ground and another, "hah!" A third whistle and we would shoot our feet out behind us and remain in a push-up position, a fourth and we would drop to our bellies, a fifth and we would flip our bodies in one motion onto our backs. On the sixth whistle blow, we reversed our previous move to return to our bellies, a seventh whistle and we were back in a push-up position, and after the eighth, we were squatting again. Whistle nine and we were back in football position, and finally the tenth whistle brought us back to a full stand where we would begin clapping. This routine would repeat three times before we would be called to the 40-yard line for the

second of the traditions.

The entire team would stand shoulder-to-shoulder and span the width of the field facing the student section of our stadium. We would unsnap our helmets and raise them high above our heads, the best marching band in the USA would begin playing "Seminole Fanfare," and we would slowly walk towards the end zone. This was the cue the fans anticipated to begin making themselves known and they would do just that. The closer we walked to the end zone the louder the fans roared until we finally broke from our walk, strapped our helmets back on, and ran to the goal line. After touching the goal line, we would about face and circle around Coach Bowden for the third and most recognizable of our warm up traditions.

The entire team, more than 100 of us, would huddle tightly around our leader and wait for his signal. He would offer a phrase or two of generic encouragement along the lines of, "let's go men," and then he would quickly jerk both of his hands to the sides of his head. Like an orchestra responding to their conductor, we would instantly mimic Coach's movement. After a second or two, Coach would quickly drop his hands and then we would follow. Again to the head, then once more to his side, until a quick up and back would signal our release to our position coaches.

We would spend about 15 minutes with our coaches before we would come back together as offensive and defensive units for a few play simulations. When the final plays had been run we would run to the center of the field, raise our helmets once more, and begin to jump repeatedly on our Seminole logo as a final sign to our fans and the opposition that we were ready to play. The significance of our opponent dictated the intensity of this moment. Were the Gators or 'Canes in town, it would be a riotous moment of vim and vigor, but for a team like Maryland, it would be part enthusiasm with another part show and tradition. Game time was just a few short minutes away and we would spend them in the locker room, while the Marching Chiefs prepped the crowd for kick off.

Coach Bowden was very matter-of-fact in his pregame speeches. He would remind us to take care of the football on offense and try to take it away on defense. He would always tell us that they might score first but not to worry about it because it was a long game. His closing remark was always the same, "seniors won't let us lose men, seniors won't let us lose." Coach would offer a prayer of protection for all the players and it would be time to hit the field.

This was the moment that the football switch was flipped for good and I became acutely focused on the job at hand. As we exited the locker room, we would smack our hands against the team's motto for the year, which was attached to the door frame. The sound altered significantly as we left the compact hallway and entered into the sound chamber that is the undercarriage of Doak Campbell Stadium. We had to take a sharp right and head down a ramp towards our tunnel, and the metal tips of our cleats would offer a distinct cadence as we neared our battlefield. As the ramp leveled out, we turned 90 degrees to our left and passed between a crowd of amped up fans being restrained by a 6 foot tall chain link fence. Our view of the stadium was limited by the garnet tunnel we would gather under, but as soon as the students saw the first of our gold helmets arrive, they triggered a wave of sound allowing us to hear what we were still unable to see. The cheerleaders were holding a 12-to-15 foot high Seminole logo for us to tear through when the time was right. Clint Purvis was standing between us and the banner waiting for Coach Bowden to pass and the television guys to signal that they were ready for us. Upon his mark we would burst forth from the tunnel like a bull at a rodeo and the crowd would roar as we did. This moment was never disappointing.

I would run the full length of the field with my arms pumping, shouting with all I had, and ever mindful not to trip. A pile up, caused by a clumsy football player, was no way to intimidate the opposing team. After both teams had taken the field, a palpable sense of anticipation swelled in the stadium. Everybody knew what was about to happen and we couldn't wait. The sight of Chief Osceola riding atop Renegade with a flaming spear lofted overhead is the most awesome spectacle in sports. Nothing compares to the moment Renegade gallops to the center of the field accompanied by the thunder of 80,000 fans. We aligned ourselves along the hash marks and held our helmets just like Osceola held his spear, and as he thrust the spear into the turf, we echoed his movement with our helmets. The fans' released an intimidating "OOOH" as the point pierced the turf, and struck the first blow of the day to the psyche of our opponents.

The Marching Chiefs would transition with the pulsating beats of the base drum, followed by the haunting melody of the Seminole War Chant. Simultaneously, the fans would begin the rhythmic chopping of their arms accompanied by their bellowing chant of the same tune being played by the Chiefs. What an awesome tradition, what an incredible privilege! It was game day in Tallahassee, and I was on the field for it all!

After the game, we would walk to the center of the field and shake hands with any of the opposition that chose to meet us there. Our chaplain, Clint Purvis, would call anyone who wanted to participate together for a post-game prayer. We would all take a knee around Clint and he would offer up prayers of thanks, prayers for any players who might have been injured, and safe travels for

our opponents. After Clint was finished, we would all get back to our feet and begin walking from midfield to our locker room. Fans have an ability to vacate a stadium at an incredible pace, so by the time we were headed off the field, the stands were nearly empty. Back in the locker room, the team would be in various stages of undress as we circled up for Coach Bowden's closing remarks. These were normally quite concise and he would lead us in a word of prayer before we would continue getting changed. Then the media would be allowed to come in. Under Coach Bowden's leadership, Florida State always maintained a very open relationship with the media. We had a crew of beat writers who hung around the stadium all week and traveled with us on road trips. Depending on what station was televising the game, or the national significance of it, we would see plenty of familiar faces from the national media as well.

They would flock to the superstars' lockers who would be forced to delay getting changed until the media was through with their questions. Some of the guys felt the freedom to continue undressing in spite of the reporters' presence, and the reporters seemed to keep a very professional posture, although it had to be awkward. The rest of us were able to get showered and dressed at our leisure before making haste for the exit. I would walk out of the locker room and down a long hallway that ended in the lobby of the Moore Athletic Center. Our families would congregate there and wait for our arrival along with hundreds of autograph hungry fans. A circle of kids would be the first to greet me, holding sheets of paper, footballs, hats, or anything they might have had handy for me to sign. They weren't concerned about my status on the depth chart, they just wanted the autograph of a Seminole, and I was the one with the marker. After signing a few souvenirs for the kids, I would find my family who were normally sitting on the steps just to my left.

There would be anywhere from two to 10 members of my family at every game I ever played, with the exception of two. My parents were standards, my younger brother, Daniel, was almost as consistent, and any assortment of my four sisters would make it any chance that they could. These games also provided an opportunity for our extended family to spend time with us. I am proud to say that family from as far as Illinois, Iowa, Colorado, and even Canada made it to Tallahassee, and whoever was in town would be waiting in the Moore lobby when I walked out of the locker room. It always felt good to see them all waiting there. Once we had all exchanged commentary on the game we would exit the stadium and get something to eat. Playing in a 3.5 hour football game can make a guy pretty hungry.

The Maryland Terrapins were the first opponent I played against in front of the home crowd. Bad news for Maryland though because the offense that struggled to find its way in California would have no such struggles in Tallahassee. Three different quarterbacks, our starter Thad Busby, his backup, Dan Kendra, and 25-year-old freshman Chris Weinke, threw a touchdown pass and had 461 yards between them. Thirty points in the first half and 50 in the game were more than enough to relieve any concerns our fans might have had with our offense because of the USC game, as we sent the Terps home with a 50-7 loss. The following Monday we went to work preparing for our next game; a game that would see one remarkable wide receiver shine above all others.

14

#9

Next on our schedule was a trip to Clemson, S.C. and a date with the Tigers. My game experience didn't change much: block for the kickoff returns, field goals, and extra points. But redshirt-sophomore Peter Warrick, turned Death Valley into a grand stage for his self-introduction to America. It was as if we were playing the game on ice and he was the only player who had skates; he was simply the fastest man on the field by a long shot. Only twice before, in the history of Florida State football had a receiver racked up 200 yards in a game. Peter made it three, because on this night he had 249 on just eight receptions. That means that every time Peter caught a pass, we averaged a 31-yard gain! He converted two of those receptions into touchdowns, with one going for 80 yards, but it was his third touchdown that had everyone talking. The score was 21-17 as we entered the fourth quarter and our defense forced the Tigers to punt. Warrick caught the ball on the ten-yard line, and very similar to Deion Sanders in 1988, he shot up the Clemson sideline. After crossing midfield, he cut back to his left to avoid the hapless punter, and continued angling across the field before crossing the goal line back on our sideline. His 90-yard punt return was the second longest in Seminole history, behind only Phil Abraira's 92 yarder against N.C.

State in 1969. It helped him stock pile 372 total yards in the game, which was the second highest total in the history of the Atlantic Coast Conference. While this was the game that put him on the map from a national perspective, our opponents had received warning in 1996 when he led our team with 21.2 yards per catch and made his first few entries into the Peter Warrick highlight archives. Of course, no one was more familiar with no. 9 than his teammates.

Without a doubt, the best athlete I have ever been around is Peter Warrick. The guy wasn't in a class by himself; there was an additional school built that he solely occupied. He was that good. I am much too ignorant to be able to explain why we aren't still watching Warrick put the finishing touches on a Hall of Fame NFL career, but I can speak to no. 9's days in the Garnet and Gold and they were incredible.

For the rest of this chapter I am stepping out of my role as a player and embracing my role as a fan because that's what I was of Peter Warrick; I think we all were. There were great athletes all over the field in Tallahassee. Some of them freakishly strong, some with world-class speed, guys who could throw a ball faster than 90 miles per hour, and 300 pound men who could do standing back flips. The FSU Flying High circus wasn't the only one in town; the Seminole football team was an athletic circus and Peter Warrick was holding down the center ring. It was evident that we were teammates with a very special athlete and thankfully we were able to stop and watch every once in a while.

It is undeniable, when you watch our games, how far superior Peter was to anyone else on the field. Even as he was tackled, you could see the sigh of relief from the opposing team that he didn't pull a Houdini act on them. We all saw the highlight plays like his zigzagging, stop-starting, whirling dervish touchdown run against Louisiana Tech, or the impossible, falling down, ping-ponging, fighting off an interfering defender, never a doubt about it touchdown catch in the 2000 Sugar Bowl. Perhaps you prefer his dress rehearsal for that historical catch when he tipped another TD to himself against Maryland in '96. Many love his touchdown pass to Ron Dugans against the Gators in '98. Everybody has their favorite plays because he made plenty of them for us to talk about for years, but it was the plays no one talks about that really made Pete special.

I would normally miss them in the flow of a game because I was blocking or following the play and Pete was displaying his unique gifts on another part of the field. But on Monday evenings, when we were watching game film, a coach would point no. 9 out to us, tell us to watch, and often say something like, "this guy is really special." Sometimes it was just Pete running a decoy route on the back side of a play, and running it so perfectly that his defender had fallen over and looked uncoordinated in the process. Other times, it would be Warrick flying down the sidelines with a safety or linebacker sizing him up and a split second before the impact, Pete would plant his foot and instantly stop. (*Go outside and try that if you aren't impressed. When you get back from the orthopedic surgeon, enjoy the rest of the book.*) The defender would catapult himself out of bounds and Peter would just skip out of bounds with a big grin on his face. It was like watching one of the X-Men. We might see him take off down the field on an apparent route and because he was so convincing, when he finally began to block, he would often knock the defender to the ground. Peter regularly produced some of the most mind-blowing, ankle-breaking, three-yard runs you could ever imagine, leaving defenders strewn all over the field. While plays like that happened with regularity in the games, it was on the practice field that some of his most alien feats occurred.

The play that is vivid in my mind happened on the defensive practice field, the field furthest from Dick Howser Stadium. We were running pass skeleton against the starting defense. As I mentioned earlier, it featured all the linebackers and the defensive backs against the receivers, tight ends, and running backs in a lightning fast game of backyard football. The defense was notorious for holding and not exactly playing authentic football when we ran this drill. Because it was passing only, they would drop into their coverage instantly, sometimes even before the snap, since there was no threat of a running play. This served to make the route running and completion of passes that much more difficult which set the table for Peter's freakish play.

I don't know the exact play or route but I know that Pete was about 20 yards down field, running parallel to the line of scrimmage toward stadium drive. First of all, the quarterback had no business throwing the ball to him because he had more defenders around him than the president of the United States. Had it been any other receiver, the quarterback might have been scolded. However; they always had the freedom to throw it to Warrick, and this play proved why. He was running full speed across the field, managing to avoid contact with the swarm of defenders shadowing him and anticipating a throw. Had I been running the route, I would have mentally checked out. Throwing into that kind of coverage just didn't happen, but Pete still expected the ball. Sure enough it came, but it was thrown behind him and the ballet began.

Warrick left his feet, and began contorting himself to fit an arm into the mass of adversaries surrounding him; he made it look effortless. Miraculously, the ball found its way through the flailing arms and hands of multiple guys, who had the advantage of facing the ball and the use of both of their hands. As if on a mission, the ball was able to find its mark as the nose of the ball drove into the open palm of Warrick. I am convinced that Pete couldn't see the ball when it hit his hand, but using the skills he alone possessed, he caught the pass and then began the hard part. Now that he had palmed the ball, he had to weave it back out from amongst the swiping defenders and manage to arrive back to the Earth without tearing a knee ligament. Like Han Solo speeding from the Death Star, Pete snuck that ball out from peril and safely tucked it to his body. Then, without losing stride, he landed part way through a 360 degree spin, continued the rotation, and not only managed to avoid being hit, but escaped all together and took it to the house!

For Pete it was about as special as eating a bowl of oatmeal, but for the rest of us it was akin to watching Spud Webb win the NBA dunk contest. Coach Andrews and Coach Amato yelled at their outmatched players but they too found themselves turning their gaze back to Pete, realizing that there was nothing their guys could have done about it. We had just come upon an athletic wonder and we all simply stopped and took it in for a second. He was a shark in the ocean while the rest of us were mere men treading water.

My favorite thing about Pete, aside from people thinking I was cool because I knew him, was that even though he was better than us as an athlete, he was one of us as a teammate. Maybe Weinke in his Heisman campaign could relate to Pete but for the rest of us mortals we had no idea what his life was like. Every beat writer, radio show host, and TV personality wanted an interview with him. He had to do photo and video shoots for the TV stations covering our games. He signed thousands of autographs and made countless public appearances. Outside the brick façade of Doak Campbell stadium, Peter Warrick was a celebrity, but once inside the walls he was just Peter Warrick. He was one of the guys doing his part to win a championship for Florida State and Coach Bowden. During any given year there were more than a hundred athletes sharing the locker room and Peter never acted like he was better than any of us. He was a legend because he was elite but he was special because he was just another Seminole... well, maybe not *just* another Seminole.

The victory over Clemson gave us a three game winning streak, which is exactly what we were going for in our next game against the Hurricanes. The win in 1996 was our first over them in the Orange Bowl in over a decade and gave us a two game winning streak. Miami came in hoping to return the favor but was outmatched from the opening whistle. The defense was smothering and the offense dynamic as we crushed the Hurricanes by a 47-0 score, which was the largest margin of victory in the history of our rivalry with them.

Over the next three weeks, we posted two, convincing, ACC, road victories over Duke and Virginia with an overwhelming, 38-0, shutout victory over Georgia Tech sandwiched in-between. The nation would be introduced to another ACC receiver the next week when N.C. State's Torry Holt almost single-handedly gave us our first defeat. The game appeared to be over after we jumped out to a 27-0 lead in the first quarter. Unfortunately for them, their defense couldn't stop the bleeding; because the Wolfpack offense mounted a torrid comeback, well Holt did anyway. He caught five touchdown passes, accounting for all of the Wolfpack's 35 points. He racked up 168 yards in his conference record setting performance. Thad Busby quietly threw five touchdown passes of his own and threw for 463 yards in leading us to a 48-35 victory.

We were 8-0 and ranked no. 2 in the country as we prepared for another game with a resident of Tobacco Road the next week. The ACC championship was on the line in our matchup with Mack

Brown's fifth-ranked Tar Heels. The game was a stark contrast to our shootout the previous week as this one would feature the defenses. There were more records set on this night, with our "D" racking up a school high, nine sacks in the game and holding the Heels to just 73 yards of total offense. It was the first time in conference history that two teams in the top 5 had competed against each other and we came out on top of that historical game with a 20-3 win in Chapel Hill.

The next week saw six different Seminoles earn touchdowns and seven different guys score, when you include Sebastian Janikowski's field goals. It was our most impressive offensive performance of the year. Wake Forest managed to get in the end zone just one time as we rolled to a 58-7 drubbing of the Demon Deacons. If you throw Torry Holt out of the formula, our defense only gave up 3.5 points per game at home in 1997, but it was giving up more than 17 on the road and our final game of the season was in Gainesville. We were 10-0 and ranked no. 1 in the country, looking to book our trip to Miami for another shot at the National Championship.

15

1:50

In two years of playing football at Florida State, we were 21-0 in the regular season and had ourselves set to play in our second consecutive National Championship game. All we had to do was beat the 10th ranked, 8-2 Gators and I knew that we would. I remember hanging out in the training room with Jeane Jeune during the week leading up to the game and debating with him whether or not we should be worried about them. Jean took the side of caution and warned that we had to take them seriously. I took the side of confidence and felt that they had no chance in the world. In fact, I thought we were going to do to them what they had done to us last year in the Sugar Bowl, and revenge was going to be sweet. If you discount the season opener against USC, our offense was averaging 44 points per game and our defense was only allowing 14 points per game. There just wasn't any chance for this edition of the Gators, without Danny Wuerffel, to defeat us. But as the old cliché goes; when rivals get together you can throw the records out the window.

We battled back and forth for the entire game. Running back Fred Taylor lit up our defense for 162 yards and four touchdowns but he was matched by Travis Minor's 142 yards and one touchdown against the second-ranked rush defense in America.

The quarterbacks had similar nights with the two-headed Gator QB of Johnson and Brindise throwing for about 100 more yards but Busby throwing two more touchdowns. We outscored them by four in the first quarter; they outscored us by five in the second. We came out strong in the third, outscored them by two and took a 26 – 25 lead into the final quarter.

The fourth was a defensive struggle that seemed to finally turn in our favor when Fred Taylor fumbled, and Sebastian Janikowski nailed a 28-yard field goal to give us a 29 – 25 lead with only 2:33 to play in the game. In typical Janikowski form, he blasted the kickoff and forced a touchback. The Gators had to go 80 yards in less than two minutes against a defense that had been clobbering them in the fourth quarter.

On first down, Doug Johnson threw a deep pass to Jaquez Green, which he caught on our 45-yard line. He made a quick cut to the inside and managed to pick up 63 yards on the play before Tay Cody brought him down on our 17-yard line. Since Sebastian had made the earlier field goal, they still had plenty of work to do, but now the clock was less of a factor. On second down, they ran a simple draw to Fred Taylor over the left guard. He shot through the line of scrimmage, made one man miss, and sprinted up the left sideline to the one-yard line. They had covered 79 yards in two plays and only took about 35 seconds to do it. The third play was a formality as Fred Taylor took the handoff and snuck into the end zone to give the Gators the 32-29 lead. They reclaimed the lead but they left 1:50 on the clock and our kicker had one of the strongest legs in all of college football, so the game was far from over.

Our ensuing drive matched Florida's in the number of plays but not in the outcome. Our first play resulted in a sack, the second was an incomplete pass, and the third was intercepted. All Florida had to do was kneel on the ball and we were forced to watch the

National Championship game slip through our fingers like the time slipped off the clock. The fourth quarter was a microcosm of the '97 season for our defense. For thirteen minutes they were completely dominating, but a three-play Gator drive would allow Florida to rob us of our national championship hopes for the second year in a row. We were one minute, 50 seconds away from another undefeated regular season, but it might as well have been three losses because the end result was the same. We were relegated to a return trip to New Orleans where we defeated Ohio State 31 – 14, and we had to watch Nebraska obliterate Tennessee in the Orange Bowl.

There was transition afoot following the season. Coach Cottrell took a job with the University of Alabama and my coach from the scout team, John Lilly, was promoted to take his place. We experienced the annual exodus of seniors which always changes the dynamic of a team, but a few specific ones with the addition of some injuries would have me learning my third position in as many years.

16

CLOSE CALL & THE PUTTY MAN

Spring practice carries with it the issue of lesser depth on the roster due to the seniors' graduation. There are always some gaps to fill until the freshman class arrives in the fall. When graduation is compounded by injuries, it can leave the coaches scrambling for help. That's exactly what happened with the fullbacks in '98, so Coach Sexton was looking for depth in the backfield. Lamarr Glenn had proven himself as the starter but was entering his senior season. William McCray put together a strong freshman season, but he was a smaller player and was being considered as a tailback. Khalid Abdullah was a significant contributor in '97, but suffered a career-ending neck injury before the Sugar Bowl. Forrest Green had lettered in '97 but was also entering his senior season. Entering spring practice, there were really only two, traditional fullbacks and they were both entering their senior seasons.

The coaches looked to solve their depth problem by asking Billy Rhodes to learn a new position. Billy was a converted defensive tackle who was 6'1" and 265 pounds, making him a massive alternative at fullback. Billy provided more depth for the upcoming season, but he was also entering his final year, so they asked me to join the fray as well. I still had three years of eligibility remaining, and I was a much bigger athlete than McCray. If I could learn the position, it would provide the coaches with some security going into the future. That was a big "if." The only experience I had as a running back was during a high school drill that left me with the wind knocked out of me and a coach saying, "Never try to jump over a defender."

At least I knew that much, as I started learning my third position. But, that was all I knew since very little of the technique I had been power-cramming as a rookie center, translated to the fullback position. The one thing that did help was that I had begun to understand our blocking techniques and assignments which would help me with my blocking assignments from the backfield. Because I was underweight as a center, taller than a traditional center, and about as strong as an old rubber band, I had yet to experience much success in the trenches. While my being about 250 pounds was a liability in the middle of the offensive line, it was an asset as a fullback. I was at least as big as the other backs and I was bigger than almost every linebacker I would be called to block. My body had gone from awkward to an asset, just by switching where I lined up and it made me that much more confident. I loved playing fullback; I stunk at it, but I loved it.

My favorite part of playing fullback was the simple truth that contact was nearly unavoidable. A linebacker has the job of tackling the tailback, which requires him to run on a line that will result in contact. My job is to be on that same line and get in the way; I was good at that part. All I had to do was run through the same hole that the tailback was going to run through and when the linebacker showed up… hit him. That was fun and I did really well right up to the point of contact. As soon as I hit the backer, I would stop moving my feet. The result would be two big people standing in a little hole that the tailback was supposed to run through. That doesn't make for a good running game. I had a lot to learn, but my development was stunted because the coaches weren't ready to give up on their plans for me at center just yet.

Long time starter, Kevin Long, played his final game in the Sugar Bowl against Ohio State. Eric Thomas and Jarad Moon both proved to be quality centers and they would wage a two-year war for the starter's job. The problem was that no one was behind them, so I was called on to provide depth there as well. Throughout the spring, I alternated periods at practice and time in meetings between the offensive linemen and the running backs. The depth issues provided me with the opportunity to learn both positions and the coaches expected me to mentally master them. It was a tall order, but I had the same amount of excuses that I had as the scout team center, zero. Get the job done.

Billy proved himself as a solid fullback and it looked like William was going to play there as well, so as spring practice ended, I was under the impression that being a center was in my future. Even though I was cross-training, I felt that I had another solid off-season and went into that summer with high hopes of seeing increased playing time in the fall. Little did I know, a lack of playing time would be the least of my problems.

The previous February, Coach Lilly put the finishing touches on the recruiting class that Coach Cottrell had engineered, and a calculated risk on their part almost cost me dearly. I remember Coach Bowden telling me that my scholarship was only for one year, and that I would have to work hard not to lose it, but I couldn't have anticipated what was about to happen.

In the world of college recruiting, there are often high school students who excel on the field but tend to under-achieve in the classroom. These kids are normally sitting on a blade's edge when it comes to their eligibility, so the coaches might recruit four of them for two scholarships in anticipation of two of them not succeeding in their efforts to qualify. In 1994, the NCAA limited the number of scholarships that a football team could hand out, at 85 per year. It's fitting that I would eventually wear the no. 85, because I represented that 85th scholarship.

As the coaches were planning their recruiting effort, they targeted a couple of students who fell into that academic grey area. Ironically, all of the kids who were border-line were on course to qualify, so the coaches were forced to make a difficult decision. The NCAA requires that institutions inform student-athletes by July 1 of their intent to renew or withhold the person's scholarship. As that deadline drew near, those incoming kids still had a chance to qualify, and they had been promised a scholarship if they succeeded. Therefore, my parents received a letter on June 23 that said:

> *"Upon the recommendation of the Florida State University Athletic Department, your athletic Grant-in-Aid (scholarship) will not be renewed beginning with the academic year 1998-99. The nonrenewal was based on your prior agreement with the Football coach."*

As quickly as I had received my scholarship, I had lost it. The letter informed me of my right to an appeal, but I had no interest in that. It was a one year deal and they had fulfilled their end of the bargain as they said they would. I was discouraged. My mom was heartbroken. She called Coach Lilly and tearfully questioned him about the process. It was his first year as the recruiting coordinator, and he wasn't in charge of the class coming in, so he could not justify any of it. He reassured her that I had not done anything to lose the scholarship, it was a simple numbers issue; just an unfortunate set of circumstances for our family.

GRATEFUL

For just over a month, we were in limbo while we waited to learn what would happen. As was the case for much of my career, someone else's struggles led to my reward. A couple of the kids ended up not qualifying and had to either enroll at a junior-college or delay their enrollment with FSU until January. When word finally came down that those kids had fallen short, my parents received a second letter on July 29, just before two-a-days:

"On behalf of the Florida State University Athletic Department, I am pleased to notify you that your Grant-in-Aid will be renewed for the academic year 1998-99 (Fall & Spring). The payment terms and conditions of your Grant-in-Aid are detailed in the enclosed information."

For the second consecutive summer, we celebrated the fact that I had been given a full scholarship to play football at FSU. The first time was a surprise and feelings of joy accompanied the news. This time was a near disaster and feelings of gratitude were mixed with feelings of relief. With scholarship in hand, I entered August practices with a renewed vigor.

Because I believed that I would be playing center, I spent most of the summer working out and eating like an offensive lineman. By the start of our preseason in August of '98, I was pushing the 280 pound mark and ready to give playing center a real shot. But I wasn't in the running for any real playing time there. I was purely an emergency plan. Not just a "one or two guys getting hurt" emergency, more like a "the entire offensive line was expelled from school and we ran out of tuba players" emergency plan. I wasn't going to see the field as a center, so the coaches continued to work me with the running backs and made sure I didn't forget how to play tight end, just to be safe.

They like to have four tight ends ready to go because of our two-tight end formations. Myron Jackson was a lock to start at tight end and Nick Franklin was secure as Myron's backup. Nick had arrived the previous January as a transfer from Southwest Mississippi Junior College. He was a highly sought after player and considered by many to be the best junior college tight end in America. The top of the depth chart was strong, but the rest of the group was unproven. Carver Donaldson was a sophomore, Stacy Davis was a redshirt-freshman, and Patrick Hughes had arrived just that August, so I continued working with them as well. For a long time, I was actually cross-training at three positions, as well as meeting with all three positions on any given day. It was during this stretch, as I was leaving a running back meeting to go into the O-line meeting, that Coach Sexton gave me the nickname "Putty Man." Sexton guffawed and said, "Wherever we have a hole, just send in the Putty Man!" He was proud at what he came up with and playfully shoved me as I went next door to meet with the big guys.

Changing positions happens all the time at FSU, and I am sure all over the country. Jeff Chaney switched from safety to running back; Wadsworth switched from defensive tackle to defensive end; and I can remember at least four high school quarterbacks (Dexter Jackson, Peter Warrick, Anquan Boldin, and Keith Cottrell) that were playing different positions at FSU. Every one of those switches requires a mental and physical adjustment, and those adjustments are compounded when it happens multiple times between multiple positions. My willingness to be "putty" and allow my mind to become putty was significant in my earning of a scholarship, and it set me in the good graces with our coaching staff. I was able to connect with guys on the team that I would not have, in the absence of my revolving positions. It is one of the reasons my story is unique.

Through the course of two-a-days, my pattern of working with the fullbacks, the O-line, and the tight ends continued. My learning curve for all three positions was steep because I wasn't getting the amount of reps that the other guys were getting. As we entered the season, and got ready for our trip to New York to play Texas A&M in the Kickoff Classic, the media guide revealed that I was buried deep on the depth chart.

At center, it said Eric Thomas or Jarad Moon. The fullbacks were led by Lamarr Glenn, with William McCray and Billy Rhodes listed as his backups. The tight end depth chart showed Myron Jackson in the starter role, followed by Nick, Carver, and Stacy. I wasn't even on the depth chart!

I did receive no. 39 and was back in my familiar roles with the kickoff return team and field goal team. I was gaining incredible amounts of whole-offense knowledge with all my switching around and frankly, after the scholarship debacle, I was just happy to still be in school and on the team. I was entering my third year at FSU, which allowed me to move out of Burt Reynolds Hall. Scholarship guys, in their first two seasons, are required to live there so that the coaches can monitor them a little more closely. Even though I only lived in Burt one year, I was an upperclassman. Because of an NCAA rule, an athletic dorm cannot be composed of 100 percent athletes, so upperclassmen had to move off-campus. Therefore it was time for me to find somewhere else to live. I partnered up with offensive guard, Justin Amman, and some of my civilian friends from the other Reynolds Hall, Jayme Johnson, Dave Perales, and Jay Miller. We lived together, in various combinations, with our dog Sable, for the remainder of our years in Tallahassee.

**Sophomore:
August of 1998
thru July of 1999**

17

SHOCKED

Forty-seven and one. Since Florida State began competing in the Atlantic Coast Conference, it had won 47 times in 48 opportunities. We had done our part in 1996 and 1997 by going 16-0 and winning the conference both years. FSU had won the conference championship every year since 1992. We were absolutely dominating within the league; we had only been behind in the fourth quarter twice in those 48 games. In 1994, the 'Noles suffered their first ever defeat within the ACC on an infamous night in Charlottesville, Va.

The Cavaliers played out of their minds that night and a raucous home crowd elevated them just enough to steal a victory. On the last play of the game, Warrick Dunn took a handoff and appeared to score the game-winning touchdown but he was ruled down inside the one-yard line. Pandemonium ensued as the fans celebrated being the first school to defeat the Goliath that was Florida State. But Virginia wasn't really a "David." George Welsh had built a strong program in the early '90s at Virginia, so as surprising as that first loss was, it wasn't unthinkable.

That was not the case when we went up to Raleigh for our second game of the '98 season. Had David been a bully when he wasn't shepherding, the Wolfpack would have been the kid he picked on. In the three previous years, the Wolfpack had accumulated 12 wins. We won 11 in 1997 alone. The last time N.C. State had won an ACC championship was 1979, while we had won the ACC every year since 1992. The Pack hadn't been to a bowl game since its 1994 Peach Bowl victory while we had played in a bowl game every year since 1979. Going into our game in '98, we were riding an 18-game ACC winning streak, where N.C. State had only won 18 ACC games in five years combined. Add to the equation that we were ranked no. 2 in America and had soundly defeated the no. 14 Texas A&M Aggies, 23-14, in the opening week and you have the formula for a beat down. The odds makers agreed and listed us as 25 point favorites. We hopped on the plane to North Carolina as confident as the English marching on Falkirk, but much to our dismay, this edition of the Wolfpack had a little William Wallace in them.

Thad Busby graduated after the 1997 season and Dan Kendra injured his knee during spring practice in 1998. Those circumstances paved the way for 25-year-old freshman Chris Weinke to take the reins. This game helps you appreciate Chris Weinke's career like 3 a.m. on a moonless night helps you appreciate the sunshine. Chris would hold the ACC record for the most consecutive passes without an interception by throwing 237 without hitting the wrong jersey, over the last eight games of 1998 and into 1999. He would graduate Florida State with the lowest interception percentage in school history with a .0289 attempts to interceptions ratio. The 2000 Heisman trophy would bear his name and he would have a nearly flawless win / loss record over his illustrious career. But, just like the hammer has to go backwards before it can launch a bullet, this game in Raleigh would be a step backwards for Chris. He made his first career start the previous week against the Aggies and posted modest numbers, completing

21 out of 36 passes for 207 yards and zero touchdowns. But his second career start got off to a much more explosive start.

The first pass attempt of the day began on the 26-yard line and ended in the end zone! Peter Warrick took Chris's first pass of the night 74 yards for a score and further added to the sense of foreboding held by the N.C. State faithful. Our second possession looked like much of the same as Weinke completed a 62-yard pass to get us into the red zone. But it was at this juncture that success excused itself from the table. That drive ended with an interception, as would two others in the first half. Unfortunately for us, the balance of the game would see Chris throw almost as many interceptions as completions while N.C. State capitalized on his struggles.

Despite us scoring a touchdown before thirty seconds had elapsed, we would find ourselves losing by six as the first quarter expired, thanks in large part to a 68-yard Torry Holt punt return. The middle portion of the game was marked by the opposing defenses. There were only three points scored in the second and third quarters, leaving the game within reach as we entered the fourth. I was on my knee watching the game unfold and had no doubt that we were going to win the game. We were only down by a score of 16 – 7 with a full quarter to play and we had proved on the first possession that we could score lightning fast. Just as the Globetrotters always pull away from the Generals, we always pulled away from our foes; we just didn't lose ACC games. But our undefeated aspirations would crumble as our quarterback faltered time and again.

Just as Peter Warrick's first quarter, 60-plus yard touchdown strike silenced Carter-Finley stadium; Torry Holt's fourth quarter, 60-plus yard touchdown set off an audible avalanche. There was still more than nine minutes to go in the game, but it was over. All the optimism and hope in the world couldn't overcome the physical insufficiency on the day. Weinke ended up setting the ACC record for interceptions by throwing six on the day. Had our defense not been so stout, we might have been pounded by much more than 17 points. We were close to being beaten by the same 25 points we were favored to win by.

As had been the case in Charlottesville a few years prior, the N.C. State fans' enthusiasm quite literally poured out onto the field. As the seconds emptied off the clock, the fans emptied off the bleachers and stormed the turf to celebrate with their giant-killing team. Just two years ago I had celebrated on our home turf with a few thousand of my closest friends, but celebrating wasn't on the agenda for this day… at least not for us.

It is a sickening feeling to watch another team and their fans celebrate a victory like that. As the time elapsed I just kept my right knee on the ground while my right hand was firmly clasped around my facemask as I used my helmet like a kick stand. Even while the fans were screaming and jumping around me I held onto the delusional idea that we were still going to win. I was actually in denial as the goal posts were swarmed with red and white clad fanatics and I moped off the field struggling with the idea that this team had just lost our first ACC game.

This disaster of a game would be to Weinke, what middle school failure was to Michael Jordan, motivation for extraordinary success. He wouldn't throw an interception for the rest of the season and would do his part to lead us back to the national championship game. Chris became the personification of confidence. He believed absolutely that he could perform at the highest level and we believed absolutely in him. He didn't misread defenses, he didn't make hasty decisions, and he threw the ball with the accuracy of Robin Hood launching an arrow. His personal excellence led to him holding lofty expectations for the rest of us; and for the most part we played up to his expectations.

Confidence can be the difference between stepping out at the one and scoring a touchdown. That can be a self confidence or a confidence in others, and you see this on display with the great running backs. Warrick Dunn would drive towards a spot on the field with the belief that by the time he arrived his lineman would supplant the defender and produce a channel for him to run through. That belief generated the necessary self confidence to squirt through those holes that were only available for seconds. Weinke's steady excellence had the same affect on us as the offensive lineman's reliability had on Warrick Dunn. We knew the ball would be where the coach drew it up, so we ran our routes with resolve. We didn't hesitate when a defender flashed across our zone because we knew that if the ball was on its way, we were open, and if we were covered, the ball was already on its way to someone else. There is a great scene in the movie, "The Sandlot," that exemplifies the relationship between Weinke and the rest of us.

Scotty Smalls was the new kid in town and he discovered a group of eight boys who played baseball every day on the Sandlot. The local boys were led by the great Benny "The Jet" Rodriguez who would go on to play for the Los Angeles Dodgers. Scotty was on the other end of the athletic universe. He was awkward, untrained, and most importantly full of self doubt. His glove was plastic, his hat featured a comically oversized bill, and baseball ignorance was a pimple on the end of his social nose. But, a baseball team needs nine players and Benny imposed his will on the situation and transformed Scotty Smalls into a ball player.

The pivotal scene began with Benny jogging out to left field for a coaching session with Scotty. "The Jet" had been leading a fielding practice by hitting balls to his teammates at their various positions and Scotty was cowering in the outfield as Benny approached. He gave Smalls a simple set of instructions, "just stick your glove up in the air, and I'll take care of the rest." As Benny jogged back to home plate, Scotty stared at the dirt with his gloved left hand held feebly above his head. The rest of the kids scoffed as Benny resolutely took his bat in his hands and prepared to do what only he could. He flipped the ball into the air with his left hand as the film transitioned to slow motion. His left hand reunited with his right, which had been firmly planted on the handle of his Louisville Slugger, and the two began their task of sending the bat into the path of the sinking baseball. A cloud of dust exploded from the collision between the ball and the miracle producing bat, as the ball began its flight towards Scotty Smalls. He never looked up. The original Sandlot team stared, mouth agape, as the ball sliced through the atmosphere on a line for the outstretched hand of the reluctant left fielder. The music reached crescendo as the ball reached Scotty's glove with a second cloud of dust. Scotty felt the impact and slowly lifted his head from the earth and fixed his gaze on his glove. He had caught the ball! Well, more accurately, Benny had placed the ball into Scotty's glove with his remarkable skill. "The Jet's" incredible ability allowed for the previously inept Scotty Smalls to become a capable left fielder. His countenance shifted from a cowardly grimace to a confident grin and he was all of the sudden able to throw the ball accurately back into the infield. He became better because Benny was so good and Weinke had the same affect on all of us.

I won't go so far as to say that the record setting failure that was that N.C. State game is what produced the Benny Rodriguez qualities that Weinke possessed, but there is no denying that the quarterback that threw six interceptions that day wasn't the same quarterback that would lead us to a National Championship. That game might have ruined a lesser player, but Weinke was unique and he viewed that valley like the base of a ramp that would launch him into greatness and he brought us along for the ride.

18

TOMAHAWKS

The following week we hosted the Blue Devils of Duke University. This was a highlight game for me because it produced a bounty of tomahawk stickers. Other than, "What was it like to play for Coach Bowden?" The next most frequently asked question is, "What do the tomahawk stickers mean?" or, "How did you earn those tomahawk stickers?" Many of you are nodding in agreement right now because you have been eagerly anticipating this chapter. There are two answers to the question and I will begin with the more obvious of the two.

The tomahawks were representative of various different forms of achievement on and off the football field. Depending on what position you played, your measuring stick for receiving a tomahawk would vary. For instance, a defensive end might earn one for a sack while a kicker might earn one for kicking a touchback. There were some universal qualifiers for the academic tomahawks and some group-wide categories as well. I earned quite a few tomahawks for being on the field-goal unit when we successfully converted three consecutive field goals. The whole defense might earn one for a shutout or maybe the offense earned one for scoring 40-plus points.

As a tight end we could earn them a few different ways.

These may sound easy but remember that as receivers, we were predominantly decoys. We would earn a tomahawk for catching a first down pass or a touchdown pass. We would earn one for three pancake blocks in a game. (*A "pancake block" is simply when you maul your opponent and drive the back of their head into the turf.*) We would earn one for grading out at higher than 70 percent for our total performance. To arrive at that grade, the coaches would evaluate every snap we participated in. We would receive a score for, 1) knowing what to do, 2) doing our job, and 3) doing our job correctly. For example, if we were to run "R 34" which was our simple fullback dive, our job would be to "drive block" the defensive end. If we actually attempted to hit the DE, we would get a "+" for knowing what to do. If we drove them off the ball and planted them into the turf, we would receive a "+" for doing the job. But, if we used poor technique like forgetting to place our head on the ball side of the defensive end, we would receive a "-" for our technique score. The coach would add up all our pluses and minuses and divide it out; if we scored higher than a 70 we earned a tomahawk.

I wasn't seeing any playing time as a tight end, but I did play on the field goal team and the kickoff return team. I was on the field for the Duke game almost as often as the starting tight end and that meant tomahawks. The first quarter was a dud but Janikowski nailed a 35-yard field goal in the second with me blocking for him, tomahawk. Then Laveranues Coles returned a kickoff 97 yards for a touchdown and because I was in on that play, tomahawk number two. Peter Warrick and Travis Minor both scored touchdowns that quarter which required the extra-point attempts. Janikowski made all three attempts in succession and I blocked for every one of them, tomahawk three. It took just eight minutes in the third quarter for us to score three more touchdowns followed by three more successful PATs, tomahawk four. In the fourth, Sebastian made a 40-yard field goal and we scored two more times, tomahawks five and six. At the end of the day, we had annihilated Duke by the score of 62-13 and I had earned six tomahawks. But, game achievements weren't the only way to accumulate the prestigious tomahawks.

Most teams that have award sticker programs probably use similar grids for the disbursement of the coveted helmet stickers. But, I doubt many have this magnificent alternative route. What I am about to share with you is a deep secret of the inner workings of the Florida State machine and must be kept between us. I am just going to say it, "not every tomahawk on every helmet was earned."

Keith Graham was the first mate in the equipment room and more importantly from the great state of Georgia. The equipment managers are the men charged with the responsibility of taking care of our hallowed gold helmets and carefully placing each tomahawk on the helmets per the coaches' order. This is an esteemed privilege to be the "tomahawk sticker sticking guy," and Keith held this responsibility during the '90s at Florida State.

I am from Augusta, Ga., and I didn't realize how valuable that was until I got to know Forest Green, who was a fellow walk-on and fellow Georgian. He shared with me the secret that old Keith was generous to the guys from the Peach State in regard to the Tomahawk stickers. Needless to say, I made haste and struck up a relationship with Keith.

It was not uncommon for Keith to befriend his fellow Georgians and lavish on them extra tomahawks. Thankfully, I became one of those blessed few who benefitted from Keith's great loyalty to the Peach State. As I write this, my helmet is sitting on top of my bookshelf in my office and I would love to believe that I earned all the tomahawks that are displayed there but in an effort of full disclosure I must admit that I did not.

I played tight end at Florida State, not some school in the Big Ten, so there is no way on God's green Earth that I would have accumulated enough "tomahawk worthy" plays to fill the back of my helmet, yet magically, even the front of mine was covered! I love Keith Graham! I am glad to say that I still consider Keith a friend, even though I haven't spoken with him in quite a few years as life has moved us around. What initially began as a lust for tomahawks and the notoriety they would earn me, blossomed into a sincere friendship and mutual respect. The guys in the equipment room are unsung heroes on a football team. That staff of guys managed ridiculous amounts of equipment ranging from shoulder pads to screw-in cleats for our shoes. They were able to accept, clean, sort, and reissue more than 120 sets of our uniforms after every practice and twice during two-a-days. Ants could learn a thing or two from our equipment managers. Those guys keep the machine rolling and my advice to any current or future 'Nole out there is to be nice to the equipment managers; you might just end up with a few extra tomahawks!

After the undressing of Duke we plowed ahead through the rest of our schedule. Southern California made the return trip to Tallahassee the next week and Hurricane Georges came with them. The rain affected the 18th ranked Trojans far worse than it did us as we dominated the time of possession by a nearly 2:1 margin, and soundly defeated USC 30-10. We were back on the road the next week headed to Byrd Stadium to play Maryland. Despite outscoring the Terps by an average of 39 points over the previous six years, they played us tough and we had to depend on five Janikowski field goals to win 24-10. Our annual, intra-state battle with the University of Miami followed and we made quick work of the 'Canes. Behind 190 receiving yards from rising star Peter

Warrick, we won our fourth consecutive game against Miami and brought our season record to 5-1.

We had moved up to no. 6 in the polls as we welcomed the Clemson Tigers for our homecoming game. This game went just as the schedulers hoped and we routed Clemson 48-0. We ran for 185 yards, threw for 312, and the defense forced 13 punts as we beat the Tigers in every facet of the game. Our next game would be a stiffer challenge because we had to go to Atlanta to face the no. 20 Yellow Jackets with the ACC title on the line.

19

DUCT TAPE

I had been on many road trips by this time in my career so I had logged many air plane take-offs and landings. I never had a fear of flying because there was never a reason to, but our trip to Atlanta in October of 1998 would make me think twice. The silver and red team bus dropped us off on the tarmac and we walked up the stairs to board the plane. I walked past first class, because the seniors had all those seats, and found my way to a window seat. After I took out my CD player and grabbed my book, I stored my backpack in the overhead bin and made myself comfortable. I chose the window seats for the ability to rest my head on the walls of the plane and that's just what I did while the plane taxied towards the runway.

We rarely had to wait for takeoff because Tallahassee has a small airport and on Friday afternoons, in the fall, the Seminole football charter is the most important flight of the day. The pilots squared the plane on the runway and we quickly began the take off process. My body was pressed against the back of the seat as the plane rapidly accelerated. The runway lights were racing past my window while I anticipated the moment we would leave terra firma. I was lost in thought until, BANG BANG BANG BANG! It sounded like someone had just beaten a tin roof with piece of rebar.

I thought an engine might have blown up as our heads were slammed forward by the sudden braking of the pilots. They brought that plane to an abrupt stop and the cabin was silent.

The airplane captain broke the silence by telling us there had been some mechanical problems and that we would have to go back to the airport to get it checked out. Now that we knew we were safe, panic set in. Many of the guys were uncomfortable on planes already and this was a proof positive for them that airliners couldn't be trusted. Upon our arrival back to the terminal, we had to wait on board the plane while the mechanics tried to determine the problem. The idle time allowed for a slight mutiny to rise up.

A group of the guys simply could not bring themselves to fly on that plane so they insisted on being able to drive to Atlanta, and Peter Warrick was one of them. They were adamant about it and watching the repairs only made things worse. Coach Bowden was still deliberating when the mechanics started applying duct tape to the plane. When the feeble flyers saw that, it was over. They were not flying on that plane. One of the guys, who was unsure, offered an interesting perspective about God's control of our lives. He reasoned that if Clint Purvis was on the plane, God wouldn't let it crash because Clint worked for Him. But if Clint took the bus, all bets were off.

All told, nine players took the five hour bus ride to Atlanta. As the rest of us arrived in Atlanta and enjoyed the police escort to the hotel I couldn't help but remember my last trip here. I thought of my teammates, still hours away just like I had been. But at least they had names on their jerseys, and this time I did too! Thankfully the airplane scare didn't affect our play in a negative way. Peter Warrick scored three times and Janikowski added two field goals but neither of them flew on the plane. Maybe we should drive more often, because we swatted the Yellow Jackets to the tune of 34-7 and moved to 6-1 on the year. The Georgia Tech victory moved us up to no. 5 in the country and we welcomed the Tar Heels to Doak the next week.

Sebastian had another four field-goal game, Warrick and Coles both caught touchdown passes and had more than 100 yards receiving, and the defense was smothering as we rolled North Carolina 39-13. We were 7-1 and tied with Georgia Tech and our next opponent, Virginia for the ACC lead. We headed into that week of practice looking to knock out another victory but it was me that would end up being knocked out.

20

KNOCKED OUT

R-34 is the first play that we install every August. It is the most fundamental play in our offense, in our most basic formation. On a traditional offensive line there would be five positions: a left and right tackle, left and right guard, and the center. We organized our offensive line a little differently; instead of left and right, we used tight and weak. The guards and tackles could line up on either side of the center which allowed us to be more specific with the athletes we had in each spot. For example, the lesser of the two tackles would be the tight tackle because he would have the benefit of the tight end to offer help if necessary. In R-34, the "R" indicated that the tight end, tight tackle, and tight guard were to line up on the right side of the ball, with the split tackle and guard on the left. The number in the play represented who would receive the handoff and where they were to run. The "3" represented the fullback, and the "4" represented the area between the tight guard and tight tackle.

We ran this play every day that we were in pads; many times in the course of a practice. The coaches loved making us run it because it forced us to drive block the man in front of us without the benefit of angles or deception. The offensive line had to cowboy -up and out-muscle the man in front of them, so it was a good test of fortitude. By this time in my career, I must have run R-34 hundreds of times. In fact, I had run it as a center, a full back, and a tight end. This particular day I was practicing as a tight end. There were no variations or nuisances to R-34, we just had to line up and block the man in front of us.

Early in practice, we were working on our running game on field three. I didn't know it when it happened but on one of the plays I was knocked out. When we watched the film the next day I saw what happened. I had fallen down on the play and as I was attempting to get back to my feet, the tailback tried to hurdle me and drove his knee into the side of my helmet. I dropped in a heap and laid still until the tape cut for the next play. Back on the field, I regained consciousness very quickly. Fast enough that no one even realized it had happened.

I jogged back to the huddle to get the next play and Coach Heggins called R-34. I found it odd that there were no objections to the play so, since no one else would, I called him out. "Coach, we don't have a play called R-34." Heggins stared at me incredulously, not sure if I thought I was being funny. He didn't budge on the play call so I asked, "What is R-34?" The rest of the line had begun their short jog to the line of scrimmage so Coach said, "Just run the play!" It wouldn't be the first time that I got help from one of my fellow linemen on an assignment so I jogged up to my spot on the line. Justin Amman was the split guard and I found my spot to his immediate left. He looked to his left expecting to see the split tackle and instead I was staring at him. He looked at me with a look of bewilderment and shouted, "Trainer!"

Everyone stopped and one of the trainers came up to see what was going on. Justin told him about my arguing that R-34 didn't exist (*even the trainers knew about R-34*) and then told them how I suddenly couldn't tell my right from my left. He and the trainer agreed that I might have suffered a concussion. My practice was over, so I spent the rest of the afternoon sipping PowerAde in the shade of the big Oak tree while my friends melted in the miserable heat. Even though I momentarily lost my capacity to recall our playbook and would have failed my kindergarten final exams, I was back to full fidelity the next day. Injuries happen all the time in football, sometimes multiple within a single practice or game. By the end of a season, everybody is banged and bruised, with tweaked knees and sore shoulders. So goes the life of a football player. But, sometimes a player receives a very serious injury and it makes all of us take a step back and drink in a tall glass of perspective. One of those situations was on the horizon.

21

THE ROOSTER

Y ou wouldn't expect to drop a rooster into a ring with a gator
and see the rooster come out on top, but that is just what
happened on Nov. 21, 1998. It is said that sometimes life will throw
you a curveball, but on an autumn day in Tallahassee, life would
toss us a knuckler.

Two weeks before the Gator game, on Nov. 7, we were
playing Virginia in the annual battle for the Jefferson-Eppes
Trophy. The trophy represents the fact that the two universities are
linked through the lineage of United States President, Thomas
Jefferson. Jefferson was the founder of the University of Virginia
and his grandson, Francis W. Eppes VII, was the three-time mayor
of Tallahassee. Eppes was also the President of the Board of
Trustees for the Seminary West of the Suwanee, which eventually
became Florida State. The trophy has two significant components; a
silver pitcher that was presented to the city of Tallahassee by Eppes
in 1842, and a wooden base crafted from the remains of UVA's
massive, "McGuffey Ash." The ancient tree was planted in 1826,
making it the oldest Ash tree in the Virginia. At 103 feet tall and 18
feet in circumference, it was the largest on the UVA campus in
Charlottesville, before it died in 1990. In 1995, FSU president Sandy
D'Alemberte, came up with the idea of exchanging the trophy, and

when the Cavaliers won that first meeting, a tradition was born.

In the fourth ever meeting for the trophy, Weinke got off to a quick start, hitting Warrick for a 79-yard touchdown and leading us to another score before the first quarter was out. Early in the second, Weinke capped the scoring himself with a quarterback sneak, giving us a 21-7 lead. Virginia would score again to cut our lead to 7, but it was a defensive play at the end of the half that would be the most damaging. All-ACC defensive end Patrick Kerney, came free on a rush and sacked Weinke. He hit him clean, but he hit him hard and drove him to the turf. As is often the case, other players fell on top of Chris in a pile. Kerney jumped to his feet to celebrate with his teammates but Chris was extremely slow to move, so Randy Oravetz and Dave Walls quickly ran to his side. Anytime a player is injured, there is nervousness in the air. If it's the starting quarterback, the air has an eerie still as the entire stadium holds their breath. Listening to a crowd of more than 80,000 people sit in absolute silence is unnerving. He had received a serious concussion but they were able to get him to his feet and help him walk off the field. Our fans nervously applauded Chris as he was being led off the field, not sure if he would return after the half. I remember watching him stagger off, relying more on Randy and Dave than his own strength. He looked dazed, bordering on unconscious. They walked him gingerly to the locker room and after a quick evaluation, they had enough information to know that Chris couldn't continue playing that day. With Weinke nursing an intense headache, we turned to Marcus Outzen to finish the game for us.

We leaned heavily on the running game and Outzen led us to even more points in the second half than we scored in the first. We retained the Jefferson-Eppes Trophy with a 42-14 victory; but we would find out a couple days later that we had lost our starting quarterback. The shot that Weinke took damaged his C6 vertebrae and required that he have surgery to fuse his C6 and C7, remove a bone fragment, and install plates on the front and back of the vertebrae. Chris had a broken neck.

I remember sitting in Chris's living room, unable to avoid staring at the halo attached to his head. A halo is a grotesque medical device that seems more at home in the laboratory of Dr. Frankenstein than the living room of a college quarterback. He was never particularly nimble, but it was unsettling to watch his methodical and delicate movements as he lay nearly motionless in a recliner. The guy had bolts anchored into his skull that were attached to a steel hoop lofted just above his head. The halo was further buttressed by long rods that were attached to a medieval looking shoulder harness. There was nothing aesthetically pleasing about the therapeutic necessity restricting Chris's motion but its practical benefit was irreplaceable. It was a miracle that Chris could move at all and we were all hopeful that he would be able to regain full mobility one day. He would surprise everyone by courageously taking the field with us again, but not in 1998. We had a season to finish and we would be led by Marcus "The Rooster" Outzen.

Marcus and I were in very similar athletic circumstances. We came in together in 1996 and there was an established depth chart to either wait out or beat out. My playing aspirations were altered by the arrival of Nick Franklin, who was a junior college recruit, and Marcus's were similarly altered by the arrival of Weinke. Chris had been recruited back in 1990 but chose to chase a professional baseball career, as opposed to enrolling at FSU. Chris wasn't able to accomplish his dream of playing in "the bigs," so he took Coach Bowden up on his offer to hold a scholarship for him. Instead of an 18-year-old, immature freshman arriving to learn from Marcus, a 25-year-old seasoned freshman arrived who was quickly labeled, "the quarterback of the future."

Marcus went from diligently working towards his potential place in the starting 11, to potentially contemplating a transfer. I don't know if he ever seriously considered a move but if he felt any of the emotions I felt when Nick arrived, it crossed his mind. As good as Nick was, he wasn't touted like Weinke. Marcus was confident in himself, but a Heisman candidate just arrived on campus and he had to notice the life similarities he now shared with Coach Richt. Mark Richt was the offensive coordinator every year that I was at FSU, but back in the day, he was an athlete for the University of Miami.

Coach Richt was an accomplished quarterback in his playing days, but very few people know Mark Richt, the football player. He had a knack for finding himself competing with particularly great quarterbacks. As a freshman at the University of Miami in 1978, he found himself behind fellow freshman and future NFL Hall of Fame inductee, Jim Kelly. When Richt's career at UM was over, he had his shot in the NFL with the Denver Broncos. All appeared to be going fine until Denver traded for John Elway, who joined Richt in Colorado. Elway also went on to become an NFL Hall of Fame inductee while Richt was cut just one week after Elway arrived. Coach Richt would have one more shot in the NFL when his hometown Miami Dolphins gave him a tryout. Unfortunately for Richt, that same year they brought in their own future Hall of Famer, Dan Marino. Coach Richt was cut for the final time with his claim to fame being that he was the backup to three, eventual NFL Hall of Famers. During Richt's senior season at UM, Jim Kelly was injured and he was able to finish his career as the Hurricanes' starter. There was no better person in the world to be in the ear of "Rooster" than Coach Richt and I'm glad he was. That precise encouragement kept Marcus grounded and focused for his potential moment, and Weinke's horrific neck injury had produced just that moment.

Marcus was going to start at quarterback for the Seminoles against the Florida Gators within the brick coliseum of Doak Campbell stadium, but Coach Richt would have to prove his mettle as an offensive coordinator for Outzen to be successful. Before the Gators though, we had a road trip to Winston-Salem and a game with Wake Forest. Coach Richt only had a couple days to reorganize the offense for the Wake game, and it showed. We had a very pedestrian performance, but still came away with a 24-7 victory. Rooster didn't throw a touchdown, but he did run for our first score of the day. Now, we had a game under our belts to learn from and a full week to install the necessary changes for Florida.

Weinke was a classic, drop-back, pocket oriented quarterback. He was 6'5", 240 pounds and he ran like it. Marcus was cut from a different mold. He won games with a combination of moxy, creativity, scrambling, and playmaking. Don't get me wrong, he could sling a football, but he didn't have Weinke's arm... few did. Going into the Florida game, Coach Richt re-oriented the playbook for a mobile passer and our offense had a new look. This game would be as much a coming out party for Coach Richt as it was for "Rooster," but it was Marcus who would become a part of Seminole lore.

The five-step drop and throw was replaced with the quarterback draw. The pocket oriented play calling was swapped for an assortment that called for the QB to be on the move. We were transformed from a predictable, blitzkrieg to an unorthodox, ambush offense, and the blue shirts didn't know what hit 'em. "Rooster's" performance was reminiscent of a Rocky fight, as he was pounded repeatedly but kept bouncing back up to scramble courageously into the teeth of the Gator defense. As is often true of players like Outzen, a little luck was present in his bag of tricks and he would use it all on one remarkable play.

Marcus had a warm-up game the previous week against feeble Wake Forest, but now he would have the privilege of playing one of the top defenses in America. We were in the midst of a 39-game, home unbeaten streak including the legendary "Choke in Doak" from 1994. To top it all off, were we to win and get lucky, we could play for a national championship; no pressure at all. The game gave the appearance early of being a long night for the us, as Florida scored on a 50-yard pass in the first quarter. After capitalizing on a couple Outzen fumbles, the Gators had a 12 – 6 halftime lead. The second half would be an entirely different script as our defense had its way and Outzen found his.

Our vaunted, and top-ranked defense played an incredible half of football, shutting out the "Fun and Gun" offense of Steve Spurrier, but "Rooster" stole the show. With about 12 minutes remaining in the third quarter, we were only 32 yards from a touchdown and easily inside Janikowski's field-goal range. We were driving into our student section and the play called for "Rooster" to roll to his left. The fans desperately wanted to believe, but thus far, disappointment was all they had tasted. As Marcus rolled out, the fans saw the same thing he did, Peter Warrick. If Marcus could just get him the ball, maybe Pete could do something special. So, Marcus unleashed a rocket towards him on the left sideline. He was so focused on no. 9 that he didn't account for the defender undercutting Warrick's route. The stadium groaned as the pass was perfectly thrown to Marquand Manuel, the Gators defensive back. It should have been a pick-six for Florida but Manuel carelessly let the ball avoid his hands and ricochet off his shoulder pads into the opportunistic hands of... Peter Warrick! The fan's heartache was replaced by childlike euphoria as we all watched Peter race to the end zone and give us a 13 – 12 lead! Just as Marcus was making the most out of another's misfortune, Warrick took what should have been an interception and turned it into a Seminole touchdown.

Even though Peter Warrick threw the game-winning touchdown to Ron Dugans on a beautifully designed and called reverse pass in the fourth quarter, and Travis Minor ran for more than 120 yards, Marcus "The Rooster" Outzen was the hero. He only threw for 167 yards, ran for just 26 yards, and he lost a fumble for a Gator safety. On any other day he might have been booed off

the field by our insatiable fan base, but not this night. Not in a game where he was courageously filling the shoes of Chris Weinke. Not against the Gators. Not when our unbeaten streak was extended to 40 games. No, this night it was simply about winning the game. It was about overcoming adversity. It was about Coach

Richt's and Marcus Outzen's lives intersecting at a specific moment in history to produce an athletic work of art. The two men, united in the shadows of greater quarterbacks, shined brightly on that day.

For 30 minutes, "The Rooster" led FSU to an improbable 17-0 half against our detested rivals the Florida Gators. In two halves, he went from "noble loser" to "magnificent champion." In two weeks, he had gone from unknown backup to unforgettable legend. One thing I know for sure, the next time I see a Gator and a Rooster squaring off, I won't bet against the Rooster.

22

FIESTA

Our improbable victory over the Gators put us in a position to hope. We had done everything we could do, and now our fate rested in the hands of two teams we had already defeated that year. Three teams ranked ahead of us had a game remaining and we needed at least two of them to lose, for us to play in the BCS National Championship Game. Kansas State was ranked no. 1 and had to play no. 10 Texas A&M for the Big XII Championship. UCLA was no. 2 and had to play unranked Miami in a game that had been rescheduled due to Hurricane Georges, and Third ranked Tennessee had to play Mississippi State in the SEC Championship game. The odds were stacked against us because all of the teams we needed to lose were favored to win in their games, but crazier things had happened.

Miami and UCLA played first and set the table for the wild ride of emotions that college football fans would savor over the next 12 hours. As sickening and incongruous as it was, the Seminole Nation was rooting for Miami to win. The 'Canes played a strong first half and led the Bruins 21-17 before kicking off in the third quarter. All of our hopes were dashed when UCLA jumped on Miami for 21 points in the third, and a 38-21 lead with only seconds remaining before the fourth. But suddenly, Najeh

Davenport took a handoff 23 yards for a TD before the quarter expired, and provided some much needed momentum for the 'Canes and hope for us. Santana Moss reeled in a 71-yard TD catch to cut the lead to 38-35 with just over twelve minutes to play. UCLA quarterback, Cade McNown scored on a 1-yard run, with less than seven minutes in the game, and reestablished their 10 point lead at 45-35. The 'Canes stormed right back. Less than one minute later, Hurricane wide receiver Mondriel Fulcher, caught a touchdown pass to bring the score to 45-42 and the defense forced a fumble, paving the way for Miami to take the lead. Four plays later, UM tailback Edgerrin James scored the game-winning touchdown and the 'Canes pulled off the huge upset. After a wild game, featuring 94 points, UCLA had been defeated 49-45 and now we only needed one of the teams playing that night to lose, and we could go back to rooting against Miami.

The Kansas State and Tennessee games were staggered because they were in different time zones, so our attention was initially focused on the Georgia Dome where we were rooting hard for Mississippi State. About halfway through the fourth quarter, the Bulldogs' Kevin Prentiss returned a punt 83 yards for a score and a 14-10 lead! We were just eight minutes away from the unthinkable happening and a matchup with Kansas State in the Fiesta Bowl. Tee Martin wasn't ready to let us go to Tempe just yet, so he threw two quick touchdowns within a minute of each other and gave the Vol's a 24-14 win. Tennessee had just punched their ticket to Arizona and the Big XII Championship Game would decide their opponent. A Kansas State win meant that they would go, but a Texas A&M win would open the door for us.

I was with a few guys in downtown Tallahassee for the annual "Jingle Bell Run" festivities. There were thousands of people down there for the tree lighting, street vendors, and a 3K run. Of course, most everyone there was a Seminole fan, so crowds were gathered in front of any viewable television. There wasn't a very hopeful feeling about the game because it appeared to be all Kansas State. They led 17-6 at the half, and they had increased their lead to 27-12 going into the final quarter. Many of us turned our attention to the festivities, in light of the Aggies being down by more points than they had scored all night with only 15 minutes to play.

As we were walking down the road, we heard a big roar from one of the viewing crowds so we hurried up to see what had happened. Branndon Stewart had connected with Leroy Hodge for an Aggie touchdown, and cut the lead to 27-19 with under 10 minutes to play. It gave us hope, but not a lot because they still had to score and convert a two point conversion just to tie the game. But our miniscule hope was enough for us to stay by the TV for the rest of the game. A second, much louder, roar echoed through downtown as Sirr Parker hauled in a nine-yard pass from Stewart to bring the Aggies within two of tying the game, with only 65 seconds to play. Parker finished what he started when he caught the conversion as well, and a celebration erupted on the streets of Tallahassee.

The game was headed to overtime and our hopes of playing for the National Championship were enormous now. The teams exchanged field goals in the first overtime to make the score 30-30. K-State got the ball first, to begin the second overtime and the Aggies held them to another field goal, giving them the chance to win the game on their ensuing possession. The overtime period started poorly for Texas A&M, and they found themselves with a third-and-17 from the K-State 32-yard line. Stewart hit Parker again on a slant route and the Wildcat defender failed to wrap him up. He raced towards the end zone with one man between him and the game-winning touchdown. The last man between Parker and us going to Tempe, hit him, but Parker managed to reach for the pylon and Texas A&M pulled off the improbable upset! The only place louder than the Trans World Dome was downtown Tallahassee as the streets exploded with joy unconfined. UCLA and Kansas State were defeated, which meant we would face Tennessee in the Fiesta Bowl and the War Chant filled the Tallahassee night.

Bowl trips were amazing experiences. Granted, we had a remarkable string of the top bowl games in America. Between our final game with Florida and our bowl game each year, we had about five weeks to get prepared. We would be given a few days off completely around finals and because we played on Jan. 1 or later every year, we would get a couple of days off to spend Christmas with our families as well. We would reunite in Tallahassee sometime between the 26th and 28th to catch a flight for our bowl destination. Following the 1996, 1997, and 1999 seasons, we rang in the New Year in New Orleans. After the 2000 season, we were on South Beach, and after the drama on Dec. 5, 1998, we spent a week in Tempe, Ariz.

We always stayed in fantastic hotels, but the place in Tempe was in a class by itself. It was a mountainside resort with architecture and landscaping that beautifully complimented the hotels' natural surroundings. We could walk out of our rooms and follow paths to various hidden hot tubs nestled around the property. There was a luxurious outdoor pool contoured to fit the mountainside, complete with custom built, naturally designed waterfalls steadily pouring water into the pool. If we wanted to get out of the pool for a while, the hotel had converted one of their large meeting rooms into a make-shift arcade by renting dozens of current games for us to play. We would have been content to stay at the hotel for the entire week, but there were always plenty of activities that the bowl committees put together for us to participate in. We got to attend dinners, entertainment oriented activities like cosmic bowling, beach parties, or tours, and special functions where we served as the honored guests. For about a week, these communities would treat us like royalty while we prepared to play in the bowl game they were hosting. Between practice and the bowl functions we would spend our time hanging out at the hotel or walking around the town taking in all that the location had to offer. All good things must come to an end, and our week of luxury did too. Thankfully, the best was saved for last as we took the field for the bowl game and soaked up their Super Bowl-esque pageantry.

This particular year, in the Fiesta Bowl, we were set to battle it out with the SEC champions to determine who the kings of college football would be for the 1998 season. It was a sloppy, hard fought game that was marred by penalties and turnovers throughout the night. The first quarter was scoreless, but the opportunistic Volunteers built a 14-0 lead in the second, capped by an interception returned for a score. We were able to answer with a touchdown and a field goal before the half and we began the third quarter trailing 14-9. The third quarter was just like the first with both teams mired in rusty play, which resulted in another scoreless frame. We entered the final quarter down by just one score and more than capable of claiming the victory. But, about halfway into the quarter, Tee Martin found Peerless Price for a 71-yard, demoralizing touchdown catch. They tacked on a field goal about three minutes later and quickly had a 23-9 lead. Rooster showed his grit and led us on a TD drive that he finished himself, with a seven-yard run. We were right back in it at 23-16, and when Brian Allen recovered a Tennessee fumble in the closing minutes, hope was alive on our sideline. Unfortunately, Outzen's first pass of the possession was intended for Peter Warrick but ended up in the hands of Tennessee's Steve Johnson. There was nothing left for Tennessee to do but run out the clock.

Once more I knelt on the sideline and watched another team celebrate a victory over us. For the second time in three years, I watched the stadium crew set up the stage for a national championship celebration that somebody else would get to stand on. I was sickened as I watched the Tennessee players hold bags of commemorative Tostitos over their heads, and heard their band blare "Rocky Top" continuously. I hated the moment in the 1997 Sugar Bowl but hated this one even more. I would have traded all the hotel amenities and bowl functions in the world to switch places with Tennessee on that night.

Sadly, this wouldn't be the last time I would watch another team celebrate on a stage that I wanted to be on. But, I wouldn't taste defeat again for almost two years. Another year complete, another national championship tantalizingly close, and another off season ahead of us motivated by falling one game short.

23

COMPETING, CALORIES, & CREATINE

The off-season of 1999 represented opportunity for me. Myron Jackson had graduated, leaving the starting tight end position up for grabs. Nick Franklin had the upper hand as he had split time with Myron throughout the 1998 season while I was bouncing around between positions. One of the position experiments was over though, my career as a center was behind me. Thomas and Moon had proven themselves at the top of the depth chart. But, the top of the depth chart was never the reason I was playing center; the concern was always with depth, and that was no longer an issue. Antoine Mirambeau was a part of the 1998 recruiting class and had already developed into a more than capable reserve. Beyond that, Josh Baggs arrived in January of '98, as a transfer from Georgia Southern, and was battling Mirambeau for playing time. Depth was no longer a concern at center, so I was free from the rigors of playing on the offensive line.

Fullback was a bit of a different story. Lamarr Glenn and Billy Rhodes graduated, leaving William McCray as the only scholarship player at that position. The emergence of Chris Weinke prompted Dan Kendra to convert from a quarterback to a fullback, but he was still in recovery from surgery on the ACL he tore in the Garnet and Gold game in 1998. Chad Maeder was the only other player taking reps at fullback, so depth was a concern for the spring.

We all knew that McCray and Maeder were a strong pair at the position and that when Kendra was ready to go, he was going to be a force, so I probably wasn't going to be playing fullback in the fall. However, the team would still need me to fill in some during the spring so I continued splitting reps between fullback and tight end.

As much as I wanted to earn the starting job at tight end, the battle was really for who would be Nick's backup. He had a strong season in '98 and was a better athlete than me. Nick proved to be a strong blocker in the running game and was fast enough to be a real threat in the passing game. I wanted to beat him out, but first I had to move ahead of the two accomplished underclassmen, Patrick Hughes and Carver Donaldson. Carver came to FSU in 1997 as the top-rated tight end in Florida and no. 4 tight end in America. He played as a true freshman, but missed '98 because of a chest injury. P-Hughes arrived in 1998 as the no. 1 high school tight end in the United States, and he gobbled up all the reps that Carver missed during his freshman year. Even though I was older than both of them, they had earned more playing time and each had at least one reception to their credit. My work was cut out for me.

While they had superior athletic giftedness, I had developed superior technique in my pilgrimage through the offense over the previous three years. Even with the technique advantage, I believe that the reason I was able to edge ahead of them was that I possessed a more complete knowledge of the offense. That knowledge translated into great confidence on the field. Not a confidence that allowed me to believe that I would succeed on every play, but a confidence that I was doing the right thing. When you aren't 100 percent sure of what you are supposed to do, it leads to a subtle hesitation or reluctance. It is nearly impossible to discern when you are doing it, but once you rise above it, you can feel the difference. That confidence helped me to have a great spring, at tight end and at fullback. I was able to surpass Patrick and Carver, and even gave Nick a pretty good run for his money. Not only did I have confidence in the playbook, now I had confidence in myself, and that motivated me going into the summer.

Nick was still listed as the starter, but I was hungry to earn the job. I knew that there wasn't a whole lot that I could control when it came to my athletic ability, but I knew that I could control what kind of shape I was in. So, I resolved to get into the best shape of my life. I was never accused of being a gym rat. Not now, not ever. You would never hear me being described as the first one on the field and the last one off; it just wasn't me. A better description would be that I would give you everything I had when I was on the coaches' time, but when their time was over, my dedication was too. Shoot, even that description is too lofty when I reflect on my weight room mentality. I was all about the social aspect of the weight room. Don't get me wrong, I did what was required of me and I did it well but I tended to take my time. My roommate, Justin Amman however, was that gym rat and I decided that I would let him dictate my pace that summer.

I had heard of Creatine before, but Justin was the one who sold me on its benefits. As I recall, it was supposed to help your muscles retain water or something, and that was supposed to help you get stronger. I still don't fully understand it, but Justin recommended it and the NCAA approved it, so I was all in. Justin also introduced me to the concept of protein consumption. He said I needed to eat two grams of protein a day for every pound that I weighed. So, even though that led to some rather un-orthodox eating patterns, I did that too. But, more significantly than creatine or protein, Justin introduced me in a whole new way, to Dan Kendra.

To say that Dan broke the mold is like saying Lebron James is good at basketball; the phrase just doesn't do the man justice. Dan didn't break the mold... Dan was from another factory, in another country, that made a totally different product. He is the most unique person I have ever met and one of the most memorable as well. He was the most muscular man I had ever seen and he completed his WWE look with the military hair cut and high top shoes. He was capable of sustaining a frightening intensity, while also being as goofy and carefree as anyone I knew. He drove a Porsche and could nearly leg press one as well. He was not your everyday college student, Dan was different.

The most glaring difference was in the way Dan chose to eat. While most of my college meals involved a microwave and the culinary expertise of Chef Boy-R-Dee, Dan's involved grilled ostrich and protein shakes. The man was the most disciplined eater I have ever known. He would even have the hotel on our road trips prepare a special meal for him to eat for our pregame dinners. We would normally have chicken breasts, baked potatoes, and a salad but Dan would have baked Salmon and brown rice. He consumed protein the way pregnant women consume pickles; he was relentless. And for that devotion to the muscle building protein, we all suffered through years of his body breaking it down, and it stunk... if you know what I mean.

Thankfully, that wasn't the principle that Justin gleaned and in turn, shared with me. Dan encouraged Justin in his pursuit of healthy and athletically aggressive eating. Dan got us excited about natural protein from our food and the manufactured protein found in our beloved shakes. However, Dan had a different budget than we did. So while he was having an Ostrich steak, we would eat a can of tuna fish. When Dan went for the lean turkey breast, we would eat a can of tuna fish. If the old adage that you are what you eat had any truth to it, I would have developed gills that summer because I ate ridiculous amounts of tuna. We also ate dozens of eggs, pounds of chicken, and drank gallons of milk, but Justin also got pretty creative.

One of his favorite tricks was to add olive oil to his protein shakes. He liked that it added the extra, good kind of fat and it also improved the flavor of the shake. Justin used to say that you don't eat for pleasure, you eat to get better, and he embodied that ideal. I remember him spiking one of his protein shakes with tuna to increase the grams he was getting in that meal. I didn't take it that far, but this was the longest stretch of time where I regularly consumed vegetables. I hate vegetables… all of them. Always have and still do today. Most of them actually make me gag, but that summer Justin made me believe that I needed to eat to get better, so I got over it. I began power swallowing servings of broccoli and chasing it with large gulps of water. I began to eat black beans frequently and also muscled down green beans with regularity. This was worse than mat drills to me. I had to psyche myself up each time I did it, but I ate my vegetables that summer because I wanted to get better.

I was eating six meals and consuming more than 400 grams of protein a day, but It wasn't all protein and vegetables. Kendra, Justin, and the rest of us also took part in a weekly reward concept known as "fat days." Well, Dan just had a fat meal, but the rest of us took advantage of the entire day. These glorious celebrations of fat and cholesterol were my saving grace. Whole pizzas, chicken wings, ice cream, hamburgers, you name it. If it was high in calories and tasted like it, we would eat it on our fat days. A favorite was when a group of us would go to a local Tex-Mex restaurant for their all-you-can-eat fajita nights. The manager had to cringe when four to six, 300-plus pound college football players took up shop for a buffet night. We didn't just go in and eat either; my dietary mentors had a strategy. Justin, for instance, wouldn't waste time and stomach space with the inexpensive elements of a fajita. He focused on the chicken or the steak and didn't stop until he had reached his gastro-intestinal capacity. Another common

The fat-day group. L-R: Jarad Moon, Ross Brannon, Justin Amman, Jerry Carmichael, & Me

strategy was to "use the restroom" partway through the carne carnage. The thought was that there would be more room after the bathroom trip, enabling us to cause further damage on the restaurant's bottom line. I don't know if that strategy actually did what we thought it did physiologically, but I know it had a positive impact on us psychologically. We believed there was more room, so we ate to fill the gap. Those were good nights. They were a far cry from our usually, conscientious attitude when it came to calories though. We always monitored the calories we ate, but one of the guys was also acutely aware of the calories he burned.

I don't know for sure if these practices were just laziness in disguise but they definitely conserved calories. Football demands an incredible investment of calories. Be it an actual practice or a session of off-season conditioning, we needed every calorie we could get to maximize our effectiveness. These end-of-practice calorie needs were the motivation for some out of the box thinking. It began with a mathematical evaluation to determine the fewest possible steps to any particular location in the house. The best example of this was seen when someone had to use the bathroom. It had been determined that it required fewer steps to go to the front porch than it did to walk to the bathroom, so they did the most efficient thing. A similar example came in the form of 2-litre cola bottles. The tops were cut off and they were kept by the bedside for any late night emergencies. Why waste all those calories and those precious moments of sleep by walking all the way to the bathroom? My favorite of all the calorie saving ideas was the shower seat. If you went in the shower in this guys' house, you might find a plastic lawn chair sitting in the tub. This was brought in to prevent the unnecessary burning of calories for something so unhelpful, in regard to football achievement, as a shower. We had a desire to become bigger, stronger, and faster, and we would do whatever we needed to, within the bounds of the NCAA rules and morality. If that meant tuna fish in a milk shake, so be it. Sitting down to take a shower, absolutely. Our guys certainly got creative and worked very hard to maximize their body's potential, but I never saw or heard of any player doing anything that wasn't on the up and up.

My shadowing of Justin paid off. By the end of that summer, I weighed about 250 pounds and had the lowest body fat percentage of my career. I could bench press 440 pounds and my vertical jump was up to 34 inches. We had guys bench pressing over 525 pounds and dudes that boasted vertical jumps over 40 inches, so I wasn't the strongest on the team, wasn't the best jumper on the team, and certainly wasn't the fastest on the team. But I was the strongest I had ever been, was jumping higher than I ever had before, and was running my fastest as well. I was in the best shape of my life. I was ready for the season to begin so that I could see if my physical conditioning would translate into success on the field.

Junior:
August of 1999
thru July of 2000

24

THE DOGG POUND

John Lilly was the ideal Guilford College Football Player. I'm not being descriptive, he actually won that award! Coach Lilly came to Florida State from Beckley, West Virginia and his story of meager beginnings to a role of significance closely paralleled mine. He came to FSU as a videographer just before I came in 1996. By the time I was on the team, he had been "promoted" to a graduate assistant and was Mickey Andrews' right hand man. He became my de facto coach since he ran the scout team offense and that's where I spent all my time in the first couple of years I was in Tallahassee. As I was transitioning off the scout team and onto the offensive unit, Coach Lilly was as well, and the "Dogg Pound" was born.

John was known to the players and staff as "Lilly-Dogg," hence his players being known as the "Dogg Pound." Our unit was unique among all the different position groups or segments. Every other segment contained a group of players who played the same position, but the "Dogg Pound" had tight ends, kickers, punters, long-snappers, and one tight end/fullback/center hybrid. Kickers are universally known to be slightly different than the position players, and at Florida State, the tight ends were marginalized on the offense. So, the "Dogg Pound" was the Seminole equivalent of the Island of Misfit Toys.

Our segment was made up of players from all over the United States and even overseas. Nick, Carver, Clay Ingram, Keith Cottrell, Sam Sprouse, and Coach Lilly's Graduate Assistant, Brannon Tidwell were all Florida boys. Brian Sawyer and Chance Gwaltney, who wouldn't arrive until the next fall, joined me in representing Georgia. Patrick Hughes made sure that everyone he ever met was aware that he was from Nacadoches, Tex. Janikowski played high school ball in Fla. but had lived in Poland until he was 15. Throw in Lilly-Dogg with his West Virginia roots and we were probably the most diverse segment on the team. Our unique blend of personalities and backgrounds kept our meetings interesting.

Some of the Dogg Pound. L-R: Me, John Lilly, Carver Donaldson, Nick Franklin, & Brannon Tidwell.

The meetings were a necessary evil for the kickers. The whole time was devoted to watching practice and game film of the tight ends, so the kickers had to entertain themselves. Janikowski was notorious for being less than interested in watching our film. He would normally set himself up a little bed in the back of the room and attempt to grab a quick nap. This often led to a "conversation" between him and Coach Lilly. These interactions were an audible fusion of Lilly-Dogg's West Virginia drawl and Sebastian's thick Polish accent mixed with a colorful dose of American slang, to create great theatre for the ears. Sebastian just couldn't accept having to waste time in the meetings and even though Coach Lilly lost a lot of coaching time correcting "38," he had to keep him in there. It was an unavoidable, daily exercise that they each enjoyed about as much as sitting in rush hour traffic around Atlanta.

I remember the first time I met Sebastian and I am not proud of it. It wasn't uncommon for me to feel intimidated in my early years as a Seminole. The first player I met was linebacker Henri Crockett, and he might as well have been the President of the United States. I didn't even know who he was but I knew he was a player, although I wasn't sure if I was yet. He was standing outside the locker room and I was supposed to be going into the locker room, so I had to walk past him. I barely made eye contact and made some stupid comment like, "hey, do you know if shoes are in there?" He looked at me like I had just said, "hey, do you know if shoes are in there?" He laughed at me and just shook his head. I hurried my pace and tried to hide in a cabinet once I got into the locker room. Not a good first impression. Looking back, I guess that was understandable. I was a kid and a walk-on, it was my first time being around the stadium, he was the first Seminole I had seen, and I was lost. It is reasonable to feel a bit intimidated in that situation. I was also intimidated by Julian Pittman and this too was totally reasonable.

GRATEFUL

Julian was a freak. Some football players are very big. Some football players are very strong. Pittman was both. As a scout team offensive lineman, I had to try to block Pittman and the rest of the monoliths we had on our defensive line. Most of the guys could crush me, but didn't make that their goal. Not Pittman, I am convinced he enjoyed throwing me and the other scout teamers around. He was built like a professional wrestler and his facial structure made him appear menacing. At 300-plus pounds and capable of literally tossing me across a room, my intimidation by him was totally justified.

Other times, I would have been intimidated by guys who might take my job away. Tommy Polley was initially slotted to play tight end. We were in the same recruiting class and I was instantly intimidated by him because he was "Mr. Football" for the state of Maryland and a heavily sought after recruit. Thankfully, they moved him to linebacker, where he flourished and went on to a career in the NFL. I felt the same way when Nick arrived on campus the past January. Nick was the no. 1 ranked junior college tight end in America and was being recruited to play tight end at FSU. I figured he must have been better than me, so I let it intimidate me a little. Again, I think all these scenarios are totally reasonable and I can sleep at night. But one day, I was in the coaches' offices and I saw a new face being shown around.

He was about 6'2" and had to weigh close to 260 pounds. He had huge legs and a bald head, and I was instantly convinced that he had come to take my job away. The job at that time, being the fourth team tight end and scout team center. My heart sunk as Coach Cottrell said hi and began to introduce us. "Ryan, I want you to meet our new kicker, Sebastian Janikowski." I guess I should have felt relieved that he wasn't after my job, but instead I felt a sense of embarrassment. I let myself get intimidated by a kicker...

A KICKER! I can't even believe I'm putting this on paper. In the real world, this would be akin to a "Hell's Angels" biker being a closet Backstreet Boys fan. It's simply unheard of and shameful. Thankfully, I never got in a fight with Sebastian but the Dogg Pound wasn't free from a little intra-pound throw down.

One such occurrence happened after a practice one day. This moment brought our team together and turned Dan Kendra ghostly white. You need a little back story before I go on. Clay Ingram and Sebastian were pretty close friends. They hung out together a lot off the field and were together all the time when they were around the football facilities as well. Keith Cottrell led a quieter life than the other two guys and had a different, more serious, approach to his craft than they did. Keith was often times the "third wheel," and was regularly on the receiving end of their comments and teasing. Such is life on a football team. There is constant teasing, sarcasm, bravado, etc., but Keith got more than his fair share. To his credit, he handled it all in stride and was an excellent punter for us and a tremendous asset to our team. But one day, he had enough of Clay's teasing and Keith called Clay to the carpet... literally.

I don't know when the gauntlet was officially thrown down, but part of the way through practice the story had circulated that Keith and Clay were scheduled to throw down right after practice, in the heart of the locker room. The excitement was palpable. We were sharp at practice that day because no one wanted to be out running gassers and miss the title bout. It was great! Clay and Keith were getting treated like gladiators during the practice, with guys telling them they were betting on them, or encouraging them to knock the other guy out, etc. When practice ended, guys were literally skipping into the locker room because of their enthusiasm. I guess to appreciate what we were feeling you could imagine going to a live taping of Jerry Springer or midget wrestling. Nobody was expecting gold gloves when the bell sounded.

Once the coaches had cleared the locker room, it was on! Clay was the first man into the "ring." He had gotten quickly out of his pads and was amped for the duel. He began yelling for Keith to get out there and the rest of the guys followed suit. The defensive guys were the most fired up and they put their enthusiasm to work. They were jumping around the "ring," cheering Clay, and chiding Keith. Not because they had any issue with Keith, but that they wanted to see the fight and it wouldn't happen without Keith entering the fray. He was stuck at this point; there was no walking away from this one. His choices were no. 1) go and fight or no. 2) quit the team and move to Alaska. Being an Orlando boy, Alaska was out of the question, so the fight was on.

He took his time getting out of his practice gear and into proper fighting attire… shorts and a T-shirt. Clay was still wearing his football pants and T-shirt, bouncing around like Muhammad Ali, and feigning as if he had true boxing skills. When Keith began his walk to the "ring," it was like a real boxing match. Keith had to make his way through the crowd of eager fans; getting smacked on the back, cheered, whistled at, booed, you name it. Keith, simply because Clay jumped in the "ring" first, had been relegated to the role of "heel" and Clay got to be the "face." He finally did make it to the ring and as quickly as he entered, it closed up behind him with a mass of humanity sealing him inside. No retreat.

They wasted no time and began circling each other like true prize fighters. At one point Clay stopped, stood tall with a solemn poker face, held his hand directly out in front of him, and waved Keith forward with the movement of just the fingers of his extended arm like Neo at the end of the Matrix. The energy in the room was off the charts; a mix of sarcasm, joy, and testosterone.

Clay and Keith, deep snapper and punter, continued to size each other up like a scene from *Fight Club,* and then suddenly the action began. Keith took a shot at Clay like a Greco-roman wrestler and tried to take Clay down. But Clay, being the much larger man, was able to free himself. Keith was left on his back with Clay standing over him.   Quickly, Keith abandoned the Greco-Roman strategy and decided ninja would be a better approach. He was a punter after all. Clay had him cornered but Keith kept taking swipes with his right foot and kept Clay at bay. Clay made a couple different attempts to get past Keith's defense, but all of the sudden there was a sense that something was happening in another part of the room. If you have ever watched professional wrestling, you will be familiar with the moment when two guys are fighting but surprisingly the theme music for another wrestler begins playing. In an instant, everyone's attention is off the fighters in the ring and is focused on the entrance. This is what happened in the locker room except our attention was transferred to the shower entrance, and the one and only, Dan Kendra. Apparently Dan missed the memo about the fight because he had hit the showers. The moment wasn't lost on him though because Dan made quite the entrance.

He was stark naked and completely white from the lather of his soap. From his toenails to his crew cut, every square inch of Kendra was saturated with soap. He bounded into the ring and began hop-swaying back and forth. He had his arms bent at the elbow with his hands in front of his body like he was getting ready to tackle someone and his fingers were spread as wide as he could possibly spread them. He just bounced back and forth with a crazy, Kendra trademark grin and began to lather himself up even more. The team erupted with laughter and the fight was quickly forgotten. As entertaining as it was to watch Clay and Keith sort of fight each other, it was like watching pinochle compared to Dan's soap commercial.

Keith and Clay found great humor in Kendra's white out and were able to make amends wherever necessary. That was certainly the last kicker fight we ever witnessed and more importantly, the last soapy Kendra too. In spite of the kicker's infighting and Janikowski's feud with Coach Lilly, the Dogg Pound was a light-hearted group thanks in large part to one Patrick Hughes.

Patrick arrived in Tallahassee the previous fall, and our segment was never the same. He was the progeny of WWE superstar Dwayne "The Rock" Johnson through television osmosis. There was never any doubt when P-Hughes was near because regardless of location or circumstance, he was not afraid to unleash a, "Know your role and shut your mouth!" While our game or practice film was running, Patrick would offer commentary in full vocal costume as, "The Rock." No player or coach was off limits from a verbal smack down from our Rock impersonator. Pat hailed from "the great state" and he constantly reminded us all of the greatness of Texas, specifically "The Nac" (his hometown of Nacogdoches). Nobody knew for sure what Pat actually sounded like because he was always impersonating someone else. He mastered the voice and mannerisms of our compliance director Bob Minnix, our offensive line coach Jimmy Heggins, and Chuck Amato among others. Pat was always "on".

When I moved into "Burt" with Carver, we got to know each other pretty well. "C.D." hailed from Tampa and loved hip-hop mogul Master-P. Carver and I were on opposite ends of the spectrum when it came to personal appearance. He was metro-sexual before being metro-sexual was cool. His clothes were sharp, with a hip-hop flair, and he kept his blond hair perfect. Just imagine a 260 pound version of Eminem and you have a pretty good image of Carver. My clothes were always casual with a gym flair and I didn't even wash my hair every day. Imagine a 250-pound version of an uber-casual college kid and you have a pretty good image of me. He was meticulous in the care of his many different shoes and actually owned clothes that needed to be dry-cleaned. I owned two pairs of shoes, my tennis shoes that were on my feet 90 percent of the time and my "dress shoes" that I wore to church. If I did own any dry-clean only clothes, I probably ruined them in the washing machine. Carver regularly tried to get me to improve my look and his area of concentration was my dingy shoes. I wore my shoes until they fell apart and when I met Carver, my shoes were in particularly bad shape. I think it irritated him. One day I came home and found him sitting in our living room with an assortment of shoe cleaning supplies and my dingy old shoes. He was working on my shoes with a toothbrush, trying desperately to revitalize them. I just laughed at him and thanked him for his efforts. My shoes ended up looking pretty good though.

We became a pretty close unit within the Dogg Pound even though groups of us were competing for the same jobs. Coach Lilly did a masterful job of keeping us focused on being the best we could be and letting the results take care of themselves. Everyone in that room wanted to win and everyone in that room wanted to be on the field as much as possible. Thankfully, we were able to maintain a high level of respect for one another and belief in Coach Lilly to have a healthy team environment within the Dogg Pound. Being able to trust one another would prove vitally important because the next two years were going to be a crazy ride.

25

WIRE TO WIRE

TWO-A-DAYS: August, 1999

The 1999 preseason marked the end of a nomadic run of position changes for me. Over my first three years, I rarely occupied one position for any length of time. Finally, I would get to settle down and develop a mastery of one position, but the previous three years of bouncing around prepared me well for success. '99 also represented the end of my pattern of constantly changing jersey numbers. My number for the '96 season was 87. In August of '97 it was switched to 65 and then two days later, 67. Before the season kicked off, my number was switched again, this time to no. 82. I kept that number until the fall of 1998. That fall I was moonlighting as a fullback, so they outfitted me with 39. Finally, over the summer of 1999, I put my two cents in and got my final number.

I always looked up to Andre Wadsworth. The guy was total class, not to mention an elite football player. So elite, that he was the highest drafted player in the storied history of FSU at no. 3 overall. Andre was also a walk-on who had matured in college and earned a scholarship. When he graduated, leaving his number available, I asked for permission to switch my number from 39 to Andre's old number of 85. Landing on that number was the start of a new phase in my career because for the first time, I was going to be able to focus solely on playing tight end and that would be the beginning of a good run for me.

Andre Wadsworth

One of the first things required of us when we reported for preseason camp, was the mile and a half run. We loathed this run. Tallahassee is brutally hot in August and regardless of how well-conditioned we were, the heat could get the better of any of us. We had to complete the run under a specific time, based on our position. Thanks to Justin pushing me hard all summer, I was able to make my run with plenty of time to spare. I didn't realize how significant it was at the time, but Nick wasn't able to make his time after the heat monkey jumped on his back. The next day it was time to hit the field, and go to work.

Dan Kendra recovered fully from his knee surgery and he rejoined the team as a fullback. His presence, along with the arrival of freshman Randy Golightly allowed me to scratch fullback off my list of responsibilities. For the first time in my career, I only had to worry about one position. I met with only the tight ends, practiced only with the tight ends, and played only tight end. It's amazing how much easier it is when you can finally stop thinking so hard and just play the game.

Jumping around between all those positions was a great thing for me because I improved as an athlete and a football player. It was also a challenge for me because I struggled to find an athletic identity and was never able to relax mentally on the field. It was vital for my development, to finally find a home at tight end. It was where I always wanted to be from the beginning and I was able to get comfortable and let all that I had learned in those three nomadic years to bear fruit.

I had a strong camp and solidified myself as the backup to Nick. He was a better football player. I knew that I had done everything possible, so I felt no shame in resolving to be the best backup tight end in the country. I still wanted to start, but it was out of my hands. Little did I know that just a few days later, everything would be flipped upside-down.

REVERSED: August 28, 1999

The opening week of the 1999 season can be summed up for me, and for our team, with one loaded word, "reversed." The first big reverse was personal. Unbeknownst to me, Coach Lilly had placed a qualification on Nick's job as a starter. Nick was told that if he failed to successfully complete his mile and a half run, he would not be allowed to start the season opener. During our post-practice talk, before we entered into our game week, Coach Lilly told the group about the condition he had placed on Nick. In a very professional, matter-of-fact manner, he told me and the rest of the Dogg Pound, that I was going to be the starter against Louisiana Tech!

This time last August I had been in turmoil. I had lost my scholarship, but was given it back a month later. I was playing three positions, but buried on all the depth charts. Just one year later, I was named the starting tight end! It was surreal. There was no fan fare or press conferences. No sooner had Lilly-Dogg made the announcement than we were off to run our gassers. It was just like any other practice. I was thrilled, but I didn't really know how to express it. I knew that it was fruit from the tree of Nick's misfortune, but it still tasted fantastic. I shared the news with my parents, which made their upcoming travel plans all the more exciting. Had it happened earlier in my career, I might have been more emotional, but I had matured a lot over the years and I knew that nothing is promised. I had to keep on doing what I had been doing and hopefully, I would help the team succeed. So, I found myself just a few days away from my first game as a starter and that game was the setting for the second big reverse, this one performed by Peter Warrick.

We began the 1999 season as the no. 1 team in America. We returned many of the key contributors from the last year's team. There were two significant reasons that people believed we were the team to beat in 1999. The first was the return of Chris Weinke, who had suffered the nasty neck injury during the Virginia game in 1998. The medical staff was very methodical with his recovery process. He wasn't even allowed to put on a helmet in the spring, although he was able to throw the ball a little. He made a full recovery and was ready to roll when the two-a-days began. He was playing as well as any quarterback in America before he was injured, and was in the midst of a streak of 228 pass-attempts, without an interception. The second reason was Peter Warrick, who had shocked the nation when he decided to return to FSU for his senior season in hopes of winning a national championship. Had he left school after his junior year, he was projected to be a first round selection in the NFL draft. His decision to return to school, and leave millions of dollars on the table was a very uncommon decision. Now as a senior, He was considered by many to be one of the leading candidates for the Heisman trophy and he didn't waste any time making his case for the award.

Our opening game was in Doak Campbell, against the Bulldogs of Louisiana Tech led by the top-rated quarterback of 1998, Tim Rattay. Tech ran a wide-open offense that was capable of scoring tons of points, but we returned the top-rated defense from 1998 and our guys weren't about to let them move the ball easily.

The game opened and our defense lived up to the billing. Tech scored their only points of the game on a second quarter touchdown pass from Rattay. Unfortunately, we struggled on offense in our season debut. We were nearly shutout in the first quarter, and the game set up for the Bulldogs to take the lead into the half. Everything changed when our free safety, Sean Key, recovered a fumble and gave the ball back to our offense for one last drive before the half. This drive was the beginning of a historical run, and was highlighted by a historical run, a reverse to be precise.

With under a minute to play, we found ourselves about 20 yards from the end zone and the coaches decided to give Warrick a chance to make a play. It was fitting that our season began with a remarkable play from no. 9 because it would end in much the same fashion. The play was a handoff to Peter and I can't remember if it was a called reverse, or a simple sweep, but the call was irrelevant anyway. Tech seemingly had the play boxed in, but Warrick provided the Bulldogs with a taste of what made him so special.

Tech had no less than 11 opportunities to tackle Warrick but he was able to thwart every attempt as he stopped, restarted, changed directions, spun, and juked back and forth all over the turf of Doak Campbell stadium. There were moments when he was actually running backwards and they still couldn't get hold of him. He finally found a crease behind the block of my summer workout partner, Justin, and was able to cross the line of scrimmage. By that time, most of the Bulldogs were laying on the field somewhere and Pete was able to make it to the end zone. In typical Warrick fashion, he didn't just run in, he had one hand on his hip as he strutted into the paint and into legend. His ridiculous run sparked the offense. and by the end of the day we had soundly whipped the Bulldogs, 41-3. The game even provided me the opportunity to make my first career reception.

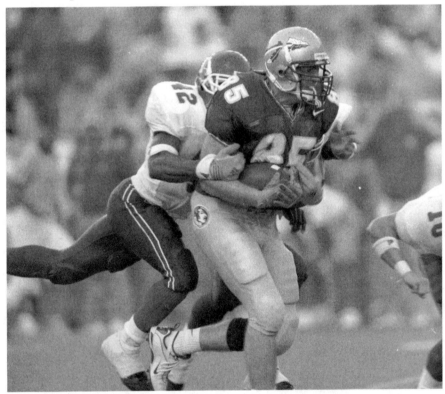

We ran a simple play called, "460 spot." The number "460" referred to the pass protection, and the term "spot" told me what my job was. All I had to do was run towards the center of the field and settle down over the "spot," at a depth of five yards. (*The "spot" represented an imaginary line, extending from the spot on the field*

where the center snapped the ball.) Because our receivers were having a big game, when I ran my route, the linebackers dropped deep into their zones. So much so, that Weinke had no choice but to throw the ball to me. It was a simple little 10-yard toss that I inexplicably jumped into the air to catch. Once I had the ball secured, I did a quick 180 and ran straight up the field. No juking, swerving, or running backwards for me. I just set my sights on the end zone and ran as fast as I could. Twenty-six yards later, a couple of Tech defenders tackled me, and my mom breathed a sigh of relief when I got up unharmed. It wasn't as flashy as Warrick's highlight run, but it was a huge milestone for me.

Two huge reverses which led to two improbable outcomes. Peter Warrick pulled off one reverse and scored a touchdown to launch his Heisman campaign. The other reverse was off the field and produced playing time and a career milestone for a projected backup. We whipped the Bulldogs 41-7 that Saturday and began another season 1-0.

ST. AUGUSTINE: August 29, 1999

After every Seminole football game, Coach Bowden would join "The Voice of the Seminoles," Gene Deckerhoff to record, "The Bobby Bowden Show." The premise of the show is just to talk through the game highlights and point out guys who played well that day. More often than not, Gene and Coach would film the show just after the game or as soon as they arrived in Tallahassee after a road trip. Sometimes that meant that they were recording the show at 2 a.m. because of a night kick off... that might explain what happened.

I always looked forward to watching the show, especially if I had made a catch in the game. Occasionally, one of the guys would point me out for a block but had I caught a pass I would definitely get a mention. For guys who were regulars on Sports Center, the Bobby Bowden show was inconsequential, but for guys like me, it was awesome. The first time Coach Bowden pointed me out to the television audience was after the Louisiana Tech game where I made my first career reception. He said something along the lines of, "There's old Sprague from... St. Augustine, Fla."

Now don't get me wrong; I can appreciate that Coach Bowden has known thousands of players from all over the country. I am often amazed at his ability to recall players and in my case, even my mom, from his vast mental database of names, sometimes years removed from their playing days. But, my friends and family took great pleasure out of Coach confusing my hometown of Augusta, Ga. with St. Augustine, Fla. I was so close to being famous, and probably quite proud of that fact. However, Coach's geographical fumble was all the fodder that those closest to me needed, to keep my head out of the clouds.

SHOOTOUT: September 11, 1999

I played a pretty solid game against Louisiana Tech and thought I might have done enough to keep my job for another week, but Coach Lilly had a different plan. After I had showered and gotten ready, he pulled me aside and told me I had played well but that he was going to put Nick back in his spot as the starter. The initial switch was based on discipline, not ability. Nick had served his time and now he was being reinstated. Lilly-Dogg was direct because he didn't want me thinking I had done something wrong when I showed up for practice on Monday and saw the depth chart. I thought that was fair... but I hated it.

The next week we were set to play Georgia Tech in Tallahassee. Our first ACC game of the year was a high-profile matchup featuring two Heisman Trophy candidates in Tech quarterback Joe Hamilton and our own Peter Warrick. We don't really practice on Mondays. Most of our time was spent breaking down the game film, before we did some light conditioning. Tuesdays, on the other hand, were full pads and full contact. Ironically, it was a non-contact drill that would change everything for Nick and indirectly for me as well.

It was during the first 20 minutes of practice, where we were running routes and working on catching passes. Nick lined up to run our "Shark" route, a simple five-yard out, and it would be his last play of 1999. When he planted his foot to make his break, his knee gave out and he tore his ACL. It was one of those freak injuries that happen and leave no one to blame. Nick went from being the deserved starter, to spending a year in the training room and on the sidelines in one wayward step. It was this unfortunate set of circumstances that moved me into the starter's role for the entire 1999 season. Coach Lilly's move to promote me to the starting position for the first game, would now bear fruit in ways unforeseen. We were set to begin our conference schedule and because of Lilly Dogg's conviction, the other 10 guys in the huddle weren't looking at a dazed, unprepared backup. Our offense was going to need a great performance to beat Georgia Tech and we had to be able to trust one another.

When two top-10 teams, with Heisman trophy contenders on the offensive side of the ball, get together, you expect a shoot out. Five hundred and ninety-five yards in the first half, proved that this game would live up to the expectations. Georgia Tech was ranked 10th in the country and led by Hamilton. The Yellow Jackets believed this was the year they were going to be able to dethrone us from the top of the ACC. But Brian Allen set the tone early, and let the Jackets know that they picked the wrong day to make a run at our throne.

Kelly Campbell was crossing the field and Hamilton found him. Unfortunately for Campbell, Brian Allen found him too and delivered a crushing blow that left Campbell on the turf with a broken jaw. It was a brutal collision that was followed by that unmistakable, "oooohhh" as 80,000 people simultaneously feel the sympathetic pain. They not only imagine the pain for the man who was the nail, but also vicariously feel the incredible rush of being the hammer. The teams traded scores for a while but we never trailed in the game. It was a thrilling game that was close until the end. One of Weinke's 16 pass completions, and seven of his 262 yards were the product of my second career reception in my second game as a starter.

Our trust for one another was growing while our confidence never waned. We passed our first real "test" of 1999, and at no point in the game was there a doubt in the mind of any player. We knew we were going to win. After a desperate comeback attempt from Joe Hamilton, the Jackets fell six points short. We walked off the field 41-35 winners, with a 2-0 record.

ALMOST: September 18, 1999

In 1998, N.C. State defeated us, which was the only ACC loss we suffered in my five years in Tallahassee. It was only the second ACC loss that the Seminoles had suffered since we joined the league in 1992. Needless to say, we had revenge on our minds as the Wolfpack entered Doak Campbell that Saturday. We had been embarrassed the year before and we hoped to return the favor this year. After already having achieved a couple milestones this season, this game would provide the opportunity for one more, my first career touchdown.

Following a Janikowski field goal, Dan Kendra scored our first touchdown of the day. But there was poor execution on the ensuing extra point, which resulted in Janikowski making a tackle instead of a kick. Instead of being ahead by 10, we were only up by nine, with the score being 12-3. On our next drive we had the opportunity to begin to pull away, but we came up four points short.

Opportunities like this don't come about very often; for most of America they never arrive. Standing in the huddle for a major college football team, playing in front of more than 80,000 fans, in front of millions more on television, and hearing your number called. It was surreal. But, I wasn't thinking about the fans or the TV cameras, I was just scared I was going to mess up.

We were inside the five-yard line, less than 30 feet from another touchdown that would give us a 19-3 lead. After a relatively sluggish start we had begun to move the ball, so everyone in the huddle had a calm confidence about them. All that changed for me when I heard the call though, a bootleg; more specifically a bootleg where I was the primary target. This is one of the simplest pass routes in the book for a tight end. We just had to release inside of the defensive end and run across the field. The only challenge is avoiding running into the umpire and the linebackers as we worked to the proper depth. Being this close to the end zone, we had to look for the ball as soon as we crossed the goal line. No cuts, no safety reads, nothing complicated at all, just running and catching. This is what makes what happened so ridiculous.

I lined up just to the left of the left tackle and squatted down into my stance. I would love to say that it felt "like any other play," but apparently I am not cut out for the clutch situations. My mind was racing.

"Will I be open?"

"Will there be pressure on the QB?"

"What am I going to say to Chris Fowler on Game day?"

In hindsight, contemplating the "Game day" interview might have been premature. On the snap of the ball, instinct took over and I deftly stepped to my right and inside of the defensive end. My release was flawless and I quickly crossed in front of the middle linebacker (*also known as the "mike"*) as I gained the proper depth and headed across the field. After successfully clearing the mike backer, I crossed the goal line and flattened my route to stay parallel to the line of scrimmage. Everything was progressing as planned. My mental preparation had taken over and I was running on pure instinct as I turned my head to the right to find the Weinke, who was running parallel to me behind the line of scrimmage.

Normally, when a Florida State tight end looks back at the quarterback, we find that he has already thrown the ball to someone else or is laser-locked onto one of the wide receivers. So you can imagine my surprise when I looked at him and he locked eyes with me! Oh, the horror. He really was thinking about throwing that ball to me. Every step that I took brought me closer to the sideline and inevitable release of the pigskin from Chris's hand. So much for mental preparation; my mind began running faster than I was and I started thinking again.

"Am I going to get hit?"

"What if I drop this?"

"I haven't prepared a proper celebration!"

But in the blink of an eye, the ball was airborne. It was only about a 12-yard throw and it got to me in a hurry. Normally this throw is a nice, soft toss to a wide open tight end, but the weak side linebacker was still in the area, so Weinke had to be a bit more precise. This is why the ball got on me like a Nolan Ryan fastball. I got my hands up just in time to see the ball whiz through them and smack me on the right side of the shoulder pads. The ball fell harmlessly to the ground as I lost all the "cool points" I had ever banked. What I saw, paled in comparison though, to what I heard.

The Seminole faithful are like sharks in the water when it comes to a revenge game. Our fans, as any good fans, don't want to just win, they want us to break records. So, when that ball was in the air and they saw the wide open tight end, the volume rapidly increased. As the ball crossed into the end zone and enticingly close to my hands, the roar was akin to an eagle on the back nine of Augusta. The fans were about to reach a raucous crescendo when the ball passed through my hands and ricocheted off my shoulder pads. The simultaneous "Awwww" of 80,000-plus, was more reminiscent of a shot into the water on the back nine of Augusta; euphoria to disappointment in a split second.

I ran back to the huddle and we ran another play, failed to score, and ended up with a field goal. It didn't affect the outcome of the game, but it stung none the less. You have heard superstars interviewed in the wake of a fantastic personal performance amidst a team loss, and they will call it "bittersweet" or "unimportant" in light of the defeat. That sentiment doesn't work the other way. In spite of the fact that we won by a score of 42-11, all I could think about was blowing it. I questioned whether or not I would ever get another chance to score a touchdown for the 'Noles, but I had to move on. My next big opportunity would be a few weeks later with much more on the line.

One of the passes I actually caught.

TROUNCING TOBACCO ROAD:
September 25th and October 2, 1999

The next weekend, we took our first road trip of the '99 season to Chapel Hill, to play the Tar Heels of North Carolina. This game was over quickly. It was a pristine, September afternoon in Chapel Hill and a perfect opening quarter for us. By the time we had played 15 minutes, the scoreboard read 28-0 in our favor and our focus shifted from victory to injury prevention. Almost every player who made the trip played in the game and after a 42-10 victory, we were on our plane headed back to Tallahassee.

The final leg of our march on Tobacco Road had us traveling to Jacksonville to play Duke. This was before the NCAA changed its rules and teams could sell their home games to bring in extra revenue. The Blue Devils were paid $800,000 to move their game from Wallace-Wade Stadium to our home away from home in Jacksonville. The stadium was near capacity and the Seminole faithful had a great time for the first 30 minutes of the game. We jumped all over Duke and didn't let off the gas until the half, leaving us with a 44-0 cushion at the intermission. Peter Warrick had three touchdowns on the day and was cruising in his campaign for the Heisman trophy. The second half was uneventful as we emptied the bench again and gave most of our team a chance to play. Including the game against NC State from the week before, we outscored three schools on Tobacco Road by a whopping total of 135 – 44. As we traveled east on I-10, headed back to Tallahassee, our minds had moved past our 51-23 win against Duke and had become focused squarely on our upcoming game against the Hurricanes. But our focus would be lost midway into our preparations by disappointing news from a local department store.

DILLARDS: *October 7, 1999*

Miami week was always different than any other, around the football program. The coaches cranked up their intensity and the players cranked up their enthusiasm because we all wanted to beat the 'Canes. Not that we didn't want to beat Duke or Maryland, it's just bigger when Miami comes to town. While we always expected Miami week to be unique, this one offered a surprise that none of us could have anticipated. Thursdays were the day reserved for a lighter practice and final tweaks with the game plan. It was rare for anything out of the ordinary to occur on a Thursday, but when Coach Bowden called the team together to announce that wide receiver Laveranues Coles had been dismissed from the team, and that Peter Warrick had been suspended indefinitely, we were stunned. Coles had been in trouble a couple of times before which is why he was dismissed. We were a veteran team and loaded with talent, but losing Coles and Warrick was a thudding punch in the gut. You just can't be prepared for that.

Warrick and Coles had been arrested for receiving an inappropriate "discount" from a sales clerk at the local Dillard's Department Store. While they didn't technically steal the clothes, the "discount" they received was apparently pretty close. Neither player denied that the incident had occurred but they didn't agree with the severity of the reaction either. When I heard about it initially, I agreed with them. I had seen my mom wheel and deal on Black Friday for years and come out of stores borderline stealing merchandise. My mom prided herself on being a shrewd shopper and hard-nosed negotiator, but Warrick and Coles were being called thieves. I didn't know all the details but I didn't like what they produced.

I wish I could say that I was mature enough to feel bad for the guys, but I wasn't. I was mad at them. Ironically though, I

208

defended them to everyone. I imagined myself at a checkout counter, being put in their situation, and doing exactly what they had done. I reasoned that most people would have, and my teammates were getting handled harshly just because they were Seminoles. At the same time, I knew in my heart that what they did was wrong. I certainly cannot judge their thoughts or motives but I think they knew it was wrong, too. So while I was as mad at the police and the NCAA for throwing them under the bus, I was mad at the guys too, especially Peter.

I hated that his choices might cost our team a chance at our goals. I can't speak for everybody, but I felt angry and selfishly disappointed. He represented my chance to play with a Heisman Trophy winner. Now, two days before we were to play Miami, we find out that he did something like this... Dadgummit!

Losing a teammate through the course of a year happens all the time, but normally it is because of an injury. William McCray was supposed to be our starting fullback but an injury had kept him out of the lineup; that's part of the game. It is one thing to lose a teammate to an injury. It's a whole different animal to lose a teammate to something like this. When a guy gets injured, the team can go through the process of rallying around him and preparing for playing without them. To lose guys like this felt like we had been cheated. It didn't happen on the field, so we didn't see what happened. We couldn't watch the film and develop sympathy for our fallen competitor, we just had to swallow it, and it was vile.

The bottom line was that we were headed into the biggest game of the year minus our top player and facing the rest of the season without our number two receiver. We had no choice but to jack the car up, throw on a spare and keep on trucking. We had to show the country that we were a great team and not just an average team with a great player. Opportunity was knocking on our door and I believe we proved to be excellent hosts.

BUT I'VE NEVER BEEN HERE BEFORE: October 9, 1999

Inside the ACC, there is no more loathed team than the Miami Hurricanes, at least for Seminole fans. We had been battling UM for decades prior to the 'Canes joining the conference in 2003, and there is a marvelous history of epic games and larger-than-life players. Outside of the Florida game, this one receives the most national attention and local hype on our schedule, and we love it.

Coach Butch Davis had the Hurricanes on the rise and they were ready to compete. They were ranked no. 19, and with our All-American wide receiver on the sidelines in street clothes, they believed they could upset us and knock us from our perch as the no. 1 team in the country.

Doak was pulsing with anticipation as the teams ran onto the field. The Seminole faithful roared as Osceola led us onto the turf and booed mercilessly as the 'Canes appeared. There is nothing quite like standing on the field and watching 80,000 rabid fans chanting and chopping their arms, while the Marching Chiefs blast the War Chant into the atmosphere. This was one of those special times when everyone was on their feet, everyone was participating in unison, and the fans' passion would have you believe that they were actually competing themselves. It was awesome! I get chill bumps thinking about it more than 10 years later. To say that we were ready to play is as big of an understatement as saying that Antarctica is chilly. It was time for kick-off and the battle was at hand.

We jumped out to a quick 7-0 lead, when Germaine Stringer caught a 48-yard touchdown pass just under four minutes into the game. Stringer was playing in the spot normally held down by P-dub. Miami answered just about three minutes later, when Kenny

Kelly hit Reggie Wayne on an 8-yard touchdown, 7-7. The game followed that pattern as Jeff Chaney ran one in, giving the 'Noles a 14-7 lead, only to have Miami answer with an 80-yard TD pass to Santana Moss. But after a fumble by Dan Kendra, Miami drove 89 yards and capped it off with another TD for Moss, 21-14 Miami, late in the second quarter.

That was the first time in the '99 season that anyone had earned a lead on us. We were 5-0 with four woodshed beatings under our belt, so to find ourselves losing, was unblazed trail for us. For the first time in 22 quarters, we huddled up as an offense, with the responsibility of regaining a lead and holding onto our national championship dreams. We began every season of my career with the goal of winning the national championship. After the Fiesta Bowl in January, when Warrick announced that he was returning for his senior season we began to expect that this year was going to be the one.

Our huddle was calm. We were excited and confident, so it wasn't a matter of if, but a matter of when we would tie the game and reclaim the lead. We believed absolutely that we were going to score on the drive; it was just a matter of who was going to be the one to make the play. We had an eventual Heisman Trophy winner at quarterback, in Chris Weinke, and multiple award-winning running backs in Travis Minor, Dan Kendra, and Jeff Chaney. Our receiver options featured All-American Marvin "Snoop" Minnis, future NFL rookie-of-the-year Anquan Boldin, the Lou Groza award winner in Sebastian Janikowski, and me.

Needless to say, I was neither Weinke's nor Coach Richt's first option when considering how we were going to defeat the 'Canes' defense. Had Warrick been in the lineup, the odds of me being involved would have been even slimmer. But because of his suspension, we were displaying a much more diversified attack evidenced by the fact that Weinke completed passes to 11 different receivers. As elite as Warrick was, his presence on the field tended to make us predictable. Not that it mattered because we scored more than 40 points a game anyway. But against Miami, he was relegated to cheering from the sidelines while we played without him.

We found ourselves looking at a third down and 10 from the Miami 18-yard line. We had to get a first down or score a touchdown on this play, or we would be forced to settle for a field goal from the, "Polish Powder Keg," Janikowski. That would have left us down by four at the half and yielding all the momentum to the team from the south. The game was on the line and Coach Richt reached into his bag of tricks and caught everyone in the stadium off guard. I don't remember the exact play that was called but I do remember that it was designed to be thrown to me. A triple reverse, throwback to the quarterback, statue of liberty would have been more orthodox for our offense than a pass to a tight end.

A post route, or "broken arrow" in our vernacular, meant that I had to release quickly from the line of scrimmage avoiding the defensive end. Then I had to navigate the linebackers while I got myself as wide as the hash marks. About 15 yards from the line of scrimmage, I was to break across the field in one of two ways. If there was a safety in the middle of the field, I would make a sharp cut across his face and into the open zone. But if there were two safeties spread across the middle of the field, I was to make a shallow cut just inside the safety nearest to me. The intent is to get me into the open zone, and more importantly, keep me from getting annihilated when the ball arrived. Miami ran a lot of "two-deep" zone, so I figured to be running the second route option.

After Weinke called the play, he looked at me and said, "Get your head around quick, the ball's coming to you!" It wasn't so much a "here's your chance" comment but more a "don't screw this up" kind of comment. I couldn't believe my ears. They were about to throw the ball to me, in this situation, against Miami! I am sure I wasn't nervous, but we'll never know because a time-out was called. "Whew, now coach Richt can fix this and call a play to "Snoop," I thought to myself. But he didn't. We had our regular old time-out routine and when we huddled back up, they called the same play. Here we go.

I released on the snap from Jarad Moon and sprinted up the field to get my width. The linebackers were dropping into zone coverage, which makes that part of the route simple, and I quickly saw that the safeties were splitting the field in their traditional two-deep look. Had they shown a three-deep, my chances for getting the ball would have lessened. But in a two-deep, I was the first read for Chris. And Chris wasn't kidding when he said, "get your head around quick," because when I did, the ball was already on its way.

It's a good thing too, because if you let me think long enough, my hands would get harder and I tended to drop passes. I was better when I didn't have time to think. I was running with my head turned backwards and as the ball neared, I jumped and turned my whole body square to the line of scrimmage to better frame the ball. The ball hit me about a split-second before the Miami safety, Ed Reed, and I'm glad it did.

I was already in the end zone when the ball entered my atmosphere and it actually slipped through my hands. But Reed's hitting me in the back, allowed me to clamp the ball against my chest and secure it for the TD, tie game! Doak exploded with roars from the Seminole fans as I lurched back onto my feet. My enthusiasm was unhindered while I performed a hybrid dance/stomp/march routine, holding the ball aloft in my right hand. I had no idea what I was doing or where I was going, I was just reacting to the fact that I had just caught a touchdown! It was exhilarating! I caught the ball near the center of the field, and I was dance/marching towards the Miami locker room, being chased by Justin Amman. He loves to remind me of this when we talk about the moment, because it appears that I am avoiding him, only to welcome with open arms, a leaping "Snoop" Minnis, who l caught and carried for a few steps. Once I let "Snoop" go, an official was waiting for me and telling me to settle down or I would get a penalty. I'm sure you have heard the purist say, "When you score just hand the ball to the ref and act like you've been there before." Well, I had never been there before and enthusiasm won the day!

It was the first touchdown I had ever scored in my life. In all my days of playing football, I had never been in the end zone with a football in my hands during a game. What better time for a first score than to tie the game against Miami on the way to a national championship? It was such a cool moment.

Another one of my roommates at the time, Jay Miller, was working for the student newspaper as their sports writer. He was in the press box working, which means that he had to maintain impartiality and professionalism. In layman's terms, he wasn't supposed to cheer. He was lucky to not have his press pass revoked because he might have been more excited than I was, and yelled along with the other fans. The other members of the press showed him mercy as he gushed my story to them about being a walk-on, earning a scholarship, and that being the first touchdown I had ever scored... ever. His irreverent enthusiasm was overlooked in exchange for the story. And the writers jumped on it.

We went on to win the game, 31-21, and our victory was truly a team victory. The defense was spectacular, especially in shutting out Miami in the second half. Everyone on the offense played great and allowed us to perform to our standards, even without no. 9 in the lineup. The special teams were excellent and our coaches called a great game. It was a wonderfully satisfying victory.

Thanks to Jay's outburst, I found my locker surrounded by members of the media, looking to interview me about the game and the bigger story of my first touchdown. There were articles written across the state of Florida and my mom got a copy of every one of them.

How did it feel? Great. The touchdown was exhilarating, winning the game made it even sweeter. Being interviewed after the game made me feel important, and I liked that. It's funny how something like catching a ball can make you feel better about yourself. I felt like I contributed, like I made a difference.

That moment was caught on camera and now resides in the 'Noles "turf room" which is in the belly of Doak Campbell

Stadium, and on the cover of this book. I get a kick out of it every time I see it. It is about 30 feet wide with a picture of Doak in the center, dominating the banner. On either side are pictures of four different Seminoles: Bobby Bowden, Chris Weinke, Charlie Ward, and me. The banner features one of the most renowned coaches in all of sports, two Heisman trophy winners, and a walk-on from Augusta, Ga. I had certainly never been *there* before... I'm glad I caught that ball.

SAVANNAH: October 10, 1999

I was from St. Augustine for quite a few weeks before somebody apparently brought the error to Coach Bowden's attention. We had come to accept the idea that I would be forever known as a resident of St. Augustine, but I held onto the hope that after the big TD catch, Coach would get my hometown right this week. As the play approached, Deckerhoff began commenting on how we never throw to the tight end, but we did on this upcoming play. Bowden said, "Yep, there's that Ryan Sprague again, from Savannah, Ga." My three-foot putt to stardom just lipped out. I made the huge play and now all the fan mail would end up at some kid's house in Savannah. Coach had placed me in the correct state but fell about 130 miles short of my hometown. He was traveling in the right direction, so there was still hope that I would eventually make it home.

DISTRACTED: October 16, 1999

Our next opponent was the Wake Forest Demon Deacons. Wake had never been very good while I was at FSU and this year wasn't any different. Our huge win over Miami the previous week, plus playing an inferior Wake team this week, with a big matchup in Clemson coming the next week, led to us playing a poor football game. Our vaunted offense was only able to muster three field goals in the first half, leaving us ahead 9-3 as the third quarter began. We weren't turning any heads with this performance.

We picked up the pace significantly in the second half, putting 24 points on the board and sneaking out of this "trap game" with a 33-10 victory. It certainly wasn't flashy, but it was a convincing win and more importantly, it set the table for the next week. The win was number 299 for Coach Bowden, which meant that the next week at Clemson was his first shot at no. 300. We found out early in the week that Warrick had been reinstated for the trip to Clemson. It's a good thing too, because we would need him.

BOWDEN BOWL 300: October 23, 1999

The 1999 season was Tommy Bowden's first year as the head coach for the Clemson Tigers, which led to this moment, the day his dad would bring the Seminoles to town. For the first time in the history of college football, a father and son would stalk opposite sidelines as competing head coaches. This piece of history was enough to create quite a buzz, but add in Bobby Bowden going for the 300 win milestone, Peter Warrick coming off of his suspension, us being ranked no. 1 and striving for a national championship, with a night game in Death Valley and you have a full blown media frenzy on your hands.

Clemson wasn't any good that year but that has never affected their attendance. They packed 86,000 fans into Death Valley that night and they did their part to level the playing field. I played around 30 games in Doak Campbell Stadium, twice in "The Swamp," and three times in the Superdome, but "Death Valley" in Clemson, S.C. is the loudest stadium I ever experienced. I was in Doak, as a fan, when we beat Miami with the famous muffed field goal and that was the loudest moment I have ever heard... ever. That was an ear drum rattling eruption of joy and relief that may not ever be matched, but as far as steady, unrelenting volume, "Death Valley" has no rival. This particular night, the Tiger faithful were in a particularly raucous mood and they brought their voices with them.

We came out slow again and found ourselves down 14-3 at halftime. The locker room at the half was as intense as I had ever seen it. Coach Bowden wanted that win bad and he made that fact very clear when he addressed us. Normally, he would matter-of-factly walk through the errors we needed to correct and the new things we needed to do and then we would go do it. On this night, he had a fire in his belly as he challenged our heart, our commitment, and our character. He wasn't about to let Tommy upset him and rob him of this special season; he was going to do everything in his power to make it right.

Thankfully, our defense responded instantly because we never really hit our stride on offense. Clemson was unable to score in the second half and we were able to scrape up two field goals, a touchdown, and a two point conversion. We escaped with a 17-14 win. Sometimes you can play a game like that and feel like you lost, but on that night when the final seconds evaporated, we celebrated like we had played a perfect game. As soon as our 60 minutes had transpired, it became about Coach Bowden.

Clay Ingram and a couple other guys hoisted Coach onto their shoulders and carried him to midfield to hug the man he had just coached against, his son. As much as Tommy wanted to win, I would bet my front porch that it was the easiest loss he ever had to accept. After the media wrapped up with him, Coach Bowden made his way to the locker room. He was presented with a 300th win plaque and reminded that the empty picture frame he had reserved for his first undefeated team still had a chance to be filled this season.

We had just been a part of one of the most historically rich games the sport had ever seen and come out victorious. But, this was just the first page that we would get to add to the history books that year.

WORLDS COLLIDE: October 30, 1999

Charlottesville, Va. was the sight of our next ACC battle, against the Cavaliers. This was a special game for me because it provided the opportunity to play against my former high school quarterback, David Rivers. I believe that it was David's high school accomplishments that opened the window and allowed Florida State to know who I was. In 1999, David was the backup QB at Virginia but he would play a pivotal role in this game.

We started very slow for the third week in a row. We didn't get on the scoreboard until there were less than six minutes remaining in the half. We were losing 10-7 at the break. I don't know why we struggled in the first half of these games but my best guess is that our confidence led to a lack of intensity, bordering on calmness, and that affected our results. Our defense was able to save the day in the previous two games and they would come up gold again this week. My offensive teammates and I took most of the third quarter to finally get back on the scoreboard. We took a 14 -10 lead, but just a few snaps later, an impossible play got us the ball back.

Our defense had knocked the UVA starting quarterback Dan Ellis out of the game, providing my friend David an opportunity to take the reins. It was certainly a tough situation for a young quarterback to see his first meaningful action. Our defense was swarming all over the field in the first 30 minutes and had ratcheted up the intensity after the half. He played as well as could have been expected, but one throw provided the highlight of the game and swung the game permanently in our favor. Corey Simon was the All-American defensive tackle anchoring our defensive line. He weighed in at close to 300 pounds and made his impact rushing the passer and gobbling up running backs. Mickey Andrews left orthodoxy in the locker room when he called a zone blitz and dropped big old Corey into pass coverage.

The move made Coach Andrews look like a genius because Rivers misread the coverage and threw it to the zone that Simon was assigned to cover. Corey made a play on the ball that would have earned him a starring role in Cirque du Soleil. He was backpedaling and as the ball was released, he broke laterally towards the throw. The ball came in very low and Corey laid out like a World Cup goal tender. He managed to get his paws between the ball and the turf, and completed the improbable interception. He had no business making that play but as coach Lilly used to always say, "Florida State players make Florida State plays."

We parlayed Simon's interception into a touchdown and a 21-10 lead and never looked back. The fourth quarter saw us add two more touchdowns and we won the game by a final of 35-10. After the game, I was able to find Rivers and have one of those cool moments you see in the NFL all the time. Reconnecting with a former teammate who represented the opposition was something I always thought was pretty cool and this was my opportunity to do that. David and I had our picture taken and then I joined my team as they streamed back into the locker room. Another sloppy first half for the offense and another dominating second half from the whole team was enough. The result was another convincing win, and a 9-0 record with just two games remaining.

AUGUSTA: *October 31, 1999*

They say that great shooters have to keep shooting and eventually they will start hitting their marks. Coach Bowden, much to his credit, kept on shooting when it came to talking about us on his show. It would have been easy for him to just say our names but he would always try to say hometowns, high schools, and even parents' names on the show too. After quite a few rimmed out, he finally found his form with me when he said, "There's old Sprague making a block. I spoke with his momma the other day; they're from Augusta, Ga." SWISH! Record books and box scores notwithstanding, I was now officially a Seminole. Coach Bowden had correctly said my name and hometown on TV, I had arrived.

HITTING OUR STRIDE: *November 13, 1999*

Being two wins away from a potential National Championship game, and with our final opponent being the fourth ranked Florida Gators, we could have suffered a letdown against lowly Maryland. In years past, the game prior to the Florida game has resulted in some pretty flat performances, but not this year... unless you were referring to turtle road kill. We were playing in front of a packed house in Tallahassee and we put together one of our best performances of the year. Weinke threw six TDs in the first three quarters, while involving ten different receivers. Warrick scored three touchdowns and the defense totally smothered the Maryland offense. We were up 28-0 at the half and 42-0 going into the fourth quarter. It's not athletically correct to look ahead to the following opponent, but there were more than a few Seminoles, fans and players alike, who shifted their focus to draining "The Swamp" in one week and booking hotels in New Orleans.

Coach Lilly, leading the Dogg Pound in prayer before the Maryland game.

UNDENIABLE: November 20, 1999

While I despise an attitude that says, "Who cares?" It might just be this attitude that made Sebastian Janikowski a great kicker. Sebastian was the most stubborn individual I have ever been around and it was hilarious. If we made mistakes in practice, we would be assigned "gassers." If you failed to make your time, usually around 40 seconds, you had to do it again. Sebastian had to do a lot of gassers again.

He could make them in 40 seconds in his sleep. The guy was an excellent soccer player so he was no stranger to running. But he insisted on not giving Coach Lilly, or any other coach, the satisfaction of seeing him work. On the whistle, we would all take off running for the opposite sideline and Sebastian would start his leisurely jog. The rest of the tight ends and specialists would dash across the finish and collapse on the turf while Sebastian would stroll across totally unfazed. Coach Lilly would write another gasser down on the card for Sebastian and after about 20 seconds, we would repeat the process. Normally, we would have four or five gassers then we would hit the showers, but not Sebastian. He was more than willing to jog those things until Coach Lilly would say mercy. Janikowski's stubbornness was second to none. But this attitude is what made him great.

After practice, the Coaches would try to create pressure situations for Sebastian. The whole team would gather on the special team's field, which is in the shadow of Dick Howser Stadium. They would line him up from 50-plus yards and lay down a scenario. Make the kick, we go inside. Miss the kick, the whole team has four gassers. Sebastian never missed a kick and it was never close. He made multiple kicks of longer than 60 yards like they were extra points. Pressure simply had no affect on him. His attitude was, "If I make it, so what; if I miss it, so what." He wasn't going to run the gassers anyway. For any other position on the field this would be cancerous, but it is ideal for a kicker.

There was not a more important series of games on the national scene in the 1990s, than Florida State vs. Florida, especially in the last half of the decade. A National Championship game appearance had been on the line every year since I arrived in 1996. Each year it was a matchup between two of the top teams in

America. In 1996, we were no. 2 when we defeated no. 1 Florida. Then in 1997, we were no. 1 and UF was no. 10. In 1998, we were no. 5 and the Gators were no. 8, and finally this year we were headed into Gainesville ranked no. 1 again, while our opponents were no. 3. Over that four year span, the average ranks of our teams when we played was 2.25 for us and 5.5 for Florida. There was no denying that the state of Florida ruled college football in the late '90s, and there would be no denying FSU a chance to go to the Sugar Bowl and rewrite history.

In 1997, we came to the Swamp undefeated with a chance to play for it all, and left Gainesville on the losing end of a 32-29 score. This represented another revenge game for us, so the team was focused, but who wouldn't be in a game of this magnitude?

The first half was pretty quiet and we took a 13-6 lead into halftime. Janikowski made two field goals in the half, but his big moment was still to come. The Gators scored first in the third quarter with a field goal, making the score, 13-9, but on our subsequent possession we would allow the Gators to take the lead. On third down, Weinke tried to hit Marvin Minnis with a pass but Bennie Alexander cut in front and intercepted it. 43 yards later, the Swamp was rockin' as the Gators celebrated his "pick 6" and their 16-13 lead. Our offense had to answer. We couldn't let momentum slip away from us and we couldn't let that crowd get any crazier.

Weinke led us, calm as ever, on a little drive into Sebastian's field goal range. Our drive stalled and we set up for a 49-yard field goal to tie the game. Sebastian jogged onto the field with his typical "who cares" facial expression and we lined ourselves up for the play. Clay Ingram's snap, Marcus Outzen's hold and Janikowski's kick were perfect, but somebody messed up. The remnant of Seminole fans were cheering the score, but were quickly engulfed by a tsunami of Gator hysteria when the official signaled a penalty and waved off the kick. We had been flagged for delay-of-game, which carried a five-yard penalty with it. We had to try again, this time from 54 yards!

I don't know if Coach Bowden considered punting in this scenario or not, but there was at least one person in the stadium who wasn't the least bit concerned, Janikowski. Coach Bowden elected to let Sebastian try to make the longer kick, so we lined up for the second attempt to tie the game. Another perfect snap from Ingram, another perfect hold from Outzen, and an even better kick from Janikowski. He smoked it! He would have made that kick from 60. I turned around to celebrate with Sebastian but he was busy. He was running around the field, mocking the Gator faithful by imitating their "Gator Chomp." It was beautiful, and vintage Janikowski.

What could have emotionally destroyed a weaker man was child's play to our uber-kicker. His will power drove coaches crazy. It kept him in the media spotlight for his antics and I'm sure made his parents nervous. But, his will power also allowed him to stare down not one, but two, clutch kicks and drill them both. Ninety thousand reptiles went home sad that day as we left town with a 30 -23 win, and a trip to the Sugar Bowl to play for the National Championship. Janikowski was like no teammate I have ever had, and I have a National Championship ring to prove it.

MISSION ACCOMPLISHED: January 4, 2000

Through the course of our journey in 1999, we had matured from Peter Warrick and the Seminoles, to simply The Seminoles. We had proven we could win with Pete absent from the lineup and become a better team as a result of it. Our opponent in the 2000 Sugar Bowl had not had the same maturing experience. We were matched up against Michael Vick's Virginia Tech squad, and as

Mike went so went the Hokies. It's a testimony to the caliber of athlete Vick was, to say that he took a good team and carried them to the National Championship game. He wasn't in the same conversation as Chris Weinke when it came to pure quarterbacking ability, but neither was Chris in the conversation when it came to athleticism and running ability.

After exchanging punts in the first quarter, we finally broke through when Weinke hit Warrick for a 64-yard touchdown. On the following Hokie possession, our defense stifled Michael Vick and their offense, setting the stage for the first special play of the night. Tommy Polley broke through their line and blocked the Hokie punt, providing Jeff Chaney the chance to scoop it up and deftly find his way to pay-dirt for a 14-0 lead. Vick bounced right back by throwing a 49-yard, right cross of a touchdown pass to cut our lead in half.

The offense came out of the corner swinging, as Weinke hit Dugans this time for a 63-yard scoring strike. As if following the same script, our special teams unit came out and managed to score for the second time that night. I am sure the Hokie coaches were thrilled to actually get the punt off this time, but irony was king as Warrick caught the punt and took it 59 yards for his second TD, 28-7 Seminoles. With his knees buckling from the body blows, Michael Vick came off the ropes for a late touchdown run just before the half, to cut our lead to 14. We went into the half leading 28-14, but Vick had conjured up some momentum that would carry over into the third quarter.

They stormed out in the second half. A field goal, followed by two Andre Kendrick TD runs, moved the Hokies into a 29-28 lead. Vick's attempt at a two point conversion after the second TD failed and we headed for the last 15 minutes of the 1999 season. For 705 minutes of the 1999 season, we had been undefeated, and now we found ourselves just one point away from making it a perfect 720. Never in Coach Bowden's 40 years of coaching had he led a team to a perfect season, but we were on the door step. We had been in this exact location and situation in the 1997 Sugar Bowl but we let it slip away. We weren't about to let that happen again and

just like our season began; it would end with Peter Warrick pulling off a mouth dropping athletic feat.

Just two minutes into the fourth quarter, we would take the lead and I would find myself in position to leave my mark on the game. In the weeks leading up to the National Championship, we had installed a two-point conversion play. In typical Mark Richt sneakiness, he devised a play that no one would expect to be called in a meaningful situation. A simple, five-yard square-out route from yours truly. The magnificence of the play was not in my route, but found in Peter Warrick's route and the assumption that the defense would be zeroed in on him. The design had me lining up on the left side of the line, with Peter splitting out wide to my left. He was to run a post route in front of the safety and because of the reduced field in the end zone, attract the attention of the linebackers as well. All eyes would be on no. 9, leaving me all alone in the end zone, and it worked like that time and again in practice. Had the play gone according to plan it would have been talked about in the same context as Boise State's statue of Liberty from a few years later… but it didn't go according to plan.

When we scored the go-ahead touchdown, we went up 34-29. Just a five point lead, presenting the perfect scenario to go for two. The play was called and I began to get nervous. The route was simple, the pass and catch would be child's play, but the circumstances were ridiculous. Succeed and we regain a touchdown lead, fail and our lead is five with momentum returning to Virginia Tech. There were no other games on TV, so every football fan in America was about to watch me attempt to make this play in Bobby Bowden's National Championship game… are you kidding me?

The ball was snapped and I was able to leave my nerves at the line of scrimmage. I cleared the defensive end and found myself in heavy traffic with the middle and strong side linebackers. As I approached my breakpoint, I leaned into the chest of the linebacker and then broke hard to my left. I turned my head toward Weinke only to see his eyes divert behind me to Pete. Upon my break, the safety jumped my route and ended up picking the corner, who was trying in vain to stay with Warrick. As Chris released his pass, I had three Hokies worried about me, the unheralded tight end, while All-American Peter Warrick was more open than sky in Montana. I began pumping my fist and shouting because we just scored. I had done my job to perfection and Peter got to be the hero. It almost felt better than scoring the touchdown against Miami because the relief of seeing the ball going towards Warrick was so sweet. As cool as it would have been to have appeared in the box score for a National Championship game, it was nothing compared to the joy I felt at that moment.

Janikowski would add a field goal to give us a 10 point lead at 39-29, but the final TD would be the one the world was talking about the next morning. Virginia Tech attempted a fake punt with about seven minutes remaining, but our special teams unit came up huge again and thwarted their chicanery. We were given the ball at the Hokies' 43-yard line with a chance to put the game away. I lined up on the right and Peter flanked our attack on the far left. I shared the responsibility of protecting Weinke with Dan Kendra. The line was able to provide the necessary time to launch a bomb to Warrick, as he bolted to the end zone. As the ball began to enter Warrick's atmosphere, the desperate Hokie defender lunged onto him and grabbed both of Peter's arms. Weinke's throw was just behind Warrick and he was only able to get his finger tips on the ball as the Hokie clung to him. Peter managed to outmuscle the interfering defender and flip the ball in the direction of his momentum, as the hapless Hokie finally fell from his side. Warrick tipped the ball once more to himself and miraculously secured it as he crashed into the synthetic turf of the Louisiana Super Dome.

I raced down the field to celebrate with Peter and the rest of my teammates. The game had a few minutes left, but we had just taken a 46-29 lead meaning Virginia Tech would have to find three scores just to tie the game. From a mathematical standpoint, the game was nearly over but after that impossible catch, the Hokies were emotionally finished. It was like a bloop single with two outs in the ninth inning of a would be no-hitter, totally deflating and rendering the remainder of the game, virtually meaningless. The celebration began before the clock ran out. Players were jumping around, saying, "hi mom," to the sideline cameras, and waving towels over their heads. The Marching Chiefs flooded the Super Dome with the War Chant while our fans celebrated their team's perfect season. When the final seconds did expire, the team rushed from the sideline and onto the field with their helmets proudly held aloft. Cheerleaders were running around with mock newspapers proclaiming us as the champs. We were being handed "National Champions!" shirts by the magical T-shirt elves, who can produce those shirts just seconds after the game ends. The joy was unbridled because we didn't have to worry about the next game, and a stage was being hastily erected within the crowd of enthusiastic Seminoles. Peter Warrick had done the unthinkable to move the

1999 Seminole team into the record books and more personally into Coach Bowden's vacant picture frame.

The post game celebration on the field was long overdue. After watching the Gators have theirs on this very field in 1997, then watching Tennessee celebrating with their Tostitos last year in Tempe, having our turn this year was all the more fulfilling. I had the opportunity to stand up on the platform and hold the crystal football which was a surreal moment. So many times I had watched other people celebrate championships by hoisting the trophy overhead, and here I was, holding a trophy I helped to earn.

I didn't have the guts to hold it over my head. In fact I was gripping it tight enough to make the Waterford people nervous. I didn't want to be the guy who broke the crystal football, and the thought ran through my analytical head. Thankfully, nobody dropped it and it now rests appropriately in Doak Campbell Stadium next to the same trophy that the '93 Seminoles earned. Coach Bowden's second national championship of the decade had marked us officially as " The Team of the '90's," and added another era to the dynasty that was ruling the college football world from Tallahassee.

Michael Vick was the best player we faced that year and he almost single-handedly kept them in the game, but we played our best game of the year and Peter Warrick owned the night. We posted our third highest scoring output behind the 51 against Duke and 49 against Maryland. We scored touchdowns by blocking punts, returning punts, and throwing passes. Our defense sacked Vick seven times and forced four turnovers. While the Hokies made it interesting in the third quarter there was not enough magic in Vick's feet to conquer us that night.

Peter Warrick said he returned for his senior season to win a National Championship. Bobby Bowden said that as soon as he won his first championship, he wanted to do it again. His whole career, Coach wanted to have an undefeated season. We wanted to finally play in a National Championship game and come out on top. When I was a goofy high school kid, Odell Haggins told me we would have a chance to win a ring every year and we did. But

thanks to Peter Warrick's legendary performance in 1999, we not only had a chance... we did it! Mission accomplished.

NATIONAL CHAMPS: January 2000

Now that we had won our championship it was time for the celebration to begin. The main award that each member of the team receives, is the ring. This year we won three of them: one for being the ACC champions, one for being the Sugar Bowl champions, and the third for being the National Champions. I was selected by the coaches, along with five or six other guys, to help design our rings that year. I had no idea that the players gave input to the ring process and now I was sitting around a table brainstorming the most important one we had earned. We entertained presenters from a couple different ring companies who were competing for the job and ended up settling on the one who seemed to grasp our vision the best. We didn't want gaudy rings, we didn't want a whole lot of colored stones on them, and we wanted to signify the school's second championship by having two Sears Trophies on the National Championship ring. The design thrilled our whole committee and the team seemed to be happy when we showed them the renderings.

It would be a couple months before we actually received the rings and the university held a big celebration in our honor when it was time to hand them out. A stage and huge black backdrop was erected on the west side of the turf in Doak Campbell. More than 20,000 fans came out to show their appreciation and see the graduating seniors one more time. We all got to watch the season highlight film on the stadium's huge TV and a few of the players were asked to address the fans. Coach Bowden also said a few words and dangled the carrot out there for us to try to do it all again next year. It was a compact, but complete, ceremony that was a fitting honor for a great team.

26

GREATNESS

It had never been done in the history of college football. Never had a team been ranked no. 1 before the season began and maintained that ranking all the way through, to being crowned the National Champions. Not only that, but never in Bobby Bowden's years as a head coach, had one of his teams gone an entire season undefeated. The 1999 football season would see both of those milestones reached and I was fortunate to be a part of it. Many people consider our team in '99 to be one of the top five to have ever played, and rightly so. Had Peter Warrick not gotten into trouble, it would have had two Heisman trophy winners on it, considering Weinke would win it in 2000. Sebastian Janikowski won the Lou Groza award as the nation's best kicker. We had multiple All-Americans on both sides of the ball, and one of the best coaches in history at the top of his game. There were teams before us and teams since that had incredible talent, yet something set us apart. There was something special about the Seminole team of 1999. We had gone beyond being good and spent six wonderful months tasting greatness.

While it isn't guaranteed that great chemistry will translate into winning, it is true that poor chemistry will lead to failure. Thankfully, Coach Bowden's second National Championship team had great chemistry. I would define chemistry as, "mutual admiration, respect, and affection amongst a group of people striving for a common goal." A team can easily have parts of that definition embodied within them but not have them all, and the chemistry is shot. If a team is committed to winning a championship, but they don't like each other, they won't have success. The reverse is also true. If a group of guys are great friends but not committed to the common goal, they will fail. Obviously, great chemistry is not all that's required, the team also needs to play the game extremely well and we certainly did that.

I cannot speak directly for everyone on the team, but I think it safe to say that we admired one another. Had there not been a Warrick to complement a Weinke, that might not have been true, but the fact that we had two elite players helped our chemistry. It was not uncommon for there to be a moment in practice that produced awe in the hearts of our team. Maybe it was watching

Pete make a ridiculous one-handed reception with a grin on his face, or seeing Chris make a read and throw a laser that a lesser player wouldn't have considered much less completed. Perhaps, it was seeing our offense execute a play to perfection, only to watch Chris Hope or Tay Cody make a super-human play and leave us with nothing. That kind of thing happened all the time; we knew we were surrounded by athletic greatness and what else can you do but admire it.

I know it was true because I never saw one of our guys back down from another. Should Warrick, Snoop, or Morgan beat one of the defensive backs, the response would be a challenge to try and do it again. If Brian Allen or Tommy Polley tackled one of our running backs behind the line of scrimmage, they would spring back to their feet ready to do it again. There was no shame in getting beat on the practice field in 1999. Our guys' admiration for one another pushed us to move from good to great because of the authentic, positive competition that it created. We weren't looking to defeat the other man as much as we were looking to improve ourselves, it was pure. Don't get me wrong, our guys could talk junk with the best of 'em and they did, but it wasn't hateful or degrading. It was as good natured as ribbing can be and pretty darn funny too.

Where you admire someone for their ability, you respect someone for their attitude. It is easy to admire a great athlete for their skill and still withhold respect on account of their attitude. As a general rule, our team had great respect for one another. I am not so biased to believe that within a squad of over one hundred college kids that we all had great attitudes; but those that didn't were few and marginalized. Even Janikowski, whose attitude towards authority left a little to be desired, held our respect. While he was insubordination personified, he didn't shirk his

236

responsibilities on the field and he did his job very well. He was simply an immature kid and he acted like it, we all did sometimes.

What didn't exist on that team was a class system where the "role players" were treated as lesser people than the "super-stars." I represent the classic example of a "role player," yet I felt as significant as Warrick, Simon, or Minor. I could understand why I would be a third or fourth option on any given passing play; that is where the admiration comes in. When I sat down to play NCAA football on the PS2 with my roommates Dave, Jay, and Jayme, I was throwing to no. 9 as often as possible. How could I fault Coach Richt for doing the same thing? Peter was a freak and our team was better when he was catching the ball. The fact that I knew how capable my teammates were and how committed they were to our goals, allowed me to embrace my role as a supporting player. It also helped that I believed that my teammates respected me too.

It would be foolish of me to expect the guys I played with to admire my athleticism, I just wasn't that athletic. I could run and jump better than most maybe, but my teammates weren't part of the "most," they were among the select "few" of elite athletes in the country. I didn't need to try and prove my athletic ability to them. My job was to know what to do, when to do it, and how to do it well. If I took care of my responsibilities and didn't hurt our team's chances to reach our common goal, then I had the respect of my teammates, and because I had their respect, I didn't need them to admire my athleticism.

The formula of mutual admiration plus mutual respect should lead to mutual affection and it certainly was true of us; our guys had so much fun together. The locker room was constantly full of laughter and playing as we were getting ready for practice or getting ready to go home. It helped that we had some genuinely funny guys like Clay Ingram, Brett Williams, Atrews Bell, and Dan

Kendra who could get guys rolling in a minute. Most teams experience closeness within position groups; offensive linemen who all like each other for example. But we had that working across the board; everybody just liked each other. It even transcended the athletes and continued into the support staff. The team had great relationships with Randy Oravetz and his army of athletic trainers, as well as Dave Delegal and his team of equipment managers.

Our support team was second to none and they were as much a part of the team as anyone else. Was there perfect harmony? Of course not, but again disharmony was the exception and not the rule. I believe that the admiration plus respect formula applied in that arena too. As gifted as our team was athletically, they were aware that their bodies were also fragile and our support guys were highly skilled at making sure our bodies were safe and well maintained. Our guys that had been through a lengthy rehabilitation were especially respectful of the medical staff and they held an admiration for their knowledge and skill too. No matter where you went, or who you were with, the chemistry around our team was evident. The guys in uniform on any given Saturday were representing a much larger team of highly trained, passionate, and gifted individuals, all united in the common purpose of seeing Florida State University earn a National Championship.

That was our goal, every year that I was there. We expected to win every game we played and win a National Championship every year, and we were justified to do so. Some teams will say that they want to win a championship but deep down they know that it is an unrealistic expectation. That was not true of the teams I was privileged to play for. The fact that in five years we only lost six games, never once finished outside of the top five in America, and played in four National Championship games, speaks to our justified expectations. We not only wanted to win, or believed we could win, we knew absolutely that we would win. We had a singular, common goal and that was to win a National Championship. By the time 1999 rolled around, we had already had our share of disappointment to provide the extra focus necessary to accomplish our mission.

At the end of the 1996 season, we were undefeated and playing in the Sugar Bowl to win a championship against the Florida Gators, who we had just defeated a month earlier. We ended up falling way behind in the second half and losing big to our most hated rival. In 1997, we were undefeated going into the final game of the year. Had we won, we would have played for the championship for the second consecutive year, but with less than two minutes in the game the Gators found a way to beat us again and keep us from our goal. 1998 was an all too familiar story. We made it to the Fiesta Bowl for the BCS National Championship game against the Tennessee Volunteers but wound up watching the Vols celebrate while we ended yet another season one game short. As we entered the 1999 season, we could easily have been the three-time defending National Champions, but instead we were being talked about in the same category as the Buffalo Bills and my beloved Atlanta Braves. It makes me sick to think how close we were to being legendary but it just goes to show how difficult it is to win every game and a national championship.

That brings us to the last part of the equation that made us great, experience. The '99 team was a veteran team that had been so close to perfection, we knew exactly what was required to achieve it. As we progressed through the season, it was rare to hear a coach yelling at the first units. We had such great upperclassman leadership that we had become a self-policing team. There were many, many times that we could joke in the huddle or at the line of scrimmage because everyone knew what they were doing so well. In the title game against Virginia Tech, Brett Williams and I were often laughing with our own little inside joke. Justin Amman was a tad uptight on the field. Brett and I were just the opposite; well, Brett was the opposite and I would have been somewhere in between. As the game wore on and the Hokies wore out, we began to tease the man who Justin had to block. We were trying anything we could to make that guy irate, so that Justin would have to deal with it. We had a ball but Justin didn't like it very much, so he began to return the favor with the guys in front of us. It was a blast! We were playing in the most important game of our lives and having a great time doing it. There was no pressure, no anxiety, and no fear of failure because we were so experienced. There were even times when one of us messed up a play, but because the other guys were so competent, they could cover for it and make it look intentional. That is a rare occurrence that only comes when a team knows what they are doing and have been doing it together for a long time.

We had it all that year; mutual admiration, respect, and affection buttressed by a stubborn resolve to win every game we played, and leave no doubt who the best team in college football was. Mix that together with all of the leadership and experience, and you have the formula for greatness. Coaches, trainers, managers, graduate assistants, and the entire football department combined with the players, to put together one of the best teams that college football has ever seen. That 1999 team was special and that would be true had we won it all or not. But the fact that we did win it all, and give Coach Bowden his first and only undefeated championship team made that year one for the history books.

27

FROM THE PEOPLE'S HOUSE...

My mom had my siblings and I heavily involved in politics for as long as I can remember, as she organized campaigns for various candidates running for various offices. I think she always wanted me to make it to the White House but I doubt she figured football is what would bring me there. Winning a National Championship brings with it the high honor of receiving an invitation to Washington D.C. to be recognized by the President of the United States of America. We made the trip to Washington and embarked on a memorable journey, rich with history and significance. The majority of the team loaded onto busses and began a tour of our nation's capital. They went to Arlington National Cemetery and witnessed the Changing of the Guard at The Tomb of the Unknown Soldier. From there, they went to the Smithsonian National Air and Space Museum where they spent time soaking up the aeronautical history of America. However, I didn't get to see any of those sights, because I was with Coach Bowden and a small selection of my teammates on a more personal mission.

It humbles me to reflect back on moments like these and consider their magnitude. Coach Bowden selected six of us to accompany him as ambassadors for the University on his trip around Washington, and I was one of those honored players. Chris Weinke, Travis Minor, Todd Frier, Chris Hope, Jean Jeune, and I became the hands and feet of our team, as we spent time with the people of Washington D.C. I considered it a high honor then, and still do today, to be chosen by Coach Bowden and to be associated with that group of my teammates.

Our first stop of the day was Eaton Elementary School for an assembly of the older kids there. We were welcomed by more than 200 enthusiastic children, eager to spend time with the National Champions. The innocence of youth was on full display when Coach Bowden offered his talk to them and opened the floor for questions. He encouraged them to stay in school, work hard, listen to their parents, and make smart decisions, but prior to that he told them a joke.

He shared a story about a hunter out looking for a bear. The hunter succeeded in finding his target but when he took his shot, the gun jammed. The bear heard the noise and began chasing the hunter, who tripped, and finding himself about to be dinner, did what most people do when death is imminent, he prayed. "God, please let this be a Christian bear." Immediately, the bear dropped to his knees, clasped his paws, and said, "God, thank you for this food that I am about to eat, Amen."

We all laughed and Coach went on with the inspirational part of his speech. When he was done and the kids were given permission to ask questions, almost every hand in the room went up. You could see the concentration on the kids' faces who didn't have their hand raised as they desperately tried to come up with a question. Coach called on a little girl and prepared himself to offer explanation for some of the wisdom he had just shared. Maybe she did work hard, but still struggled in school and was eager for encouragement. Perhaps her parents weren't around and she was being raised by an aunt, so she had a deep question about what "listening to her parents" meant to her. Or maybe, she was worried about the bear.

"Why did the hunter want to shoot the bear?" the soft-hearted little girl asked. I doubt if he gets that question at an elementary school in Alabama, but we were in the big city, where all the food comes from the grocery store. Bowden offered an answer and quickly called on the next eager child. A little boy offered, "Why did the hunter's gun jam?" Coach chuckled and offered some kind of practical reasoning before quickly moving on again. A third child, who was desperately concerned, asked, "did the bear eat the man?" Bowden laughed again and the principal tried to redirect the kids. "Does anyone have questions that aren't about the bear or the hunter?" he asked. Almost all of the hands dropped, but the kids furrowed their brows again while they conjured up more questions, and in a matter of moments the room was filled with waving arms again.

We left Eaton Elementary and went over to the National Rehabilitation Hospital to visit spinal cord injury patients. This hospital, full of people in wheelchairs or bedridden, was a sobering contrast to life around a college football team. We spent our time working on becoming excellent players, while these folks spent their time re-learning how to walk or hold a cup. What we took for granted every day of our lives, these courageous folks were striving to achieve. It was difficult for most of us to grasp but not Weinke. Chris had been in the same situation that these people were in and he might have been the reason we visited. They had the opportunity to meet a person, just like them, who shared the same type of injury and same kind of scars. Chris was the personification of hope to a group of people who needed it terribly. Seeing someone who has overcome provides hope for the patient, for the physical therapists, and for the loved ones of the patient, who need hope like we need food. Hope is the driving force for people striving to overcome and Chris gave them a full dose of it.

Our tour continued to the Hospital for Sick Children (*now the HSC Pediatric Center*) to spend some time with the kids there. The HSC is a place where kids who need long-term rehabilitation, or are transitioning from a life-altering surgery, can come with their families for the necessary care. There were kids there with varying types of disabilities, including Cerebral Palsy and other brain injuries. We were at that hospital to offer hope, just like our last stop, but more necessary here was diversion and laughter. None of us could really put ourselves in these kids' shoes, but we could enjoy their company. We signed autographs, gave out all kinds of Seminole stuff, and even threw a football around in the hallway. But the best thing we did, was to sit down and talk with them. Some of them were able to interact with us and some of them could not, but we spent time with each of them just the same. Some of these kids were fighting for every breath they took and it forced us to appreciate how comparatively easy our lives were.

I am struck by the reality that as a college kid, I had the opportunity to visit a spinal injury hospital to offer hope, before visiting one a few years later looking for hope myself. On March 11, 2006, my sister, Gina, was thrown from her car and suffered an injury to her spinal cord. Most of my family gathered at Craig Hospital in Denver, Co. to be with my sister as she endured surgery and began her rehab. The initial outlook was grim and we feared that she would never walk again. Rehab from a spinal injury is more about the mental aspect than the physical, which is what makes hope so significant. It can be depressing as they struggle to perform menial tasks that they once did without thinking. Having to learn how to walk again is humbling and hope is what kept my sister working. Thankfully, she is now an example of someone who is overcoming! She can walk around again and is participating in many of the things that she did prior to her injury. But for me, the remarkable foreshadowing of that Washington trip didn't end at the National Rehabilitation Hospital.

On Feb. 16, 2004, my wife and I welcomed our first child into the world. About nine months later, we learned that our little boy, Caedmon, had Cerebral Palsy. I had no idea when I was walking the halls at the Hospital for Sick Children, that one day my son would need the same services. As a father, my appreciation goes beyond the confines of mere words when I think about what happened at that hospital. Caedmon is six now and he is the biggest Seminole fan in the world. He loves going to games with me and wearing his 'Nole gear. He shares a room with his brothers, Jackson and Andrew, and their walls are adorned with Seminole posters and pennants to reflect their shared love for Florida State. If Caedmon had to spend a prolonged amount of time in a hospital like the one we visited, he would only be more excited by visiting family, than the visit of a Seminole.

I couldn't appreciate at the time what it meant that we were at that hospital because my life experience was insufficient. I always felt foolish to be acknowledged or desired just because I played football. I couldn't grasp the significance of what being a Seminole meant to someone who didn't have the opportunity to be one. It was just playing football to me, but now I know that it was so much more than that. When I put on that uniform and took my place on the field, I became the representation of the dreams of thousands. Some of those dreams were in front of their dreamers, as kids imagined themselves in my shoes; while others' dreams were far gone as men wondered what it would have been like to be in my shoes. We were to a child in a wheelchair, what the glider was to Orville and Wilbur Wright; the realization of a seemingly impossible dream. I am glad we got to share a moment with those kids and their families.

We left the Hospital and were delivered to the United States Capitol and led into Statuary Hall. There was a reception being held there in our honor and attended by Seminoles from the Washington area. We spent a little time there shaking hands with people and talking about our season before being ushered away to reunite with the rest of our team. They were waiting for us at the last stop on our respective tours, the White House.

We were fortunate to be visiting "The People's House" on the 200th anniversary of its construction. For 200 years, this American marvel has hosted presidents, world leaders, major political summits, and now for the second time, the Seminoles. We were escorted into the East Room to wait for our opportunity to shake the hand of the leader of the free world, the 42nd President of the United States, William Jefferson Clinton. The team loitered in the opulent hall while the coaches and support staff went into the speech area and waited. After some time, President Clinton arrived and each of us had the privilege of personally shaking his hand. Democrat or Republican, liberal or conservative, the honor of being face to face with the President of the United States is profound. Our time with the President was brief and we were transferred into the presentation area and arranged four deep, in long rows on a platform. We looked like the heaviest choir in the world. We were facing an audience of our support staff, various members of political offices, and a small crew of media with our bodies angled just a little so that we were all facing the podium at the center of the platform. Once we were properly arranged, the final three participants entered the room from a door directly across the room from us.

GRATEFUL

Sitting FSU president Sandy D'Alemberte, Bobby Bowden, and President Clinton entered the room, walked down the center aisle dividing the audience, and joined us on the platform. President Clinton addressed the room first. He welcomed everyone and acknowledged a few people before talking about the reason we were all there. After listing off our accomplishments from the championship season, he turned his attention to Coach Bowden specifically. He described him and the program he built very well when he said, "I have watched him (*Coach Bowden*) be gracious in victory and gracious in defeat, which is more difficult. 'Course, it's easy when you don't lose very much." He mentioned a cool bond that Coach Bowden and he shared in that the 1993 Seminole championship team was one of the first that he welcomed to the White House and now our team would be his last. He wrapped up his statement and President D'Alemberte said a few words before turning the floor over to Coach Bowden.

Coach Bowden had the room eating out of his hand from the word, "go" and had President Clinton in stitches for much of his address. His opening thought was a reference to an old coaching proverb that it isn't far from the outhouse to the penthouse and vice -a-versa. Coach said that our season had added a new wrinkle to the idea, as we went from the outhouse, to the penthouse, to the White House. He thanked President Clinton for having us as his guest and offered a quip about us being the team that would usher him out of office, "we just had a better year than you did." Coach Bowden's charm and wit set the mood for everyone and he handled himself like he had been there a hundred times. Todd Frier had the privilege of addressing the room and presenting the president with a no. 1, garnet, Seminole Jersey complete with a Nokia Sugar Bowl patch. The president accepted the gift, held it up to himself and joked that he was going to have to bulk up. With that, our trip to the White House was complete and we boarded the busses to head back to the airport. Our long and fulfilling day in the nation's capitol was complete. We had seen the sights, met the president, and offered hope to some people who needed it. All because for a season, we excelled at the game of football. It was a great day to be a Seminole.

28

... TO THE PEOPLE'S ELBOW

My final off-season as a Seminole was exactly what it should have been, extremely positive. We lost a great deal of talent to graduation and the N.F.L. Draft including four All-Americans: wide receiver Peter Warrick, offensive guard Jason Whitaker, defensive tackle Corey Simon, and our kicker Sebastian Janikowski. Though not All-Americans, we also lost three All-ACC players: center Eric Thomas, defensive tackle Jerry Johnson, and corner back Mario Edwards. Not to mention our second leading receiver, Ron Dugans, our starting fullback and free safety in Dan Kendra and Sean Key respectively. Beyond the major statistical contributors, we also lost key elements of our collective heart with the departure of guys like safety Todd Frier, linebacker Bobby Rhodes, and long snapper Clay Ingram. Every off-season presents this issue and its result is a great opportunity for new leaders to step in and fill the void.

The first opportunity for new leadership came in the form of mat drills. I won't go so far as to say mats were a breeze, but they were certainly the easiest of my five attempts. As a senior, in the eyes of the coaches, I was able to share a line with fellow dependable teammates who were rarely forced to repeat a drill. Therefore, we were able to spend more time encouraging the underclassmen while they took their turns being sent back. We were now the examples to follow, and not being made examples of. It also helped that Coach Amato accepted the head coach position at N.C. State. As much as the guys loved him, he wasn't missed during mat drills, neither was his little black book.

The 2000 version of spring practice was probably the most upbeat string of practices of my career. We were coming off the undefeated season, the team was very mature, and the new freshmen weren't with us yet, so very little time was wasted on discipline issues. We were able to go out and play football, and it was fun. The previous season, we were carrying the bullseye of being no. 1, along with the swelling pressure to get Coach Bowden his first undefeated season. Now, for the spring anyway, it was just us. No polls to worry about, the BCS computers were irrelevant, and no winning streak to continue. The coaches still worked us like dogs, but for this stretch of practices, we were back to simply playing a game with our friends. Practices concluded with the annual Garnet and Gold Game, which is an intra-squad scrimmage held in Doak Campbell Stadium.

Because I spent almost every Monday night watching wrestling with Dave, Jay, Justin, and my brother Daniel (*he had enrolled at Tallahassee Community College earlier that year*), I concocted a plan for a touchdown celebration that would pay homage to our favorite wrestler, The Rock. He had a "signature move" that he used on his opponents to finish off a match. These "signature moves" are an industry standard, to help the personalities create an identity and excite the fans. The Rock's was particularly effective on both fronts and it was called, "The People's Elbow." It went something like this. After knocking his fellow combatant to the mat and leaving him in a dazed stupor, he would stand over his victim's head and stare down at him. The crowd would be abuzz with anticipation, waiting for the drama to unfold. After a dramatic pause, The Rock would suddenly shoot both of his arms out to the side, turn his head to stare at the crowd to his left, and raise his trademark left eyebrow. After a prolonged survey of the crowd and sufficient time for them to go crazier than teenage girls at a Beetle's concert, he would slash both arms across his chest and tear the pad off of his right elbow. Then he would run to left, ricochet himself off the ropes, cross back over the ring, leaping the poor soul on the mat, bounce off the opposite ropes, and come to an abrupt stop at the right shoulder of the man about to be pummeled. He would shoot his right leg straight out in front of his body and swing it over the top of his opponent. Once his leg had cleared the man below, The Rock would snap himself towards the mat and, like a guillotine, drop "The People's Elbow" across the grill of his soon to be pinned opponent. Were I to score a touchdown in the Garnet and Gold Game, I was going to drop "The People's Elbow" on the football and I even wore a medically unnecessary elbow pad for added flair.

I was on the Garnet team, and we were winning 14-7 when Malcolm Tatum intercepted a pass to give us the ball back. We ran a couple plays before Weinke threw me a pass that I caught right at the goal line. I dove for the end zone as a couple of defenders converged on me, so I had to wait for the officials' signal to know if I had scored. He came running towards the pile with both hands extended overhead in the classic touchdown position, so it was show time. I always believed that the Garnet and Gold game was for the fans, and because it didn't count for anything either, I was willing to put my plan into action. This would have never happened in a live game situation.

I grabbed the football, ran to the corner of the end zone, and placed the ball at my feet. Then, just like The Rock, I stuck my arms out to my sides and stared up into the stands. With the drama unfolding in my mind, I swung my arms across my chest, tore my costume elbow pad off, and threw it aside. Imagining the crowd going ballistic, I stuck my leg out in front of me, swung it over the top of the football, and BOOOM! I dropped "The People's Elbow" on the poor football. As soon as I dropped the elbow, the referee dropped the penalty flag, and the Garnet team received a 15-yard penalty for my "excessive celebration." We missed the extra point and it could have cost us the game, but the Gold team missed one

too, and the game ended in a 27-27 tie. However, if you count "cool points," we won by a thousand!

Despite my theatrics, the coaches gave me a couple of awards at the conclusion of spring ball. I won the "Second Effort" award and the "Most Dependable" award for the offense which I considered high honors. The positive vibe of the off-season continued through the summer, especially in my personal life.

When workouts were over, I spent most of my free time hanging out with a pretty little co-ed named Jeni Rudzik. We met through the FCA group, and spent our spring break together, with a few friends, at my Uncle Paul and Aunt Nancy's house, skiing in Colorado. She was interning with the youth ministry at a Tallahassee church so I spent a lot of time at Killearn United Methodist working with the high school students of our community. She was also attending a little church called King's Way Christian. It was another cool glimpse into my future, as Jeni would eventually become my wife, ministry would develop into my career, and King's Way is where I am now a pastor. With my last off-season as a Seminole behind me, it was time to reenter the world where games mattered and our quest to repeat as National Champions would reign supreme.

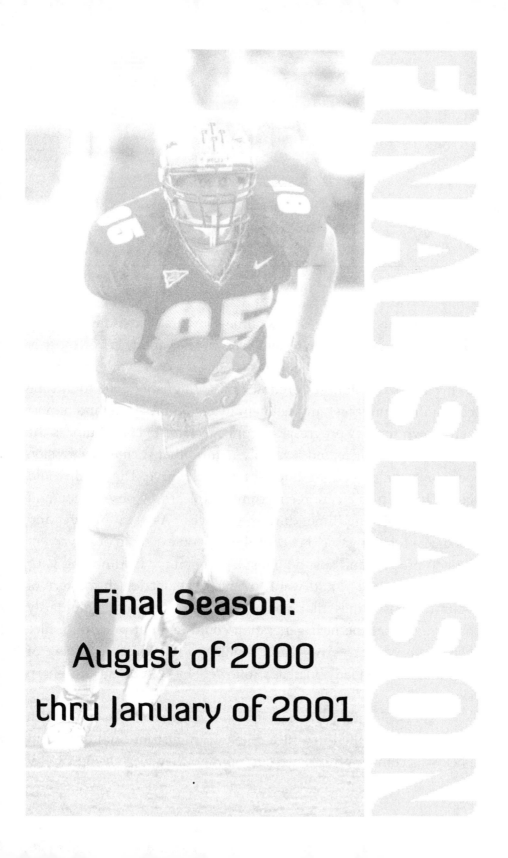

Final Season:
August of 2000
thru January of 2001

29

40:31

In relation to football responsibilities, my first two-a-days and my last two-a-days couldn't have been further apart. While most of the month of August in 1996 was spent on a knee, with my helmet in my hand and almost bored at times, August of 2000 found me constantly on my feet, my helmet always on my head, and almost zero down time. A progression from spectator to contributor is the desire of any athlete and it is only natural that such a progression occurs. Actually, you are hoping for a bell curve. The ideal would be to show up as a carefree freshman, to learn by observation and occasional playing time during practices. As you mature and become a regular game day contributor, you expect to observe very little in practice and spend almost all day on the field honing your skill. Finally, you would want to have developed such mastery of your responsibilities that you could step aside and voluntarily observe so that the next generation could learn at practice; a nice bell curve. My curve was more similar to the value of a share of apple stock, a steady increase followed by a sudden and sharp skyrocketing.

Nick Franklin was labeled as a co-starter with me, which should have resulted in a nice relaxing August for both of us. But Nick was coming off of knee surgery and they were being careful with his participation at practice. Carver Donaldson was listed as the third team tight end but the heat affected him pretty severely as he battled cramps for much of the time. Patrick Hughes was set to take a redshirt, so he was encamped with the scout team. That left me as the only, completely healthy, tight end in camp and we had a National Championship to defend, starting in just a couple of weeks with a trip to Jacksonville to play BYU.

Just like when I was thrown to the wolves as a wiry freshman on the scout team and allowed no room for excuses, I would find no sympathy in 2000 either. No excuses, no whining; I was expected to do my job and do it well, regardless of the circumstances. It wasn't easy but I was able to anchor myself to a Bible passage found in the Old Testament book of Isaiah. Clint Purvis was our team chaplain and he would regularly give out little gifts to encourage us in the development of our faith. One such gift was a simple bookmark containing these words,

"but those who hope in the LORD will renew their strength. They will soar on wings like eagles; they will run and not grow weary, they will walk and not be faint." - Isaiah 40:31

I didn't know it at the time but those words would become like water to me as I fought through those demanding practices. The physical language of the verse resonated with me. I was an athlete after all, and the idea of being able to "renew my strength" and "run and not grow weary" was very appealing to me. When camp began, I had the verse in the back of my mind. But when Carver began battling the leg cramps and dehydration, and I began to shoulder the lion's share of the load, the back of my mind wasn't good enough. After practice one day, I grabbed a black marker and wrote, *"Isaiah 40:31,"* on the toes of both of my shoes. I figured that when I got tired, I would be bent over and it would be easier to read my shoes than to hold up my wrist to read something written on some tape. The process of thinking about the verse and writing it on my shoes allowed me to commit its words to memory and I would dwell on them as practice wore on.

Coach Lilly became my other source of encouragement through the oppressive August grind. He was familiar with the verse and he was aware of the effort being asked of me, so he would often remind me of it as we ran from drill to drill or while I was gulping water between plays. He made no excuses for me either. If I let fatigue control me and I dropped a pass, slipped running a route, or got beaten on a block, he would be on me like that verse was on my shoes. He wouldn't let me reduce my focus or effort just because I was tired. That just isn't acceptable for a senior at Florida State, nor is it acceptable for a person professing to follow Christ. Jesus didn't quit when things got hard; Coach Lilly wasn't going to let me quit either. I wrote a verse of God's Word on my shoe. It couldn't just be a lucky charm or gimmick idea. If I was who I claimed to be, I had to let those words affect my life.

One particular day, during the afternoon practice, a combination of heat and gravity got the best of me. We were up on field three running a passing drill with the defense and we were running our plays towards Doak Campbell. On one of the plays, I ran a dig route over the middle of the field. A "dig" requires that the route runner plant and make a 90-degree turn to continue his path towards the center of the field. The ball was thrown a little high and I jumped to make the catch. As the ball met my hands, a safety met the back of my legs and I fell to the ground. Because I was in the air when he hit me, I fell onto my back, and because I was so tired, I failed to support my head allowing it to slam into the Earth. I didn't know it when it happened, but I had just received a nice concussion.

The trainers came and checked me out but attributed my not

popping right back up to fatigue. I did get up and I told them I was fine as I jogged back to my place next to Coach Lilly. Randy Oravetz had trained his staff well and his right hand man, Dave Walls, kept a close eye on me. I must have looked a little wobbly as I ran because when I turned around to face the action, Dave wasn't far behind. As he approached, he asked me a bizarre question, "Why are you crying Ryan?" I didn't even know I was crying! I wasn't feeling physical pain and I certainly wasn't feeling emotional pain, but apparently I was crying. That was enough for old Dave to wave his hands like a fight official ending a boxing match and take me off the field. I spent the rest of the day under the big oak tree sipping PowerAde while the offense worked on our four wide receiver formations.

The concussion was very mild and I checked out fine after practice, so I was back in the huddle the following day. The most difficult part of practice was when we worked on the passing game. Under normal circumstances, a player runs a route and then while they are jogging back, the backup runs the next play. For many of these sessions I was both players so after I completed a route I would hustle back to the huddle to get the play and go run it again. As my feet pounded the turf, and my panting echoed inside my head, I would repeat the words of Isaiah 40:31 one syllable at a time, between each desperate inhale.

"But," inhale, "those," inhale, "who," inhale, "hope," inhale, "In..."

Then Weinke would call the play, "Pass 44 Demon, Pass 44 Demon, on two, on two, ready, break!" I would jog to the line, listen to the cadence, and on the second "hut" I'd run my route. The ball would go to Snoop and then I would continue.

"The," inhale, "Lord," inhale, "will" inhale, "renew," inhale, "their," inhale, "strength..."

Back in the huddle I would hear Outzen say, "460 shark, 460 shark, on one, on one, ready, break!" I would repeat the process with the second team and this cycle continued all day long.

I didn't experience superhuman strength, nor did I go throughout the practice absent of feeling weary. I was tired the entire practice, so much so that I ended up receiving the concussion. But, that verse of scripture represented belief and produced perseverance. I believed that no matter how tired I felt or how hot it was, I wasn't going to die. I would survive, so I might as well push as hard as I could. This was where the perseverance showed up. I was able to perform well beyond my own expectations and I'm sure beyond the realistic expectations of the coaches as well. I believe absolutely that God enabled me to do that.

The verse had become a part of my identity as a football player, so I felt it only appropriate to include it whenever someone asked me for my autograph. I would attach the reference for that verse, "Is. 40:31," just underneath my name, to the left of my no. 85. It represented who I had become and provided much more of the story than just my name and jersey number.

The two-a-days portion of camp came to a close and we transitioned into game prep. Only one practice a day with plenty of time to renew my strength afterwards. Nick was cleared for full participation and we began to share the load more fully. As a team, we picked up the 2000 season right where we left off the last year. We soundly defeated Brigham Young in the Pigskin Classic, then survived a little scare up in Atlanta before rattling off three resounding victories in a row over North Carolina, Louisville, and Maryland by a combined score of 153-21. Chris Weinke had thrown for just under 1,500 yards and 12 touchdowns in the opening phase of his Heisman campaign. We were 5-0, had won 17 straight games, and were headed to Coral Gables, Fla. carrying the familiar no. 1 ranking. That game provided us the opportunity to become a part of an infamous Seminole tradition, our own edition of "wide right."

30

WIDE RIGHT III

In 1991, Florida State was ranked no. 1 going into the game against no. 2 Miami in Doak Campbell Stadium. After 59 minutes of football, the outcome was on the foot of Gerry Thomas, but his field goal attempt drifted wide right and the Hurricanes stole a 17-16 victory. In 1992, the location changed and the kicker changed, but the result didn't. The 'Canes were the defending National Champs and ranked second in America, while the 'Noles were ranked third and eager to avenge the loss from '91. Florida State was leading in the fourth quarter but Miami staged a late rally and took a 19-16 lead with 1:35 to go in the game. Charlie Ward led the 'Noles right back down with Matt Frier, making a fabulous fingertip catch and converting an unlikely fourth and 12, with a pass to Kez McCorvey. The game seemed to be going the Seminoles' way as Dan Mowrey lined up for a 39-yard field goal. Despite the fact that Mowrey was 3 for 3 on his field goal attempts that day, his fourth try floated wide right and Miami celebrated a 19-16 victory. When we squared off against the 'Canes in 2000, our fourth quarter would follow an eerily similar script.

It was unnaturally hot for an October day in Coral Gables. South Florida is never cold but the weather was sweltering that day. The third largest crowd to ever see a home game for Miami crammed into the Orange Bowl, to see what I think was the most exciting game in all my years at FSU. The Hurricane fans couldn't have dreamed of a better first half as we struggled mightily on the offensive side of the ball. Weinke threw two interceptions just six feet short of the end zone and even though we averaged scoring 42 points per game, we headed into the half trailing 17-0. The last time a Seminole football team was shutout in the first half was in the 1988 game against these same Hurricanes. It was unthinkable that FSU could go 12 years without seeing a first half shutout and then have one of its most prolific offensive teams do it twice in one season. That second thirty minute shutout wouldn't happen for a couple months. In the meantime, Coach Bowden managed to rein the guys in and we came out swinging in the second half.

Our opening drive led to an 18-yard Matt Munyon field goal that helped to relieve the mounting pressure. We were within two scores at 17-3 but we would quickly cut even further into that cushion. About three minutes later Weinke found Anquan Boldin for a 48-yard touchdown and despite our miserable opening half, we were within seven points of Miami. Before the quarter was out, Miami added a 37-yard field goal and we began the momentous fourth quarter, trailing 20-10.

It was a defensive struggle for about 10 minutes but with 3:15 to go in the game, we were given hope when Weinke hit Boldin again for a two-yard touchdown, and we were within three at 20-17. On Miami's ensuing drive, one play would generate misery and then euphoria, in a matter of seconds, for Seminoles everywhere. The 'Canes wanted to run as much time off the clock as possible, so they gave the ball to running back Najeh Davenport. They had a chance to knock us out, but Tay Cody forced Davenport to fumble and Brian Allen jumped on the ball, giving it back to our offense on Miami's 48-yard line. After a nightmare beginning, we found ourselves down by just three, with the ball, and less than half the field between us and victory. It didn't take long for us to break the hearts of the Hurricanes as Weinke found Atrews Bell on a post pattern and hit him for a 29-yard score. Following Munyon's extra point, we had overcome the 17-point deficit to take a 24-20 lead, with only 97 seconds remaining in the game.

Just like in 1992, the Hurricanes found a way to reclaim the lead. Ken Dorsey led them on a hectic drive towards the end zone. The final play of their 68-yard drive, was a 13-yard touchdown pass to Jeremy Shockey. So, with 46 seconds to go in the game, we were back down by three with a punchers chance to score. Just as Charlie Ward led his team into field goal range on this same field, Weinke led us on a drive of his own. On that day, Chris threw for 496 yards and three touchdowns, and our offense accumulated 565 yards of total offense. The only thing hotter than the air that Saturday were the team's offenses, as they combined to rack up more than 1,000 yards. But, the game would once again be decided by a Seminole kicker.

Weinke managed to get the ball to the 34-yard line, so Munyon would be attempting a 49-yard field goal. I remember getting into my position on the left side of the line and having a very peaceful spirit. It was easy for me to think, but I had no doubt that Munyon would make that kick. He was only 3-7 on his attempts up to this point in the season but distance wasn't his problem. He had plenty of leg. I would imagine that most of the fans were having flashbacks to '92 which would have left the 'Canes hopeful and the 'Noles full of dread. History wasn't lost on Matt either. You cannot be a kicker at Florida State and be unfamiliar with the notorious history associated with the Miami game. He had his mind made up that he was going to rise above the moment and write his own history.

He struck it pure. The ball launched off of Matt's foot and it was clear from the moment it passed over our heads that it had plenty of distance. From my vantage point, it looked to be equally accurate as well. The ball was in the air for just a matter of moments, but those moments were flooded with emotion. At first, I felt a sense of accomplishment, joy, and pride as the ball appeared to be heading through the uprights, but those were replaced with feelings of disappointment and sympathy for Matt as soon as the official signaled that the kick had, in fact, sailed wide right. Matt dropped instantly into a catcher's crouch and clasped his hands around the back of his hanging head. The Orange Bowl erupted with a sadistic joy as they witnessed yet another Seminole kicker fall from glory.

I jogged back to Matt and hugged him around his head. As painful as it was to lose that game, it was nothing compared to what Matt had to feel. We didn't lose the game because of him but he felt the complete burden of the defeat. Our defense allowed more than 450 yards and a game-winning touchdown drive in the final minute. Our offense turned the ball over three times and failed to score any points twice in the red zone. We lost the game as a team. We also fought our guts out as a team, outscoring Miami 24-10 in the second half. It was up and down, back and forth, excellence and errors; it was football. We battled a great Miami team to the bitter end and wound up on the short end. The Seminoles and the Hurricanes have one of the most memorable and meaningful rivalries in college football, and it's classics like this one that make it so. Adding a chapter to the wide right saga was not how our team envisioned making history. Our goal was to go 13-0 and repeat as National Champions. This loss ended our 26 game, regular season winning streak and prevented us from going undefeated but we still had a chance to defend our title, so we hit the practice field the following Monday focused to do just that.

Poor old Duke had to come to Tallahassee the next Saturday and we unleashed our frustration on them. We scored 28 points in the first quarter, 42 in the first half, and won the game by seven touchdowns at 63-14. Weinke continued to make his claim for the Heisman Trophy by throwing for 536 yards and throwing five TD passes to four different receivers. Our record was now 6-1, we were undefeated in the ACC and ranked no. 6 in America. Our goals were still very much in front of us as we prepared to play Virginia.

31

TORN

For reasons unknown to me, our annual matchup with the University of Virginia always seemed to be eventful. If you remember, in 1998 Patrick Kerney sacked Chris Weinke which resulted in Chris's season being over and replacing his helmet with a halo brace. In 1999, our defense knocked Dan Ellis out of the game with a concussion, allowing my high school quarterback David Rivers to play the second half and throw the memorable interception to Corey Simon. The matchup in 2000 would prove to follow a similar storyline, with different characters.

Nick Franklin and I had been exchanging series all year long. He would play a drive or two, then I would do the same. Occasionally, one of us would be in particularly good form and might have an extended stretch, but that was rare. As the offense headed onto the field for a drive, Nick was taking his turn at tight end. Unfortunately, it would be his last drive of the regular season because of another freak injury.

A reverse was called to Atrews Bell and the play was supposed to go away from Nick. Our assignment was simple; just keep the defensive end from being able to track down the play from the back side. However, due to the defense's quick reaction, the play moved back towards Nick. A lesser player might have disengaged his block by then, but Nick was still locked up when Atrews came close to him. While Nick was still blocking, a player fell into his right knee and Nick dropped to the turf writhing in pain. The training staff hurried out to him and began to work with his knee. It was obvious from Nick's grimace and the trainers' body language that it was bad, so I walked out to them. I was going to have to go into the game anyway, but I felt terrible for Nick and wanted to try to offer some sort of comfort. I remember kneeling with him on the field unsure of what to say or do while the trainers prepared to take him back to the locker room. Here I was again, watching Nick's season drift away due to another knee injury and wrestling with the reality that I was the one who would be taking his place. I really felt awful for him, while at the same time I knew that as soon as Nick had been taken off the field, the officials would restart the game and I had to play. He ended up with another torn ligament, and just like in 1998 when Weinke was injured in the Virginia game and Marcus Outzen had to come in and lead us, I had to step in for Nick to finish the 2000 season.

It proved to be a big day for the tight ends, as both me and my Virginia counterpart Chris Luzar, were named the "Chevrolet Scholarship Program Players of the game" by the television broadcast team. Weinke and Outzen were generous enough to connect with me four times, which resulted in 87 receiving yards. Both numbers were career highs for me and unfamiliar territory for any FSU tight end since Melvin Pearsall left in 1997. The last reception I made, late in the fourth quarter, was the best of my career as far as difficulty goes. In Super Bowl XLII, David Tyree made his memorable, circus catch on a crucial third down late in the fourth quarter. He was streaking down the center of the field and Eli Manning's pass floated a little, requiring Tyree to leap for the ball. He was fully extended as his hands found the ball, but

Rodney Harrison was draped all over him trying to dislodge it. As he fell to the turf, he had to keep the ball over his head due to Harrison's invasive right arm, and finally secured the ball against his helmet as it came perilously close to touching the ground. The replay confirmed that he had made the improbable catch and the Giants went on to win the Super Bowl.

My catch was not that good. I too had run down the middle of the field and my pass had also drifted, requiring me to leap for it. But the acrobatics and the drama were lacking. We were winning by more than four touchdowns, with no Super Bowl on the line. Even though I was in heavy traffic, I was able to secure the ball with both hands, no helmet required. While I would like to think that I was David Tyree before David Tyree was cool, the truth is that it was a pretty good catch in an insignificant moment, but it still felt pretty sweet.

Ironically, setting two career highs, making a relatively memorable catch, and earning the "Player of the Game" made my parent's sick. Had I played an uneventful game and failed to be a part of anything special, their absence wouldn't have stung so much. My parents made the trip to every game of my career, with the exception of the opening game of 1997 in California. Because of that commitment and an imminent arrival, they were torn between making the trip to Tallahassee and staying in Augusta. Really, it was a simple decision to stay home and my parents made the right one. My oldest sister, Jennifer, was expecting her fourth child. So, in spite of a string of 43 consecutive games in the stands, my parents watched the best performance of my career on TV. Our game was on the 21st, but Bennett decided he was quite comfortable and didn't arrive until the 27th. Because I had a memorable performance and the anticipated baby didn't arrive, my parents felt like a contestant on "Who wants to be a millionaire" that stopped playing and ended up knowing the next answer.

Catching a few footballs pales in comparison to the potential birth of a child but there was still significance in that Virginia game. I only caught four passes in a game one other time, I was never close to 87 yards, and certainly didn't win another "Player of the Game" award. My mom and dad would have had a blast cheering with the jersey wearing, tearful, proud, nomadic community known as the "parents section." Instead, they shared the day with an even prouder group, watching a son on TV and anticipating the arrival of a new grandson. Maybe one day Bennett will benefit from Chevrolet's contribution to the scholarship fund that they generously donated in my honor; that would be pretty amazing! Even though it was the first time in three seasons that my parents watched a game in Augusta, it was still a joyful day in the Sprague family. At the same time, the Franklin family experienced one of their saddest.

Nick's football career effectively ended that autumn Saturday. Where Oct. 21 will represent life and joy in our family, it is an anniversary of shattered dreams for the Franklins. The game of football can be fickle and heartless. One day you are the starter, and the next you are having surgery that could end your career. Or in my case, one day you are a backup and the next you are a starter. The history of the game is full of stories like mine; of guys being granted playing time due to the hardships in someone else's career. Sadly, for every story like mine there is a story like Nick's. A player who possessed great potential as a football player but it never worked out for him, due to injuries on both knees. His career could have been marked by great athletic achievement but instead was marred by two unfortunate ligament tears, and it really was a shame. I loved being able to start and make a meaningful contribution on those great Seminole teams, but I sincerely wish it had been under different circumstances.

At the end of the 1999 season Chuck Amato left his position at Florida State to become the head coach at his alma mater, N.C. State and the week after the Virginia game had us traveling up to Raleigh to play against our old coach. Chuck ignited the Wolfpack fan base upon his arrival and reconstruction of the attitude around the N.C. State program. His first big coup was to convince high school phenom quarterback, Phillip Rivers, to come to Raleigh from Alabama. Rivers was given the reigns from the start and would lead his team against us that Saturday. The fans were boiling over with the enthusiasm that Amato had infused into the program and over 52,000 showed up, believing that they could pull off the shocker. Two years earlier, we had been beaten by N.C. State and the aftertaste of that monumental upset was still fresh in their mouths. Unfortunately for them, it was fresh in ours too.

Coach Amato and Rivers had the Pack ranked no. 21 in the country. They came into the game with a 5-1 record and a realistic shot to win the ACC if they could beat the odds one more time. The first quarter gave the impression that it would be a defensive struggle, as the enraptured fans savored a scoreless opening period. Fifteen minutes later, the stadium had a drastically different feel as we piled on four touchdowns and took it to the half with a 27-0 lead. Chuck was always loved by the guys on the team, in part, because of his reckless passion for the game. He must have tapped into that passion at halftime because his team came out with hope renewed.

Amato gave Bowden a taste of his own medicine by running a fake punt from the shadow of his own end zone and converting it for an 81-yard touchdown. Carter-Finley Stadium was pulsating with belief and intensity when Chuck called an onside kick for the ensuing kickoff and the Pack recovered. The burst was short lived because our defense smothered them on three consecutive plays, forced a punt, and dashed their hopes for a quick comeback. With the crowd still hopeful that their defense could keep them in the game, we rattled off 24 consecutive points and put the game to bed. It was 51-7 at that point and any belief that the fans maintained had been doused by a heavy dose of reality.

It was fitting that I had another one of my better games when we played a team led by Coach Amato. He was notorious for neglecting to pay attention to tight ends in practice, or in games for that matter. I never heard him say it, but my assumption was that he'd rather a tight end have the ball than a tailback or a wide out. So, Weinke found me in some pretty wide open spaces three different times for 50 yards. I was tied with Snoop for the most receptions in the game and only 10 yards shy of being the yardage leader. That didn't ever happen at FSU and maybe it was Amato's familiarity with our tendencies that allowed it to happen on that night. The uprising was calmed for another year as we improved our record to 8-1, but our next game would bring Coach Bowden against an opponent even more familiar with him than Amato; Bowden Bowl II, against his son Tommy.

32

GOTCHA

I have often used board games as a way to help people understand what makes a good offensive coordinator. Anybody can play checkers, but to excel at chess you have to possess a different mind. Chess requires strategy. To have a plan mapped out in your mind five or six moves in advance and anticipate what your opponent is likely to do, is beyond me. I can think one or two moves ahead, but even then I get lost. Chess is for particular people with particular skills and I would bet that Mark Richt can play chess.

An offensive coordinator thinks much the same way. Calling a game is not as simple as, "run right then throw deep." It is a strategic art that requires a particular mind. The great ones will study film and discover tendencies in the opposing team and game plan accordingly. Even greater still, are the coaches who can force the other team to do something and then exploit it. Because he knew Amato tended to ignore tight ends, the previous week he leaned heavily on us in the game plan. Tommy Bowden didn't have the same tendencies, but he did have them, and I was able to be on the field for one of the great plays in the history of FSU football. It happened because Coach Richt was one of those particular minds.

Early in the week, we would sit down as an offense and get

a scouting report on the opposing team. Each week, a different coach is assigned the task of evaluating tendencies, formations, blitz frequency, etc. They would then walk the offense (*or the defense*) through those tendencies in the form of a notebook. Those notebooks were about 50 pages thick and full of all kinds of facts that stat guys love, but we didn't pay much attention to them. Those graduate assistants slaved over those things but I think the QBs were the only ones that really paid them any mind.

This particular week, Coach Richt let us in on a little secret. It was like getting a behind the scenes look at a magician performing his tricks! He pulled up a series of plays run by different teams where they lined up in the same formation. He had noticed a tendency that the Clemson defense had, although it was more than a tendency, it was a certainty. Their opponents would line up in an I-formation with two tight ends and a wide receiver to the QB's left. Prior to the snap, the quarterback would send the wide out in motion towards the ball. Coach Richt pointed out the safety over the tight end, to the receiver's side.

Every time those other teams got in that formation and sent that receiver in motion, it was a strong side run. The Clemson safety had picked up on that pattern and as the receiver motioned, he would start sneaking closer to the line of scrimmage and would attack when the ball was snapped. He was a pretty smart player and it proved to be effective, but he was a checkers player caught in a game of chess.

Coach Richt told us the plan. We would get in the same formation and run the same motion but Weinke would play-action fake, Snoop would fake a block and then go deep. That was it, nothing more to it than that. But you don't have to be complicated when you're smart, and Coach Richt proved to be brilliant on this day. He was smirking like someone about to pull off a world-class prank as he said, "if we get in the right situation, we will run this play."

That situation came very early in the game and set the tone for the evening. We had kicked a field goal on our opening possession and our defense came out strong to force a punt on Clemson's first attempt. The Tigers were fired up after their punter pinned us down at the two-yard line, but they didn't know that they had just thrown Brer Rabbit into the briar patch. We were in the Marching Chiefs end zone facing the student section 100 yards away from us, and lined up on the right hash. We were on the sideline waiting for the play call and the coaches were like little kids hearing gossip, as news of the play filtered through to Weinke. Sure enough, we were going to try it.

I lined up on the right side, and Carver Donaldson was the tight end on Snoop's side of the field. I had a goofy grin on my face as I ran up to the line of scrimmage. The poor Tigers had no idea what was about to happen to them. My stance was terrible because I was so curious to watch the play unfold that I totally disregarded all my technique. I had my eye on that safety.

Weinke sent Snoop jogging into motion and they played right into Coach Richt's hands. I would have loved to have been on a headset while this was happening. My guess is that they sounded like someone who had bet on the long shot and their horse was about to win. Full of wild anticipation, yet hoping that nobody messed anything up.

I was not peeking, but staring at the safety. When he began sneaking closer to the line of scrimmage I began laughing out loud... We had 'em! At the snap, I dropped back into my pass protection but I was watching Snoop and the safety. Bear in mind that it wasn't that long ago that Chris had broken his neck on this field. But this day, he pulled off the gutsiest play fake of his career to perfection, and when I saw Snoop sprint by the Tiger defender, I began sprinting too!

Weinke hit him in stride and Snoop flew down the field totally untouched. I chased him the whole way and ran the fastest 100-yard dash of my life, and didn't feel it at all. It might have been the happiest moment of my playing career. I was jumping, pumping my fist, laughing, high-stepping, and who knows what else as I chased Snoop into the end zone. He barely had time to turn around before I caught up to him, along with Carver, and we celebrated like it was a game-winning score. In reality, we had gone up 10-0 and there were still more than seven minutes remaining in the first quarter. Clemson mustered up a score of their own to make the score 10-7 as we entered the second. Weinke went off for 521 yards and 2 touchdowns as we outscored them by a 44-0 count over the next 3 quarters.

The first Bowden Bowl was a nail biter and even though the Tigers lost, I believe it was an acceptable loss in Tommy's mind. His overachieving team nearly pulled the upset but instead, his dad got win no. 300 and an eventual undefeated season. I don't think this one was as easy to swallow. At the end of the day, we had won 54-7. The second Bowden Bowl went convincingly to dad. The announcers might have called it a romp or a white-washing, but I would call it check-mate. We were no. 3 in the country, boasting a 9 -1 record with two games remaining in the regular season.

33

FATHERS

The 1999 and 2000 Clemson games brought a spotlight onto the family aspect of Coach Bowden's legacy. He was the only father to coach football against his son in a Division-I competition. The scope expanded to his other son, Terry, who had been so successful at Auburn and his son Jeff, who coached the wide receivers at FSU. Family was a top priority for Coach Bowden. He modeled it himself and he made it easy for his assistants to keep that priority as well.

A few years after I graduated, I considered the idea of getting into college coaching, so I called Coach Van for some advice. "You have to understand, Ryan, that Florida State is utopia. You won't find the atmosphere you saw in Tallahassee anywhere else." His comment was referring to the way Coach Bowden maintained his priorities of faith, then family, then football, and how it wasn't like that anywhere else in the country. Coach Van knew I had a couple of toddlers at the time and he was warning me of the incredible time sacrifice that is required of college coaches to maintain successful programs. Coach Bowden made similar sacrifices but somehow, Coach Bowden was able to make those sacrifices while at the same time making sure his family was a priority, and that it was a priority for his coaches, too. One of the ways he did that was family nights.

One day a week was family night in the Seminole football department. Because the coaches didn't eat dinner at home during the week and stayed out way past bedtime for youngsters, Coach Bowden invited the families to the facility around the end of practice to hang out through dinner. We were able to experience Coach Andrews, the Bear Bryant protégé and drill sergeant coach almost every day, but on family night we saw behind the curtain at Mickey Andrews, the loving husband. He would smile and laugh, tell stories and tease us, but he would pay even more attention to Diane, his bride. We were able to see him in his primary role as a husband and that helped bring the legend down to Earth. I heard the story of one of the women in a support role at FSU and how family nights changed her perception of Mickey as well. She had always viewed him as unapproachable because of his natural scowl and laser focus when he was around the stadium. It would be easy to have that opinion of Coach Andrews if you didn't know him, but on one of these family nights, her perspective changed. He was hanging out with his grandkids this particular night and the scowl disappeared. His laser focus was aimed at enjoying his grandbabies and he became very approachable. From that night on, she viewed him as Mickey Andrews the man; the grandfather, and she was able to engage in a good relationship with him. Such was the power of these family nights. But the most memorable thing about family night was not eating dinner with the Andrews, it was watching Coach Richt and his kids.

It was one of my favorite scenes each week when practice would officially end and the Richt boys, John and David, would race across the field to hug their dad. John would have been around nine, while "Davy" was about five. Coach Richt would melt into dad faster than Clark Kent could become Superman as he dropped his practice cards and squatted down to hug those boys. I used to love to watch him take off the coach hat and put on the dad hat so effortlessly. I was no longer watching the hottest name in the world of potential head coaches, I was watching a man love on his boys who could care less what their dad did for a living. Actually, I think they did care. In fact, I think they loved that their dad was a coach at FSU and they loved all the perks that came along with it. How cool must it be for a 9 year old boy to have free reign of the most dominant football program in America? That is what made it so special. John and David wouldn't have had that access at most places, but Coach Bowden's insistence on family allowed them that freedom.

Once or twice, I had the privilege of sticking around while Coach would have John run routes and throw passes to him. Sometimes, Weinke or Outzen would hang out and QB for John while Coach Richt would just sit and soak up the moment. Most times, little Davy was wearing a caped costume and was more interested in saving the day than running routes. But John would run routes over and over again as Katharyn Richt, Coach's wife, looked on, wearing a big smile. While John was returning with a ball, Davy would take the opportunity to tackle his dad and Coach Richt would head straight to the ground to let his little boy in a superhero costume wrestle with his personal superhero in a football coach's costume. They did a lot of wrestling. It was a frequent happening to be on our way to meetings or to a coach's office and find Coach Richt in a two-on-one wrestling match against both of the boys in our indoor gym. Those boys were unrelenting and Coach Richt never hesitated to give them his undivided time and attention. It didn't matter if Peter Warrick or Corey Simon was walking by, the most important people in the room were Katharyn, John, and David.

I would think often of my teammates who never experienced a positive father in their life when I would see Coach Richt being a dad in front of us. My dad was always around but I'm afraid I was in the minority. A few of the guys were dads themselves, and as someone who has spent most of his adult life working with teenagers, words are lacking in regard to how appreciative I am for Coach Richt's example. But it didn't stop with just being a loving father to John and David. Coach and Mrs. Richt made an awesome decision for their family, and for two little children from Ukraine, when they chose to adopt Anya and Zach.

Their stories are incredible and their adoption was magnificent. Little Anya was injured due to difficulties associated with poor medical facilities. I remember meeting Anya and being so impressed with Coach Richt and the willingness of their family to offer their family to these kids. It is no small feat to adopt a child, much more adopt one from overseas, even greater still to adopt one with health concerns. I mentioned earlier that we are blessed with four wonderful sons, and to think that a family like the Richt's would choose to adopt our little boys if my wife and I were not around, oh that they would be so blessed!

One of my greatest influences as to being a father is Coach Richt. His willingness to give those boys his undivided attention, and to bring Zach and Anya into their family, motivates me to this day. My wife and I hope to adopt one day and Coach Richt was one of our inspirations. Thankfully, he is still offering that example to the young men he coaches at Georgia. If you were to show up on a Monday night to the Bulldog football complex, you would probably run into Zach or Anya playing with their dad just like Davy and John did 10 years ago at FSU. It's all a part of Bobby Bowden's legacy.

Coach Richt wasn't the only coach setting a great example of being a husband and father; Coach Van's example was much the same. Van had the advantage of teaching many of us at the weekly FCA huddles. He would often use that time to talk about his role as a husband but outside of FCA, we got to see him be dad. His son Matt was hanging around all the time, as well as his daughters Julie and Danielle. The girls normally just came on family night but Matt, being a boy, found much more enjoyment around a football facility, so we saw him more often. Coach Van was the same with his kids as Coach Richt, except that Van's kids were older, so there wasn't as much wrestling. Van continued the adoption tradition as he and his wife, Michelle, adopted Michael from Ukraine in December of 2000, just before the Orange Bowl, and then adopted Katelyn from China in 2004. Anya and Zach Richt, as well as Michael and Kateyln Van Halanger, have been given a better shot at life. From being poverty laden orphans on the other side of the world, to beloved sons and daughters in the heart of college football country was an incredible journey. Just as their adoption gave them a new outlook on life, being able to observe these men being devoted husbands and fathers gave me and my teammates one as well.

Sure, Coach Bowden is one of the winningest coaches of all time, sure he had an incredible dynasty run at FSU, and sure he revolutionized the game of football in his prime, but those are not his true legacy. His legacy is found on Monday nights at the University of Georgia. It was found in Tony Dungy having his kids with him at the "office" and with him on the road. It's found in the reality that four orphan children were given parents, siblings, and a home. More importantly, it's found in guys like me who want to be better fathers because of things like family night. Coach Bowden is a man who lived out his priorities. First God, then family, then football. You may or may not have liked his methods, but you cannot argue with his results; men of faith, men who are strong husbands and fathers, and some pretty darn good football too.

34

SENIOR DAY

There were only two weeks left in the regular season and we were in a battle with the University of Miami to see which of us would play Oklahoma, for the National Championship. This week, we had to go to Winston-Salem to play lowly Wake Forest and regardless of the outcome, we would take a hit in the computer rankings. Chris Weinke was quoted after the game saying, "It's gotten to be that the expectations are so high with this team, that if we don't win by 50, we didn't do a good job. Winning by 29 is still nice, but we know it's probably going to cost us." It's a crazy reality of the state of college football and the era of computer polls, that teams are now compelled to shame teams by running up scores so that it will impress a hard drive in New York. Miami only won its game by 28 points, but Pittsburgh was considered a higher caliber opponent than the Deacons, so a 29 point victory might have proven inadequate. In the game, I had a couple more receptions and Snoop caught three touchdowns, while Chris continued his march on the Downtown Athletic Club with 324 more yards. It was a typical Wake Forest performance for us as we entered the fourth quarter, only leading 21-6. For some reason, we struggled when we played up in Winston, but we cranked it up in the final frame, and scored two more touchdowns en route to our 35-6, unimpressive victory. When the polls came out, we learned that Miami had surpassed us in the BCS rankings, but we had a game against the fourth ranked Gators the following week. A good showing in that game might be just enough to convince the Macs and PCs to let us play in the Orange Bowl.

Nov. 18, 2000 was the last time for me and the rest of the 1996 recruiting class to play in front of the home crowd. In five years, we had won every time we played in Doak Campbell and we had one final test against the Gators. We had beaten them twice on this field before and once in their stadium, so we weren't intimidated. We had also played in plenty of huge games and in front of enormous crowds, so we weren't nervous. But none of us had ever played in our final home game, so some of us were nostalgic. It was senior day in Tallahassee and 83,042 people had packed the friendly confines to see us off. There was a significant game to play and a national media to impress, but prior to all that, there was a more intimate opportunity at hand. The tradition at Florida State is for the seniors to be introduced over the PA and escorted onto the field by their families for a brief moment with Coach Bowden. After watching me play on this turf more than 20 times, my dad and mom had their opportunity to experience things from my perspective.

We were in our traditional home uniforms of gold pants with garnet jerseys. I met my parents under the north end zone bleachers. My dad was in a suit and my mom was wearing one of my jerseys from a previous year, under her garnet outfit. I think my mom began crying the night before because by the time we all locked arms for our walk out of the tunnel, her eyes were bright red. On any other Saturday, I would have been in the locker room focusing on the game at hand; thinking over play variations, visualizing my assignments against potential formations, and mentally preparing for the three hour grind I was about to endure. But this Saturday I was just smiling. I wasn't thinking about the Gators or the game plan, I was just soaking in the magnitude of the moment. The last five years of my life had been incredible and sadly, it was nearing its conclusion. I felt like a recruit again, standing with my parents in the locker room, giddy with enthusiasm at seeing the word "Sprague" on a locker name plate. It wasn't that long ago that a thousand of my peers booed me at my first pep rally and today, more than 83,000 fans who didn't know I existed five years ago, would cheer for me. What a crazy ride.

Our PA announcer, Nick Menacof, spoke into his microphone as his amplified voice echoed throughout the stadium, "Number 85, tight end, Ryan Sprague." Upon his herald, we began our walk from the tunnel and into the end zone. One parent was on either side of me as the three of us walked up the field towards my legendary Coach, Bobby Bowden. I felt so proud. Not a self-inflating pride but a corporate pride, similar to what a member of our armed services might feel. I felt proud to have been a part of something so transcendent, proud to have served under such a magnificent leader, proud to have worked alongside such a dedicated group of players, proud to be a Seminole, and proud that I was sharing this moment with my two biggest fans. In 1996 we became Seminoles, and for the last five years we had given ourselves to Florida State University. But before that time, and in this moment, we were first and foremost a family.

Coach Bowden reached out and shook my hand, and I imagined all the people watching who would do anything to change places with me at that moment. I was humbled. I don't remember exactly what he said to me, but it was something like, "well done son, it was good to have you as a part of this team." It was never lost on me that I was a part of something special at FSU. Every year about 25 kids get the call and become Seminole football players and I was one of those extremely fortunate kids. For five years I had played football for Bobby Bowden at Florida State University. I knew then that I had more in common with the guys who played basketball for John Wooden, than I did with my peers playing college football. Sure, we all played the same game, but Coach Bowden is bigger than college football and I got to play for him. Forty-eight times I was able to strap on my gold helmet adorned with our trademark spear. 48 times I put on the garnet and gold and represented Florida State on the gridiron. But the time for nostalgia was over, because it was time for no. 49 and the Gators were in for a long night.

Florida scored one touchdown in the first quarter and that was it; the rest of the night belonged to us. We kicked off and our defense, charged by the electricity in the crowd, smothered them. After a punt, our offense took the field and from the outset, we expressed our dominance. We drove straight down the field and Weinke hit Atrews Bell for a 14-yard touchdown giving us a 7-0 lead. The Gators answered with a TD of their own, but 56 seconds after they tied the game, Snoop Minnis hauled in a 34-yard touchdown and we never looked back. Neither team scored in the next quarter, but we received the second half kickoff and used that possession to double our lead. A seven minute, 80-yard drive capped off by a William McCray touchdown, gave us a 21-7 lead. Later in that same quarter, Weinke found Minnis again, this time for 51 yards streaking down the visitors' sideline. The fourth quarter was all about our defense as they killed two Gator drives with interceptions. Chris Hope nabbed the first one, then Tay Cody got his second of the night and returned it 58 yards. We capitalized on Tay's pick with a field goal, giving us the 30-7 victory. Maybe a 29-point victory over Wake Forest wasn't good enough, but a 23-point victory over the fourth ranked Gators sure should have been. Our fans sure thought so because when the game clock expired, oranges rained onto our field like ball caps after a hat trick in the NHL.

They believed, and we did too, that we had done enough to merit a trip to the Orange Bowl to defend our championship. After our post game prayer with Clint, I jogged over to the student section in the north end zone and climbed up into the stands. I was joined by a few other guys, as we celebrated with our classmates the sound drubbing we had just laid on Florida. We finished our careers undefeated at home. Once the computers had it all figured out, we learned that our 50th game for Coach Bowden would be in Miami against the Oklahoma Sooners.

With over five weeks separating the final whistle of the Florida game and the kick off of the Orange Bowl, Seminoles everywhere turned their attention to the Downtown Athletic Club in New York City, for the presentation of the 2000 Heisman Trophy. Three quarterbacks were the frontrunners for the award: Oklahoma's Josh Heupel, Purdue's Drew Brees, and our own Chris Weinke. Chris had a remarkable year, as he led the nation with 4,167 passing yards and threw 33 touchdowns as well. He became just the second quarterback in NCAA history to throw for over 9,500 yards in his career and win a National Championship. When the voting took place, Chris was the FSU and ACC career record holder for passing yardage and touchdown passes, not to mention holding the longest no-interception streak in ACC history as well. As the first quarterback to start for three seasons under Coach Bowden, he led us to the National Championship game every year, compiling a 32-2 record along the way.

My wife used to always say how much more fun cheering for the 'Noles became when she got to know so many of the players. I know this is true, because December 9, 2000 was my favorite Heisman presentation ever. This was the first time I had ever known one of the potential winners and knowing him made the moment much more memorable. It's almost silly to write, but I was proud when they announced that Chris had won the 2000 Heisman Trophy. His parents had to have been overwhelmed with emotion. At 28, he was the oldest player ever to win the award, and his story of stepping away from baseball to enroll as a 25 year old freshman is wonderful. Coach Bowden promised him that a scholarship would be there for him, and Chris honored Coach Bowden's faithfulness by making him only the 9th coach in NCAA history to coach multiple Heisman winners. It was only fitting that the two of them would lead us to the National Championship game, in the Orange Bowl, where FSU's first Heisman winner, Charlie Ward, led his team to Bowden's first championship.

35

SCURVY

For every David there is a slain Goliath, and my last game as a
Seminole left me with bruises on my head. We went into our
Orange Bowl matchup against the Sooners as 10-and-a-half point
favorites, even though they were the no. 1 team in America. We
were ranked third. Our offense was averaging more than 540 yards
and 42 points per game, and our defense was pretty strong in its
own right, led by NFL first round draft pick, Jamal Reynolds. We
were heavily favored for a reason and had we played up to our
standards, we could have easily won the game. But in college, we
are students as well as athletes and an academic "injury" would be
a foreboding sign of things to come.

Marvin "Snoop" Minnis had been named to the All-
American team and was headed to the National Football League at
the end of the season. Unfortunately, he left his academic career
behind a little early as he ended up failing a class. There would be
no chants of "Snooooooooop" from the Seminole faithful in Miami
because Snoop's poor choices required payment in the form of
being suspended from what would have been his final game as a
Seminole. Many have criticized Snoop since that occurred, but I can
assure you that no one paid a higher price than him and no one felt
worse about it. He was a great support to us during our

preparations but things just weren't the same without Snoop on the field.

I'm not about to make excuses for our performance though. As good as Snoop was, this situation was no different than when we lost Peter Warrick the year before. In that game, our team rallied and we played our most complete game of the season; there was no reason we couldn't repeat that feat. We still had Javon Walker, who played in the NFL for many years, Anquan Boldin, who would be the NFL rookie of the year and make the Pro Bowl, and Atrews Bell, who had come out of nowhere to be a game changing receiver for us. We had plenty of skill playing wide receiver, even with Snoop on the sidelines. Athletically, we were fine. Our deep athleticism and previous experience should have had us quite prepared, but there was more to the story.

Before we were finished with our Orange Bowl preparations, we learned that our offensive coordinator, Mark Richt, had accepted the head coach position with the University of Georgia. It was a great move for him and that is when the big programs make their hires, so I really don't blame him for the choice he made. But his choice did affect us. The players liked Coach Richt and while it didn't impact the seniors, the underclassmen were now faced with uncertainty as their season was coming to an end. The issue facing the 'Noles that January was not one of missing athletes; athletes were plentiful in Tallahassee. The issue of the day was of a team and a program beginning a long transition, and it proved to be too much.

The game was as hyped up as any game I had played in. South Beach was swarming with media and celebrities who were there to be seen. The eye of the American sports world was focused on Miami and this National Championship game. The Heisman trophy winner was matched against his runner-up in Oklahoma's

Josh Heupel. Oklahoma, the team of the 1970s, against FSU as the team of the 1990s. Oklahoma's Head Coach, Bob Stoops, was the former defensive coordinator of the Florida Gators, and Seminole nemesis. The game was rich with story lines, but much to the nation's disappointment, it wasn't rich on points.

The game was surreal. We had been down before, even by 17 to Miami on the road, but not once in my career did I ever doubt we would win a football game. This was almost solely because of the calm confidence possessed by Weinke; the guy was unflappable. He totally believed he would succeed and we totally believed him. It was this fact that made the Orange Bowl so strange. Torrance Marshall intercepted a pass intended for me, in the first half and that play was a microcosm of the entire game, in my eyes. Our defense had just forced a Sooner fumble and gave us the ball only 47 yards from the end zone. It was a scoreless game midway through the first quarter and Coach Richt dialed up a pass. Weinke had been throwing the ball well thus far, but on this particular play, something went very wrong. I was running a "broken arrow" route which was the same route I ran when I scored against Miami the previous year. This was one of our staple routes that we had run for years, not something we game planned into the playbook for Oklahoma. My job was simply to release up past the line backers, read the safeties, and depending on their coverage, break my route across the field in one of two ways. The linebackers were supposed to be a non-factor because the route is a deeper route designed to find space between them and the safeties. As I ran the route, I read the Sooners to be in a two-deep shell so I was going to run a "skinny" route just inside the safety ahead of me. Chris apparently read the Sooners to be in a three-deep shell, expecting me to cut my angle much more sharply across the field. After I began my break, I knew I was open but as I turned my head back to look for the ball I saw Torrance Marshall, the line backer, flash in front of me and pick it off.

As soon as I saw him running the other way I began to chase him. I was focused on the football in his right hand. I intended to hit him from behind and strip the football so that we could get it back. He cut to his right to avoid being tackled. I hit him in the back and knocked him down but couldn't dislodge the football. As we were jogging back to the sidelines, I asked Chris what happened and he told me I was supposed to have cut underneath the safety. I just remember staring back at him and saying, "Chris, that was the linebacker."

I haven't gone back and watched the game but as I have heard others talk about it, they remember that Bob Stoops had devised an excellent game plan. They ran a zone all night long and moved Marshall all over the field to confuse us and they succeeded. I would swear to you that I ran that route correctly but as people have pointed out that fact about Marshall, I wonder if I missed something. Did they have him lined up at safety? Was he at middle linebacker instead of strong? I am not so confident anymore and I really don't want to watch that game again, so I will leave it to you to sort out. I do remember that for the first time, I doubted whether or not we would win and I wonder if Chris doubted it too.

Oklahoma put together a little drive that ended with a 27-yard field goal and they had a 3-0 lead. As the first quarter was drawing to a close, Tay Cody intercepted a Heupel pass and returned it about 20 yards. The next play, Weinke completed a pass and we were in business again near our 45-yard line. We couldn't move the ball much after that and we had to punt. Cottrell sent a rocket down the field and our punt coverage team forced a fumble inside their 20 yard line. The ball managed to travel close to 15 yards and bounce out of bounds before we could get it, and the

Sooners dodged a bullet. That kind of thing happened to us all night long. Later on in the second, we drove down to inside the 20 before Minor was tackled one-yard short of the marker on third down. We were only down by three and set up in the center of the field for a simple, 30-yard field goal. Inexplicably, we missed it and the pressure built.

For the second time that year, after going 12 years without it happening, we were shutout in the first half. Miami had done the same thing to us earlier in the year but we came out after the half and scored 24 points to nearly win. That game was also in Miami, so we played four quarters of first half football in Miami that year and failed to score a single point. Sadly, the second half of the Orange Bowl would look a lot like our first 30 minutes. We never found a rhythm, and despite our defense playing a magnificent game and forcing numerous turnovers, we couldn't get out of our own way on offense and we let the Seminole Nation down.

The game continued down this path into the fourth quarter. Weinke would throw a great pass and a receiver would drop it. One of the receivers would break free and Weinke would under throw the pass. We would call a screen play when Oklahoma was dropping eight men into coverage. It just wasn't our night, and the final act in our career ending tragedy was when Weinke was stripped from behind, on what would have been a first down run. The Sooners recovered the fumble and converted it into the game's only touchdown.

We were able to avoid being shutout in the game as our special teams scored a safety when their long-snapper sailed a snap over their punter's head. At the end of the day we were defeated 13 -2 in the worst offensive performance I had seen in my five years as a Seminole. We were humiliated. As fulfilling as winning it all the year before had felt, losing in this manner was even more deflating.

This loss hurt worse than that win felt good... and it wasn't close. We didn't know it then, but that game marked the end of an era at Florida State and in college football.

My fellow seniors and I only lost six games in our career and three of them were National Championship games. We played for the championship four times in our five years and won the ACC every single year. As the years go by, I can appreciate more and more how special those years were, but losing our last game leaves a bitter taste in my mouth. We finished the year ranked fifth, continuing the unprecedented run of 14 straight seasons ranked in the top five. Unfortunately, that would prove to be the last year of that run. Coach Richt went on to Athens and took our strength coach, Dave Van Halanger with him. Jeff Bowden replaced Richt as offensive coordinator, and FSU began a stretch of years marked by coaching turnover and defeats like FSU had not seen in over two decades.

Losing that group of seniors, including the Heisman trophy winner, losing our long time offensive coordinator, and losing that Orange Bowl were the three stones that felled the Goliath that was Florida State football in the 90's. We left Miami heartbroken and searching for our identity, while Bob Stoops and the Sooners left Miami with a national trophy in one hand and a sling in the other.

36

Macaroni & Cheese

After college, my wife, Jeni, and I spent a year in Hawley, Minn. and then six years in Highlands, N.C. Highlands is one of the most beautiful places in the United States and many people spend millions of dollars building homes in those western Carolina mountains. While serving as a pastor at Community Bible Church I met a lot of people and some of those people were very well off. One night my wife and I invited a couple down to the house for dinner, and they happened to fall into that "well off" category. This couple is as jovial and down to Earth as they come and we loved spending time with them, but this was the first time in five years we had invited them over. We were intimidated by their wealth and let that establish an artificial barrier between us. We felt that a family who owned an expensive steakhouse and ate there often wouldn't want to come to our house and eat macaroni and cheese. That night at dinner, we apologized for not being hospitable and told them about our macaroni and cheese fear, to which they simply replied, "We like macaroni and cheese." Jeni and I learned a lesson that night that I wish I had known while I was at Florida State, because I had a very similar experience with Coach Bowden.

In Tallahassee, Fla., Bobby Bowden is a big deal. His name or appearance is coveted for advertising and marketing space.

Every church in town wants him to fill their pulpit on Sunday in hopes of drawing a larger crowd. We live in the capitol of Florida, but Coach is bigger than the governor or any congressman as far as Tallahassee is concerned. He is larger than life, iconic, and someone that people just want to get close to. People will wait in line for hours to get him to write his name on a picture or a football. I didn't have to wait in line; I had direct access to him but I was never quite confident enough to take advantage of it. He always said that his door was open and that if any of us players needed to talk, he was there for us. It's not that I didn't believe him, but I never felt like I had something important enough to say. I was a player and all, but seriously, who am I that I should occupy Bobby Bowden's time? All my pretense was trumped one night when I selfishly took the initiative to go to Coach Bowden's house to ask for an autograph, and I ended up receiving much more.

I had agreed to get the autograph as a way to impress my future in-laws. They knew I played football and had seen my games, but I felt that if I could go to Coach Bowden's house, unannounced and return with an autograph, I would really show them something. In hindsight, it probably wouldn't have been that impressive because Coach was as approachable as the mailman, and as hospitable as a Motel 6. I had been to his house once before when I hosted Randy Golightly for his official visit, but even if I hadn't made that trip, I still would have known where his house was. Most of Tallahassee knows where the Bowdens live because they had been there ever since Coach began at FSU in 1976. Coach Bowden's house had a half-circle driveway and at both intersections, between the driveway and the road, there were twin white columns with globe shaped lights on the tops. The Bowden house was nice but not opulent, featuring two stories, a brick façade that has a subtle, gold hue, and an elegant front door at the top of an equally elegant concrete staircase. We pulled right into their driveway and I led Jeni up to the front door to ring the doorbell. I did my best to remain cool, but I was scared that Coach Bowden wouldn't recognize me and I would be humiliated in front of the woman I wanted to marry. My pride was stronger than my fear on that particular evening, so I rang the bell.

Ann Bowden, affectionately known as Miss Ann around Tallahassee, answered the door and before we could even explain ourselves, she invited us in to sit down. We followed her into their living room and sat down on a couch. I have always observed people's book shelves when I have entered their homes to learn about them and find ways to engage in conversation. The first thing I noticed on Coach Bowden's shelves was war books. As I was racking my brain for old history class facts so that I wouldn't look stupid if I asked about the books, Coach Bowden walked in and very casually said hi and sat down. He was wearing a pair of shorts and an FSU T-shirt, the same thing I would normally wear around the house. Thankfully, he remembered me and graciously broke the ice by noticing that we had come bearing gifts that were not for him and asked, "Do You need me to sign somethin' for ya?" I handed the items over to him and he quickly signed them and handed them back. As Miss Ann walked back into the room, Coach asked about Jeni and me and after our answer, Jeni asked them about how they met which began our evening with the first family of college football.

We spent over an hour listening to the two of them talk about how they met and eventually got married. They shared stories about coaching at Howard and then South Georgia with toddlers and newborns to care for. Miss Ann talked about being a coach's wife and coach's mother. We heard about their modest home that overlooked the practice fields and Coach talked about having his boys with him while he worked with his teams. I asked about all of the war books and Coach gushed for a few moments about his love of strategy and leadership found in some of the great military minds. As the conversation began to taper off, Coach got up and told his bride that he was going to his room. He told each of us good night and headed up the stairs. Miss Ann filled in the blanks by telling us that his "room" was his film room and that he went up there most nights to study game film.

It was after 9 p.m. when Miss Ann finally led us to the door and we said our goodbyes. I had my autographs but more importantly, we had spent an evening getting to know the man who had so heavily influenced my life. I never dropped in on Coach Bowden again and I regret it. More often than not, I let the aura of Bobby Bowden create an artificial barrier between he and I that I was unwilling to climb. I am afraid that I missed out on allowing a great man to make an even deeper impact on my life. We learned that those two icons of college football were just regular people with real stories. I was vividly reminded of that truth from our dining experience with our friends in North Carolina. Had I known then, when I was playing for Coach Bowden, what I know now, I bet I would have learned that he liked macaroni and cheese too.

With autograph in hand, Jeni and I made our way back to her parents' house. We were experiencing a mixed assortment of emotions ranging from a feeling of, "are you kidding? We just hung out with the Bowdens!" to, "that was really nice, I am glad we got to spend some time with them." We expected to be there for 30 seconds to a minute and ended up sharing the evening, because they wanted to spend time with us, surreal.

37

PLAYING FOR COACH BOWDEN

When people learn that I played football at Florida State, without fail, the first question I hear is, "What was it like to play for Bobby Bowden?" It would be my first question too. Coach Bowden is one of the rare figures who transcend the game. You have your great coaches within all the different sports; men who had great runs, won championships, or changed the game. Sure he did all of those things, but Coach Bowden was bigger than that. He led the Seminoles to 14 consecutive years finishing in the top 5, winning two National Championships, and inventing the shuffle pass, among other things. Coach Bowden is one of the greatest coaches of any sport, college or professional. His name belongs in the same category as Bill Walsh, Phil Jackson, Tommy Lasorda, and John Wooden. These iconic men are coaching personified and Robert Cleckler Bowden is one of them.

I have to admit, I didn't know much about Coach Bowden when I made up my mind to play for him. I could tell you about Knute Rockne, Dan Devine, and Lou Holtz because I loved Notre Dame so much, but my football knowledge didn't extend very far from South Bend. I knew Bowden was the coach and knew that he was successful, but I had no concept of the fact that I was going to be playing for a living legend. When I arrived in Tallahassee, the reality of who he was began to sink in. The football facility was adorned with historical memorabilia, most of which had to do with Coach Bowden and his teams. If someone I met found out that I was on the football team, I would get asked the "What is it like..." question. I didn't have a full appreciation, but I had enough of an awareness to be star struck whenever he was around.

In team settings, being around him was totally normal. It felt just like being around any other coach on any other team, but the idea of talking to him scared me. I wouldn't even say hi to him when he drove past or walked by; I would just shy away or pretend I didn't see him because the idea of having to speak to him made me sick. I just couldn't get over the fact that he was a legend and carried far reaching fame while I was a faceless walk-on trying not to get cut from his team. When I saw the relationship some of the other, more accomplished guys had with him I was jealous and also very aware of my place at the same time. I must say though, it really had nothing to do with a player's accomplishment, but everything to do with their willingness to approach him. I was simply unwilling to make that effort, so I never benefitted from a close relationship with him.

With the other coaches, relationships were almost unavoidable. This was the result of Coach Bowden's leadership philosophy; to coach the coaches and let the coaches do their jobs. He held the primary role of overseer and public leader while his assistants handled the work on the field. I was able to strike up an off-the-field relationship with all the other coaches, simply due to the fact that I spent time with them every day in practice. Coach Bowden wasn't ever the one correcting my hand placement on a block or my footwork on a pass route; Coach Lilly, Sexton, Heggins, Richt, or Jeff Bowden took care of that. Therefore I felt more comfortable interacting with them off the field. There was one exception to this rule though. Even though I spent time on the field with Coach Andrews, I still had the same sense of awe around him and I struggled to get over my issues and strike up a relationship with him, as well. In Tallahassee, Coach Andrews is nearly as iconic as Coach Bowden, and I was intimidated by their celebrity.

During my years there, our teams achieved incredible levels of success. More importantly, we were able to continue an even more incredible run of excellence that began about a decade before I arrived in Tallahassee. Our team in 2000 was the last team in a 14-year run that finished in the Top 5 in America for Coach Bowden. No team had done anything like it before and I doubt that any team will ever come close to doing it again. The University of Southern California teams from 2002 – 2008 were expected to give Coach Bowden's dynasty a good run, but ended the 2009 season ranked no. 20, terminating their streak at seven years. As dominating as they were for a while, they were only able to accomplish 50 percent of what Coach Bowden and his teams accomplished. Unfortunately, the NCAA found out that USC had not been above board and stripped them of their victories from the 2004 and 2005 seasons. They also took away their 2004 national championship. The dynasty that Coach Bowden established was staggering and with every passing year, I appreciate that I was a part of it more and more.

He is simply bigger than the game. No one ever asks me, "What was it like to play at Florida State?" The question is always in relation to Bowden. In a part of the country where football is the biggest thing going, Coach Bowden is at the beginning of the conversation. He is a legend. There are other names in the elite legends of southern football, well one other name, Paul "Bear" Bryant. But not even Bryant, with all of his astounding success was able to accomplish what Coach Bowden did. Bowden even did it under tougher circumstances, after the NCAA imposed scholarship limitations.

While we continued the most important streak, the Top 5 finishes, we let one streak end on our watch. The 1997 Sugar Bowl against Florida was the first bowl loss in 11 seasons for Coach Bowden. For 11 consecutive years, the seniors won their last game, the fans celebrated on the last weekend of the year, and the historical run was extended. That just doesn't happen.

Had I played for Coach Bowden in 1970 or 1980, my experience might have been totally different. Maybe I would have had more time on the field with him or perhaps I wouldn't have been so awed by him. But I didn't play then, I played in the twilight of the golden era of Florida State football. I was on teams that were benchmarks for greatness and milestones in an illustrious career. There have only been two teams in the history of college football to win a 300ᵗʰ game for a coach at their school, and I played on one of those teams. There has only been one team in over 100 years of college football to go undefeated and maintain a no. 1 ranking from the preseason all the way to the championship, and I played on that team. The very first time that a father coached against his son in a college football game was in 1999 when we played Clemson, and I was on that team. Our teams never lost a home football game. Our five year stretch was part of a larger 10-year run of 37 consecutive home wins and 54 consecutive games without a loss (we tied Florida in 1994) inside Doak Campbell Stadium. Almost every year I was part of a historical team, so my experience with Coach Bowden is tied to the history.

So, what was it like to play for Bobby Bowden? It was an historical, humbling, awe-inspiring, privilege. Beyond the historical significance of playing for him, my years at FSU also provided me with incredible personal milestones. Nothing compares with a Saturday in Doak Campbell Stadium, but I had the privilege of playing in some fantastic football stadiums. Death Valley in Clemson, S.C., Los Angeles Memorial Coliseum in California, The Meadowlands in New York, the Louisiana Superdome in New Orleans, the Orange Bowl in Miami, the Swamp in Gainesville, Alltel Stadium in Jacksonville, Fla., Sun Devil Stadium in Tempe, Ariz., and historic Bobby Dodd Stadium in Atlanta, Ga. I was granted the opportunity to accomplish a list of firsts outside the game of football, including my first trip to New York City and the Statue of Liberty, my first trip to California, my first trip to Washington, D.C. and the White House, and my first trip to Miami, FL. I was able to play alongside a collection of great players, including multiple All-Americans, a Lou Groza winner, a Johnny Unitas Golden Arm winner, multiple NFL pro-bowlers, a couple ACC players of the year, a group of NFL first round draft picks,

306

and a Heisman Trophy winner. It was during my years at Florida State that I met a local girl named Jeni Rudzik, who agreed to become my wife in 2002. The most significant moment of my life was when I came to believe that the Jesus of the Bible was real and that what He said was the truth; and that happened because of the leadership and authenticity of Coach Bowden.

When I pause and reflect back on all that transpired during my 60 months in Tallahassee... all the people, places, and moments... the game days, road trips, and practices... the honorable men who influenced my life, the great friendships I developed, and thousands who offered their support every Saturday... only one word feels adequate to express the way that I feel...GRATEFUL.

EPILOGUE

***

$\mathbf{A}$s a high school student, I never imagined myself playing football in college, yet following the 2001 Orange Bowl, I had a realistic optimism that I might play in the National Football League. I had one more game as a college player because I was invited to participate in the Gridiron Classic in Orlando, Fla. There are a couple of different all-star games following the college football season, and it is a rare honor and opportunity to be invited to participate. The game is billed as Florida vs. the USA and involves athletes who played high school or college ball in Florida, vs. players from the rest of the country. I was on the Florida team with my teammates Justin Amman, Jarad Moon, and Keith Cottrell. The game was unique because it was coached by former NFL coaches and they made every effort to prepare us for a professional pace. Of course, having Disney involved made the entertainment aspect of the week particularly enjoyable. The game was dominated by the defenses, but I had a big game and scored the game's only touchdown. While I was in Orlando, after the game, I made my first professional decision.

I signed with my agent, Russ Campbell, and I thought that was about the coolest thing I had ever done, partly because of the simple fact that I had an agent, but even more so because he was also Coach Bowden's agent! I don't know why, but signing with an agent just felt so "NFL" to me. I felt like I was already in the league, or at a minimum, that playing in the NFL was inevitable. They had to take me; I had an agent after all.

I quickly began my preparations for a potential invitation to the NFL Combine. My agent was based in Alabama and he had a speed coach that he sent his athletes to, near Tuscaloosa. I spent a couple of weeks working on my start and form, to minimize my 40 time. I had never spent that kind of focused time working on my running technique and I actually believe that it hurt my chances. My coach was excellent and he had a history of helping guys improve their draft status, but I began thinking too hard and it had a negative impact on my time. I wasn't fast to begin with, so I don't believe it affected my draft value.

Every spring, scouts from every NFL team make the trek to Tallahassee to evaluate the senior Seminoles. They ran us through a battery of tests to determine if our athleticism was worth their considerable investment. I had a good pro day, but not good enough because I didn't receive an invite to the Combine. Not being invited to the Combine was a bad sign, in regard to my being drafted but I held out hope. I camped out in front of my TV and watched almost every minute of the 2001 Draft. I knew I wasn't going on the first day but I had fun watching some of my friends get selected. Jamal Reynolds was the 10th overall pick and went to Green Bay. Derek Gibson went no. 28 to the Raiders, and Tommy Polley went to the Rams in the second round. I believed that day two was going to be my day. Surely, someone would want the tight end from the team that was so dominant over the last two years. I watched as a few more of my friends were drafted, including Tay Cody going in the third to the Chargers, Snoop Minnis to the Chiefs, Brian Allen to the Rams, Travis Minor to the Dolphins,

Chris Weinke to the Panthers, and finally Charron Dorsey to the Dallas Cowboys. After the seventh and final round concluded, I began to believe that there wasn't a team that wanted me. There was, they just didn't want to use a draft pick.

About five minutes after the draft concluded, I received a call from my agent. I was thrilled that he called! Even though the draft was over, I knew he had connected me with an NFL team. He greeted me with, "Congratulations! You're a Buffalo Bill!" My unenthusiastic response was, "Cool but, Do I have a say in that?" I was hoping that since I wasn't drafted, I would have options. Call me picky, but I just didn't like the idea of playing football in Buffalo. My first choice was to play for my hometown Falcons, next would have been the Panthers, followed by Tampa Bay. We talked briefly about the process, and he brought me back down to Earth as he explained that no other teams had expressed an interest. But I pleaded with Russ to see if any other teams would rescue me from the land of cold weather and hot wings. About 10 minutes later, my phone rang again and he had much better news.

"Well, how do you feel about being a Pittsburgh Steeler?" I was thrilled and eagerly jumped at the chance, "I'd love it!" As far as I was concerned, Russ had worked incredible magic by securing this deal. I had just switched from the land of four Super Bowl losses, to "Title Town" in Pittsburgh. Not only that, but he managed to get me a five times greater signing bonus! The only thing better would have been a slot with my Falcons, but I quickly got over that and became a Steeler fan. My future father-in-law was already a huge fan, which I think made him feel that much better about providing his consent for me to marry his oldest daughter.

Very soon after the draft, I joined the other rookie Steelers for a weekend orientation to Pittsburgh. We toured the facilities, received physicals, met our coaches, and received our workout programs. After a few weeks in Tallahassee, I moved up to Pittsburgh for a couple of months. We had workouts and run-through practices as part of the off-season preparations and I loved them. Pittsburgh is an awesome town and the Steelers are an incredible organization. The head coach of the Steelers, at that time, was Bill Cowher but my position coach was Ken Whisenhunt, now the head coach of the Arizona Cardinals, who was also from Augusta, Ga. As it turned out, the Steelers drafted Kendrell Bell out of the University of Georgia and he too was from

Jeni & I on Heinz Field.

Augusta. I was totally convinced that I was destined to make the team; how could they not keep the Augusta trio together?

The mini camps were cool, but the preseason camp was where it really got fun. We spent most of camp in Latrobe, Penn., the home of Arnold Palmer. I tried to get as involved as I possibly could in the whole experience, so I led a Bible Study for the players while I was there. We met once a week and worked through the New Testament book of Philippians. In the back of my mind, I felt that I might be compelling God to keep me on the team. I know it was a silly thought now, but at the time, I really thought that my spiritual contributions would translate into athletic returns.

EPILOGUE

The training camp experience was so rich. The folks in western Pennsylvania love their Steelers and they showed their support all through two-a-days. There were thousands of fans at every practice which made the whole experience fun. One day, there was an air show being hosted by the Latrobe airport and we had fighter jets and trick planes buzzing our fields. Another day we got dressed for practice and went through our stretching routine, before Coach Cowher called us in and dismissed us for a trip to the movies. They had reserved an entire theatre for us to invade. We had our choice of films and an open concession stand to provide the necessary snacks. That was the coolest football practice of my career. Another one of my most memorable moments wasn't so positive.

We were having a scrimmage at a nearby high school and the stadium was packed with Steeler fanatics. As we got off the bus, there was a man waiting with his Harley Davidson motorcycle sporting a custom Steelers paint job. He asked me to autograph his bike and I declined. He insisted, so I made sure that he knew I was a scrub and probably going to be cut any day; but he still wanted me to sign it, so I did. It was closer to an act of vandalism than an autograph, but it was his desire. Later in the scrimmage I had my bittersweet moment. I was in when a play was called that involved me running a deep post route. I ran the route perfectly and caught the ball about 30 yards downfield. I was walking tall as I jogged back to the huddle and thrilled when Coach Cowher said, "Great catch Sprague…" He knew my name! But his statement continued with, "too bad it didn't count." He was right, I had flinched before the snap and would have been called for a false start. So much for my defining moment.

When it came time for the preseason games, I was excited to be playing my first ever NFL game in Atlanta at the Georgia Dome.

This trip presented a stark contrast to the first time I made the trip to Atlanta for a football game. Not only did I get to travel with the team and have my name on my jersey, I WAS IN THE NFL! I was putting on the same uniform that Terry Bradshaw, Lynn Swann, Franco Harris, Mel Blount, Jack Lambert, and Mean Joe Greene all wore. Not to overlook that I was playing with Jerome Bettis, who became the Steelers second leading rusher of all time. The moment went from great to magnificent because there was a group of more than 40 of my family and friends in Atlanta for the game. I was able to play about five snaps in the game, and it was exhilarating. It was awesome to know that they were there cheering me on.

That was a special day, but the sprinkles on the ice cream were getting to play in the inaugural game in Pittsburgh's new stadium. Historic Three Rivers Stadium had become a parking lot and the Steelers were beginning a new era in the state-of-the-art Heinz Field. My family, my fiancée, and her family all got to be there with the raucous Steeler fans. Those passionate fans treated it like it was a playoff game and I couldn't have been more proud to record a fourth quarter reception from the hand of Kent Graham. I made the box score! After the game, Jeni jumped down on the field and we were able to take a picture together with me in uniform.

The next day, I was called into the general manager's office and informed that I was being cut. Apparently, the leverage of the Augusta trio, my leading a team Bible study, and my ability to produce in big games wasn't enough to convince them to keep me. Honestly, I expected it. I had hope, but I also had my eyes open and it was apparent that the veteran guys were going to keep their jobs. Just like that, my NFL career was over. I was put onto a plane and I flew back to Tallahassee to meet up with Jeni and begin to figure out life without football.

Much to my surprise, part of the way through the season, the Jacksonville Jaguars called and invited me over for a workout. I met their coach, Tom Coughlin, and he and his staff worked me through some drills before quickly deciding to pass on my talents. I was not terribly disappointed by my not making it, because I had long since believed that I had been called into vocational ministry anyway. I had begun to make a different plan and the first part of that plan was to get married, which we did in March of 2002. Next was to get a job. I accepted a position to serve as a youth pastor in Hawley, Minn. A year after that, we moved to Highlands, N.C. to serve in the same capacity where we began adding kids to our family.

Our team was invited back, in 2009, for a pregame ceremony to honor the undefeated, National Championship and I was thrilled to be able to share that moment with all four of my sons: Caedmon, Jackson, Andrew, and Toby. Jeni and I are season ticket holders now and try to make it to as many games as possible. I get asked all the time if I miss it and my answer is always the same. I don't necessarily miss the game, but I do miss being on the team. I still love Saturdays in Tallahassee, but they are different now. I still love the War Chant, but it's different now. I still love being in Doak on game days, but that's different now too. It's funny, now I am much more anxious on game days than I ever was as a player, and that sick feeling after a loss lingers for much longer. I've traded my helmet for a cap, my jersey for a T-shirt, and the sidelines for a seat in the stands. I no longer share the experience with the guys in the locker room. In the place of those men are four little boys. Little boys that I have been given to lead, teach, and love. My sons are the beneficiaries of my being led, taught, and loved by Coach Bowden and his staff. So, if the school decided to cancel the football program and close the baseball stadium, if they no longer offered classes or produced world leaders, no matter what may change or how many games might be lost, my years as a Seminole football player can never be taken away. I sat at the feet of one of the great leaders and mentors of this generation and my life is exponentially better in light of it. Because of that truth, beyond the football and the education, I will always remain a true Seminole… Unconquered and Grateful.

ACKNOWLEDMENTS

This book is a product of my life, so the thanks are many. First of all, Glory be to God for putting a mind in my head and thoughts in my mind; for giving me a story to tell and the means to tell it. I am humbled when I consider that God chose to communicate to His creation in the form of a book, and allowed me to share in the joy of creating a book of my own. To God be the glory, through Jesus Christ.

Larry and Candi Sprague, aka Dad and Mom: You made the sacrifice to get me through my first year at FSU and made the commitment to be at almost every game, home and away, for 5 years. Thanks guys!

Daniel, Gina, Stacey, Angie, Jennifer and Tom, Bennett, Emily, Alex, and Carly: Thanks for sharing this ride with me. Having you guys at so many games made the journey so much more fulfilling.

Greg, Becky, Lisa, Steven, and Amy; you guys joined the party late, but made it that much better!

To my family and friends: You traveled from Iowa, Illinois, Colorado, Canada, New Mexico, North Carolina, Pennsylvania, and Georgia to attend my games. You invested time and money to support me and I am so appreciative. You guys are awesome!

Brent Moody: You were my inspiration to write. I consider it no coincidence that we reconnected after all these years. Your own journey as an author and your persistent encouragement to me on mine has been invaluable. Had you not pushed me, this book would not exist. Thank you for helping me to find a new way to express myself.

Jayne, Lis, and Will: The computer that served as my "quill" was the computer that you so generously gave to me. Thanks so much!

GRATEFUL

King's Way Christian Church: Your willingness to bring my family to Tallahassee and your commitment to us provided the time freedom and support necessary to write this book and that was vital to this book becoming a reality, Thanks!

Bob Thomas: Your willingness to work with me was a great motivation to getting this done. Thanks for your expertise and connecting me to your friends.

Rob Wilson and the Florida State Sports Information Department: Thanks for all of your support. I am very appreciative of your willingness to house me for all those hours of sorting through pictures, and taking your own turn to sort and scan. You made the book better!

Bill, Colin, Ross, and Ryals: Thanks for taking great pictures and thanks for sharing them with me for this book.

Jerry Kutz and the Seminole Boosters, Thanks for all of your support. You do great work for the university and have been a tremendous encouragement to me!

I don't know how I would have completed this book without the assistance of a few websites. Warchant.com, nolefans.com, and Seminoles.com were the source of mountains of information for me to fill in my mental gaps.

Jim Crosby: Thanks for your encouragement, and for writing "You can't become a football overnight." It helped give me a deeper appreciation for the players and coaches who came before me and built the tradition that I have come to love.

Stratton Glaze: Thanks for having lunch with me and having the humility to lead me to Matt.

Matt Thompson: Thanks for your belief in me and this project to so quickly jump on board and offer your expertise. Your help has been invaluable, and your friendship appreciated!

ACKNOWLEDMENTS

Jared Pervis: Thanks for volunteering to share your creative talents and designing a great cover!

Darlene Melcher: Thanks for partnering with me on this project. Thanks for your patience with me and working so hard to make the interior of this book beautiful.

Steve Crislip, Bruce Gaddy, Randy Hill, Jon Johnson, and David Machovec: Thank you for investing four years of your life into trying to coach me into a football player and mold me into a man, while I awkwardly went through Lakeside High School.

Ronnie Cottrell: Thanks for taking a risk and recruiting me. Thanks for helping me transition to Tallahassee and become a Seminole.

Florida State University: Thanks for allowing me to represent you on the football field by providing for my education.

John Lilly: Thank you for being my coach! Thank you for being my continued friend!

Bobby Bowden: Thanks for having enough belief in me to give me a scholarship. Thanks for being authentic and treating me as a young man, not simply a football player. I am honored that you would offer your name and your thoughts to this book in the form of your foreword. I am humbled to have had another opportunity to work with you.

Mrs. Sue Hall and Mrs. Ann Bowden: Thanks for helping me track down Coach Bowden!

Jim Henry, Nita Woodard, and my wife Jeni: Thank you so much for editing this book. I respect your willingness to tell me what I needed to hear, even when I didn't like it. I am appreciative of your thoughtful encouragement of my writing, in spite of the errors in syntax. The best gift I can offer you is a rest for your weary eyes after all that proof reading. Thanks team!

Caedmon, Jackson, Andrew, and Toby: You guys are incredible! Thanks for loving me, playing "Sorry" with me, and wrestling with me. Thanks for sharing my love for the 'Noles! You are my four favorite guys in the world!

How can I express enough appreciation to my wife and pseudo-editor Jeni? You tolerated the incredibly late nights and subsequent late mornings. You showed remarkable belief in me and this project; I never doubted that I had your support. Thank you for reading this whole thing, more than once, and lending your talented eyes to this effort. This book is better because of your contributions, but not to the extent that I am better for being married to you. I love you.

About the Author:

Ryan has spent the last 10 years of his life communicating to groups of students and adults. He has addressed church congregations, youth groups, high schools, athletes, and various community groups. Ryan is a dynamic speaker who captivates listeners of all ages and has the ability to articulate ideas with a unique and fresh perspective. He embraces the opportunity to encourage, motivate, and educate others through a wide range of topics.

If you are interested in having Ryan come and speak to your group, go to www.ryansprague.com to learn more and make a request.

SEMINOLE

You fund the Winning Edge

Your contribution to Seminole Boosters -at any level- funds a portion of the FSU athletic budget, the winning edge.

Membership, which starts at just $60 per year, pays for scholarships for our men's and women's teams, supplements coaches salaries and budgets, and fan-friendly events throughout the year.

Tax-deductible membership comes with many benefits including ticket, parking and event priority. Your participation, and that of thousands of other avid Seminoles, gives FSU the winning edge.

For information or to join:
seminole-boosters.com | (850) 644-3484